THE COLLEGE OF LOUIS-LE-GRAND

THE SCHOOL
OF THE FRENCH
REVOLUTION

A documentary history of
The College of Louis-le-Grand
and its director, Jean-François Champagne
1762-1814

Edited and Translated by

R. R. PALMER

Princeton University Press, Princeton, New Jersey

Copyright © 1975 by Princeton University Press
Published by Princeton University Press
Princeton and London

Library of Congress Cataloging in Publication Data
will be found on the last printed page of this book

Publication of this book has been aided by a grant
from the Whitney Darrow Publication Reserve Fund
of Princeton University Press

Composed in Linotype Janson and printed
in the United States of America by Princeton
University Press at Princeton, New Jersey

Acknowledgments

Since the present work forms part of a larger plan, my obligations are greater than the small dimensions of this book may reveal. I should like to thank the John Simon Guggenheim Memorial Foundation for a fellowship which freed my time in the latter half of 1973, the National Endowment for the Humanities for related assistance, and the Rockefeller Foundation for a month's residency at its study center at Bellagio, Italy, where most of the translations were actually made. The stay at Bellagio gave a rare chance for my wife and me to work on a project together, and I am indebted also to her. It seems fitting to add, since this book is so largely about scholarships, that it all began with the scholarship funds of the University of Chicago, of which I was the beneficiary almost fifty years ago.

R. R. P.

Contents and Chronology

THE COLLEGE OF LOUIS-LE-GRAND

PRINCIPALE COUR

Dessiné et Gravé par F.N. Martinet.

Du College de Louis le Grand.

THE old print on the facing page shows the main courtyard of Louis-le-Grand about 1780. The boys are at play during one of their "recreations." On the ground floor to the left were two dining halls; at the far side from left to right were the rooms used by the Physics, the Fifth, and the Sixth classes; and along the right-hand wall from rear to front were the Second, the Rhetoric class, and the chapel. The round-topped doorway at the right rear can be seen in the two pictures and in the ground-plan shown in the following pages.

The next page reproduces a section from a perspective drawing made by a Paris engraver in the 1730's. He drew the streets as wider than they were in reality, so as to give a better view of the buildings. At the bottom of the picture is the dome of the Sorbonne church. Above it, facing the Rue Saint-Jacques, is the college of Louis-le-Grand, here called the Collège des

Jésuites since the engraving was made about thirty years before the Jesuits were expelled. The main courtyard is clearly visible, but the rear courtyards are very foreshortened Adjoining Louis-le-Grand is Plessis college, and two other full-program colleges, Montaigu and Lisieux, are within the scope of the picture, as well as two small colleges, Sainte-Barbe and Cholets. The building marked "Jacobins" is not the site of the Jacobin club of the Revolution, but simply one of the houses belonging to the religious order of that name. The area shown is the heart of the Latin Quarter, and makes the urban setting of the Paris colleges very apparent.

Facing this engraving is a ground plan of Louis-le-Grand and Plessis colleges in 1793. At the right, along the long side of the page, is the Rue Saint-Jacques. The small rectangles

Continued

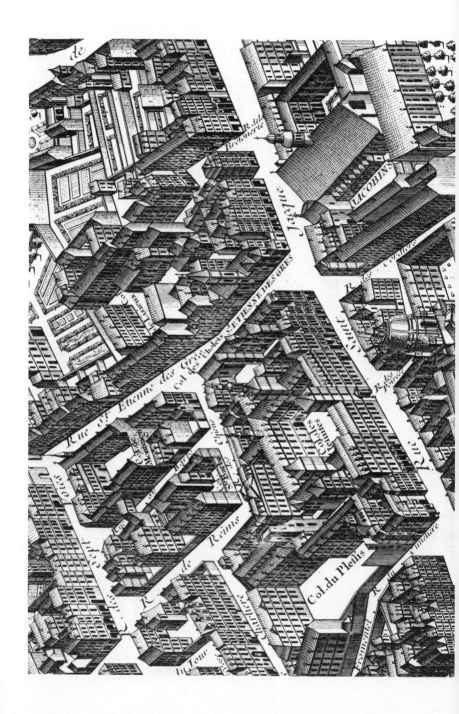

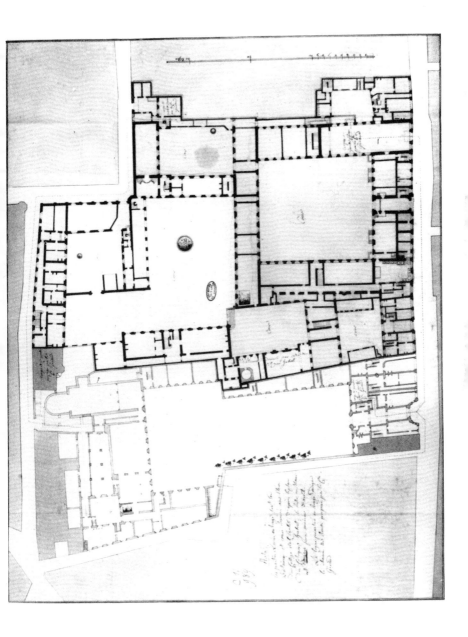

along the street were occupied by shopkeepers. The moderate sized rectangles were classrooms and dining halls. The largest rectangles were open courtyards, which may be compared with those shown in the preceding perspective drawing. In the plan, Plessis college with its single large court is on the lower third of the page; the larger Louis-le-Grand has no fewer than six courts, large and small. The two sets of buildings were combined shortly after 1800 to form the quarters of the Imperial Lycée.

During the Terror, on 19 Nivôse An II (January 8, 1794), a letter accompanying this plan ordered that the shaded part, that is, the front half of Louis-le-Grand, should be "reserved for public instruction." The rear half of Louis-le-Grand was joined with Plessis college to form a place of detention for political prisoners. Even the front part of Louis-le-Grand, however, was converted in 1794 into a work-shop for national defense, and in general the years 1793-94 saw a rearrangement of rooms, breaking through of walls, and opening of new entrances, as described by Champagne in his letter of August 1795 (Item 33).

The last of these illustrations is a bird's-eye view of Louis-le-Grand in the 1860's. Except for the demolitions that have begun in the lower left-hand corner, the college must have looked very much like this at the time of the Revolution. The dome of the Pantheon, completed in the 1780's, is in the distance. The main courtyard, with its round-topped door in the far corner, and its two low flanking towers, are as in the perspective drawing of the 1730's and the print of 1780. Most of what is seen here disappeared after 1870, when, in the wave of educational construction of the early Third Republic, the present buildings of Louis-le-Grand were erected.

Introduction

THIS BOOK is about a single institution and one man who was its head. The institution is the College of Louis-le-Grand, long considered the leading lycée of France, which still stands in the Rue Saint-Jacques, in the heart of the Latin Quarter, across the street from the Sorbonne. Most of what we see today dates from the end of the nineteenth century, as does the visible Sorbonne itself, but some of its buildings and courtyards are older, and were the scene of events described in the following pages. The man in question is Jean-François Champagne, who as a schoolman or educator deserves more than the oblivion into which he has fallen. He spent half a century uninterruptedly in the college, first as a scholarship student, then as a teacher, then as its director during the Revolution, and finally as the first head of the Imperial Lycée, as it was called under Napoleon. Louis-le-Grand, under a variety of names, was the only college in Paris never to close during the Revolution, even at the height of the Terror. It is the only such place with a connected history from the *ancien régime* into modern times.

The book may therefore be of interest to anyone concerned with either revolution or education. It is a new book on an old theme. So much has been written for over a century on education in France, and so much of it is inconclusive when not clearly polemical, reflecting the long conflict between Catholic-conservative and republican-revolutionary-liberal schools of thought, that it has seemed most useful to present simply a collection of original sources, together with such explanations as seem necessary. None of the documents assembled here has ever been translated

9

or published in English. Most of them are equally inaccessible even in French.

At first glance the subject seems so specialized that one may ask whether the translation has been worth the effort, since those who work primarily in French history would rightly prefer to see the documents in the original. References are given by which they may be traced. The present book is addressed, however, to a wider circle than those who have an easy knowledge of the French language. The impact of revolutionary events on a particular institution may arouse the curiosity of students and general readers. The history of education is now an expanding field, and those concerned with American or British schools and colleges—or Russian or Japanese—may find their range of vision enlarged by a collateral knowledge of a famous school in Paris. Comparative education is a timely subject; its difficulty is that few people can know enough languages to pursue it, and for them the materials offered in this book may also be welcome.

In fact, thanks to the attention of the royal authorities before 1789, and of the revolutionary authorities thereafter, Louis-le-Grand must be one of the best-documented eighteenth-century schools or colleges to be found anywhere in the world. There seem, unfortunately, to be no surviving letters of students, nor autobiographical memories. The sources take the form very largely of regulations, proposals, and reports. That such materials do not exactly describe reality is well known, but they may be as credible as sporadic literary recollections, and in any case, properly used, they allow us to visualize the daily and inner workings of a large residential school. We can tell, for example, that the boys and young men went to classes at the sound of a bell, until Napoleon replaced it with drums, and that they ate with silver implements on tablecloths, at least until the silver was confiscated in the Revolution.

Though dealing with one institution and one individual, the book should throw light on many matters of more general interest. It should illuminate, for example, the origins of the peculiarly bureaucratic and regimented structure of French education, and suggest that this peculiarity is not to be attributed to Napoleon only, but goes back to the monarchy, and to a desire for planned reform as much as to any crude love of domination. It should be useful to the history of what is nowadays called meritocracy, or the idea of careers open to talent. It tells us something about access to education and the social origins of students, who more at Louis-le-Grand than in most places were of fairly modest social levels. The reader may even feel, after perusing some of these documents, that a certain excess of education, or production of educated young men beyond the capacity of society to find places for them, may have been a contributing cause of the French Revolution. There is much in the book on the history of scholarships and student aid, and hence of college endowments. The meaning of "public" education in the eighteenth century should become clear, in a way suggesting why private schools in England are still called "public." The whole dichotomy between endowed education on the one hand, and a system supported or paid for from tax funds on the other, should be elucidated.

We get a glimpse of student radicalism during the French Revolution, and learn that a great many professors in the old colleges were not so stultified as they have often been portrayed as being. Some teachers were fairly radical: Champagne himself might pass for a sans-culotte in 1793, or at least was a member of the revolutionary committee of his section assembly; but he was essentially a practical man who favored certain reforms in education, and was above all concerned to keep his college going in a time of political turmoil. To know that he gave up his religious ordination (as sub-deacon, not a priest), married, and translated Aristotle's *Politics* at about the same time enlarges our view. We may conclude that professors or professional teachers, as a class, though they lacked the social standing to make themselves heard, had as much to say on education that was worth listening to as most *philosophes*, free intellectuals, and orators in the Revolutionary assemblies. Finally, the book may give body to that phantom concept of a "bourgeois revolution," for the College of Louis-le-Grand and J. F. Champagne were very bourgeois indeed, if we once agree that education, or the aspiration to education, is at least as good a sign of bourgeois status as is the possession of property.

It is necessary, if Louis-le-Grand is to be seen in its proper context, to begin with some observations on what a "college" was. This involves the meaning of words, which in turn involves problems of translation.

At the time of the Revolution there were several hundred "colleges" in France. Their number has been estimated as high as 900; Champagne himself gives 320, and he was in a position to know. The uncertainty arises because a *collège* was only one among various kinds of schools. It was not a small school giving only elementary work. It was not a "private" school, operated by an individual schoolmaster, expiring when he died or changed his occupation, and leaving no records. The number of such private enterprises, called *maisons d'éducation*, or educational houses, or simply *pensions* because the schoolmaster took boarders (*pensionnaires*) seems to have been multiplying in the last years of the monarchy. This fact alone will make it forever impossible to know what proportion of French youth was receiving some schooling, of a kind that we would call secondary, on the eve of the Revolution, or whether the proportion was rising or falling. It has been argued that the proportion was actually falling, and it may be true that there were fewer "colleges" than in the time of Louis XIV, but the growth of the private sector makes the argument doubtful, and in any case there were certainly a great many educated men in France at the time of the Revolution. There were also a great many educated women, though women's education remains one of the great unexplored areas.

A college was a public school. There is a sense in which a comprehensive public school system, from elementary to university levels, is, so to speak, an invention of the French Revolution. It is the sense in which the system is planned, maintained, supervised, generalized, and in the long run paid for by the state. But "public instruction" was an old expression in France long before the Revolution. It referred primarily to teaching in the colleges. A college was a place that had public support, and a life that went on beyond the lives of individual teachers. Some colleges had endowments, some were subsidized by town governments, some enjoyed both kinds of income. It was usual for town governments, or trustees responsible for endowments, to reach agreements with groups of men in religious orders, or of "secular" priests who belonged to no order, to carry on the actual teaching and conduct the boarding facilities. The boarding school in later times became a place of special advantage for the well-to-do. Formerly, before the state provided locally accessible secondary schools, only those boys who lived within walking distance of such a school could live at home; others had to be boarded at or near it. Hence some colleges had many boarders; and "masters" of *maisons d'éducation* or of *pensions* would set up near the college, board the pupils, give elementary instruction themselves, and assist their boys or young men in work actually done in the college classes.

Endowments, or grants made by towns or other corporate bodies, usually took the form of maintenance for such boarders. That is, they were scholarships (*bourses*), and there is much about such scholarships in the following pages. Endowed scholarships drew on the income of funds given at various dates from the fourteenth century to recent times. They existed all over France, and many places maintained scholarships in the Paris colleges so that local boys might be sent there for an education. Some were family scholarships, in which the living head of the family had the power to nominate the candidate. Others were founded to assist boys of a given town or province. In such cases the power of nomination might lie with the bishop, an abbey, a town council, or other such body. Favoritism, nepotism, local pride, and chance might all play a part in the distribution of such awards, but a strong college could refuse nominees who did not meet its requirements. The regulations of 1769 for the College of Louis-de-Grand, abridged as Item 5 below, show how admission was becoming increasingly subject to systematic examination. Once admitted to his scholarship, however, the scholar enjoyed a kind of tenure, a fact that was to raise problems during the Revolution.

If teaching was actually in the hands of the clergy before the Revolution, it was because most families wanted it so, and because among the laity there were not enough grown men of any ability who would make the teaching of children and adolescents a lifetime occupation. The development of a lay teaching profession is indeed one of the phenomena of the Revolutionary and Napoleonic years. There were lay teachers, and married teachers, before 1789, either as private schoolmasters or working in organized colleges alongside members of the clergy, to whom they would be subordinate. It is correct to say that teaching before the Revolution was controlled by the clergy. But the first step in clarification is to recognize that neither the "clergy" nor the Catholic Church was a monolith. Many teaching clergy were not priests; Champagne was only a sub-deacon, and the famous Fouché, Napoleon's chief of police, was a lay brother teaching physics in Oratorian schools until 1792. Many took priestly orders only as a means to a teaching career, somewhat as in the United States today there are those who take a doctorate and engage in research although they are mainly interested in college teaching. If we see the matter in this light, it is less surprising that so many "clergy," who were really professional teachers before 1789, abandoned their clerical status during the Revolution, sometimes married, and emerged as lay teachers in the Napoleonic lycées. Catholic polemicists called them apostates; our view can be more charitable. In any case it was usual in all countries for education to be in the hands of the clergy. Fellows and tutors at Oxford and Cambridge were ordained, and the presidents of American colleges (where there were few other professors) were also clergymen.

Of the several hundred colleges in France before the Revolution, some had an existence apart, and some were affiliated with one of the twenty-two universities. In the latter case, the one or more colleges in a university constituted its Faculty of Arts. A complete university, such as the one in Paris, had three "higher faculties," in Theology, Law, and Medicine, below which the Faculty of Arts, though usually the most populous and flourishing, constituted a kind of undergraduate branch. The Faculty of Arts granted a degree of master, or *maîtrise ès arts*, which was necessary for entrance to one of the three professional schools. This constituted a great advantage for the university colleges. Students in other colleges or "educational houses," if they wished to go on in law, medicine, or theology, usually had to take their final year or two at a university college in order to obtain the master's degree. On the other hand, the youth who had no such intentions could obtain his education in his small-town college or "private" school; he could study for as many years as he or his family wanted; there were no drop-outs, because it was not expected that everyone had to take the whole course or obtain a degree.

The colleges differed also in that some, though far from all, were conducted by religious orders. Thus the Jesuits had over a hundred colleges in France until 1762, and the Oratorians at the time of the Revolution had thirty-six, of which seven had once been Jesuit. It might happen, in this or that university in the provinces, that one of the colleges of the Faculty of Arts was Jesuit (before 1762) or Oratorian. On the whole, however, these Jesuit and Oratorian colleges constituted complex systems of their own, apart from the universities, and were organized in their own way in that the order selected and trained young men as teachers, and then appointed, promoted, and transferred them within its system. The University of Paris, resisting such outside control, never in the seventeenth and eighteenth centuries allowed any religious order to maintain a college within it. Its colleges were operated by secular clergy.

The colleges of the French universities had originated in the same way as had those of Oxford and Cambridge. Founded mainly from the thirteenth through the fifteenth centuries, they had at first been residential halls which gradually acquired teaching functions. Their program of study reflected the old medieval trivium, or a sequence of grammar, rhetoric, and philosophy. At the close of the Middle Ages the ways of the English and French universities began to diverge. In England, the "grammar," or studies for younger boys, became concentrated in grammar schools, and the colleges at Oxford and Cambridge received only older youths who had already attended such schools. In France, the colleges as they developed in early modern times took in boys from the ages of eleven or twelve to those of eighteen or nineteen. Hence developed a French academic parlance which is sometimes literally translated in the following pages. The youngest boys in the college were called "grammarians," those of fifteen or sixteen were "rhetoricians" or "humanists," and the oldest were called "philosophers." The youngest studied mainly Latin grammar, with more attention to French as time went on. The oldest studied mainly moral philosophy and logic, but the term included natural science also.

The highest level, just before the *maîtrise ès arts*, was called simply Philosophy. It consisted of two years of study, and embraced both the older logic and moral philosophy, and a general treatment of the newer natural sciences, especially physics. The next year down was called Rhetoric, and the year below it the Second and so on down as far as the Seventh. Sometimes the Second and Third were grouped in Rhetoric and called the "humanities." In full usage the phrase was, for example, *la seconde classe*, which however would commonly be called simply the Second; and this usage has been preserved in translation. Thus Champagne in 1790, before he became director, was Professor of the Second. A regulation of 1784 in effect set maximum ages, or at least norms, for the colleges of the University of Paris. Pupils in the Second were to be no more than sixteen to compete for university prizes, in the Third no more than fifteen, and so on down to the Sixth, where they were not to be more than twelve. No age limits were set for students in Rhetoric and the higher levels.

Each class had its own *professeur*, though the teacher of the Seventh, dealing with boys who might be only nine years old, was not dignified with that title. Many boys entered college well above the Seventh, and others left before finishing their Philosophy, so that size of the classes could vary considerably. To the "professor" in charge of each class were added "masters" and "assistant masters," usually recent graduates of the college. They were assigned to assist in particular classes or age-levels, to preside at particular tables in the dining halls, and to watch over particular parts of the dormitories at night. These subdivisions of the dormitories were called "quarters." Masters also supervised the hours and places of study, and helped students to prepare for recitations which they were to make to professors in the actual classes. In the language of the day the terms *professeur* and *maître* were sometimes interchangeable, and both might also be called *régents*, but at other times the distinction was clearly made; our translations attempt to follow the meaning of the originals.

In addition to this body of younger boys, or what might

be called undergraduates, a strong college, in Paris or elsewhere, might also have older students. In this case it functioned as a residence hall or living center, from which the young men went out to hear lectures in one of the higher faculties of law, medicine, or theology. If such students were numerous enough, there might be a kind of adjunct professor of one of these subjects, attached to the college to assist them. In the 1780's about a third of the students at Louis-le-Grand were such older youths studying in the professional schools.

As a result a big French college was a complex institution. Champagne's report for the year 1792, reproduced as Item 29 below, though written at a time when many teachers and students were absent because of the war and Revolution, describes an organization having, for about 500 students, eight professors, two adjuncts in law, twenty masters, a chaplain, a doctor, a consulting oculist, a library, an infirmary with four attendants, three porters, two watchmen, various kitchen employees, and no fewer than twenty *garçons de quartier*, or "quarter boys," whose function was probably to clean up the quarters into which sleeping and living accommodations were divided. Adding the professors and masters together gives a student-faculty ratio approaching sixteen to one, which is more favorable than the best American colleges of the time could have shown.

The range of age-levels, however, creates pitfalls for any attempt to compare the French colleges with those of America, or of Oxford or Cambridge. It is true that in England and America no standardization of ages by school year had yet occurred. In general, boys entered and graduated at earlier ages than later became the rule. But if averages were lower, the range was very great. In American colleges, in the 1790's, the age of students extended from fifteen to twenty-five. Students in American colleges, however, like those at Oxford or Cambridge, remained only for a four-year course. A student in an active French college might remain for as long as twelve years, if he entered in the

Seventh or Sixth and remained through three years of professional training. A French college, therefore, might in theory be three times as big without serving, statistically speaking, any larger a clientele. It is therefore somewhat irrelevant to remark, although it is true, that Louis-le-Grand alone, only one of the Paris colleges, had in the 1780's more students than Harvard or Yale, and almost as many as all the colleges of either Oxford or Cambridge.

The same differences in ages of students complicates any attempt to compare the content or level of instruction. We do know that a young Frenchman, on finishing Philosophy at his college, was supposed to be educated and could proceed directly to his advanced or professional studies. It is hard to estimate the attainments of students at the moment of entrance. It may be that John Adams, when he entered Harvard College, not quite sixteen years old, after a short examination in Latin, knew about as much of this language as a bright boy in France of the same age who was beginning his Second. The Marquis de Chastellux, an officer in the French army, visited Princeton in 1780 and talked to its president, John Witherspoon. He was favorably impressed, and concluded that the work at Princeton corresponded to the Rhetoric and Philosophy of the French colleges. It is probable that the French *maîtrise* and the American bachelor's degree signified about the same level of scholastic achievement.

Until 1763, the Faculty of Arts of the University of Paris contained no less than thirty-eight colleges. All were old if not strictly medieval foundations, with one exception. The exception was Mazarin College, also called the College of the Quatre-Nations, founded by the cardinal's will in 1661. All were crowded together in the Latin Quarter, again with the exception of Mazarin, which was on the Seine half a mile away, in buildings occupied since Napoleon's time by the Institute of France. Only ten of the thirty-eight colleges, however, were operating with full vigor. They were the *collèges de plein exercice*, called "full-program colleges" in our translations, because they offered the full series of classes outlined in the preceding paragraphs. Others were the "small colleges," which were able to offer only a part of the program, usually the most elementary. A few offered no instruction at all, and had become ineffectual boarding establishments, if indeed their *bourses* or scholarships had not turned into sinecures. Either such colleges had begun with very small endowments, and had failed to grow; or their endowments had wasted away through mismanagement, malfeasance, neglect, or simply the declining value of money since the fifteenth century. The small colleges, in short, were in a state of decay. Planted squarely among them in the Latin Quarter was a healthy intruder, a Jesuit college which did not belong to the university at all, since, as noted above, the University of Paris refused to allow any of its colleges to belong to a religious order. This college was the old Louis-le-Grand, founded by the Jesuits in 1564 as Clermont College, and renamed after "Louis the Great" in 1682. It did not belong to the University until after the Jesuits had been driven from France.

Two dates before the expulsion of the Jesuits were very important for the University of Paris, and in particular for its Faculty of Arts. After 1719 tuition was free. In that year the government undertook to pay the salaries of the professors in the ten full-program colleges. The arrangement came about because the university surrendered its own mail service, which had been developed since the Middle Ages for the use of its students, and which had become a source of income; and the government in return granted to the University an annual sum equaling one twenty-eighth of the proceeds of the newly developing royal post-office. As the mail service expanded this annual grant increased, reaching 300,000 livres at the time of the Revolution. Since the livre is often mentioned in the following pages, it should be noted here that after 1726 it had the same gold content as the franc created in the Revolution. Comparisons with eighteenth-century sums stated in English pounds can be made by dividing by twenty-five, and for American dollars after the 1790's by about five. Thus a grant of 300,000 livres a year would correspond to about £12,000 or $60,000.

In return for this grant the Paris colleges agreed to charge no tuition fees—with various consequences. The colleges prided themselves on being public institutions offering free instruction, and on their independence from parental or other pressures because of the security of their salaries. The professors, though virtually all clergy, were salaried men paid by the state, and long before the Revolution we find regular salary scales and provision for retirement pensions, the salaries running from 2,000 to 2,500 livres a year. For expenses of board and room for students, and for support of masters and accessory personnel, a college drew on its endowed income so far as it had any, and on student boarding fees. Funds for scholarships or "free places" went for the same purposes, without having to be used for professorial salaries. Average expense per student was regularized before the Revolution at about 450 livres a year, and scholarships were set at that figure. That is, in a rough comparative view, it was possible to attend a Paris college for about $100 a year, or have a scholarship of that value. There were colleges in which rich boys could pay more for better accommodations, but the exact differences in social tone among the Paris colleges remains unclear. All we can say is that sons of both the highest nobility and the lesser social ranks were to be found in the colleges in Paris.

The other important date was 1747. In that year, from a legacy it had received, the university instituted an annual contest among the ten colleges. The awarding of prizes became a grand event, not unlike an American commencement of the time. It was patronized by the public authorities and attended by parents, in an assembly which listened to student compositions and declamations, read aloud in poetry or prose, in Latin or French. Colleges competed to have the highest number of prize-winning students. The students, or the best of them, were aroused by a spirit of emulation, a word that we find everywhere in the educational writings of the time, and that can be translated as "emulation," "rivalry," or "competitive spirit." A sociologist might call it an orientation toward achievement. The last such *concours général* of the ten colleges occurred on August 4, 1793, in the hall of the Jacobin club, with a delegation from the National Convention present "at this august ceremony," reinforced by numerous lesser officials, and with the galleries full of *citoyens* and *citoyennes* "whose great multitude added a brilliant touch to this interesting celebration." Two months later all the Paris colleges except Louis-le-Grand were closed.

The great event of French education of the eighteenth century, however, was the removal of the Jesuits from their colleges, which took place in a series of steps from 1762 to 1764. In the latter year the Jesuit order itself was expelled from France, as it was from other Catholic countries at about the same time. The buildings, facilities, and endowed properties of their hundred-odd colleges passed under the administration of various authorities in various parts of the country. In Paris there was only one Jesuit college, though a large one—Louis-le-Grand. The history illustrated by the documents in the present book begins at this point. Explanation or comment accompanies each document, as needed. What is said here is to keep Louis-le-Grand in more general perspective.

The expulsion of the Jesuits, coinciding with the general movement of thought in intellectual circles, was accompanied by a great outpouring of writings on education. The best-remembered is Rousseau's *Emile*, published in 1762, which, however, in setting up a hypothetical single pupil and single teacher, had little direct bearing on organized education. More relevant to schools was La Chalotais' *Essai sur l'éducation nationale* in 1763. Its very title signalized a new era, in which "national education" became a slogan or watchword. The words "nation" and "national," accompanied by "patriot" and "patriotic," from this time until the Revolution, took on an exciting, broad, and forward-looking significance, somewhat like "the new society" or "the great society" in America at a later time. "National education" was to prepare men as social beings, effective and participating members of a modern society, and not, as was alleged of existing schools, as souls destined for an after-life or mere passive devotees of dead languages. It opposed "monks" and priests as teachers, and wanted lay-men instead. As expressed by its most insistent proponents, it attributed social ills to wrong education, and assumed an almost total plasticity of human nature, by which a prop-erly ordered environment, and especially the right kind of schooling, would produce a better or indeed perfect so-ciety. The idea of national education reverberated for thirty years, became widely accepted in both moderate and ex-treme forms, and heightened by the enthusiasm of the first year of the Revolution, appears as the dominant note in Champagne's plan of 1790, presented to the National Assem-bly, and printed as Item 53 below. A good many professors in the colleges, in addition to independent writers like Rous-seau, took part in all this discussion. Among the most in-teresting of such works is a reply to La Chalotais, written by J.B.L. Crevier, and a little book written by the Abbé Garnier, director of the College of France, called *L'éduca-tion civile*, of which a few pages are given in Item 3.

The wave of writing was accompanied by attempts at practical reform on the part of the government. Throughout the country various royal officials and the high provincial courts, called *parlements*, busied themselves with measures of innovation, primarily for the former Jesuit schools, but with a view to restructuring education as a whole. In the capital, the College of Louis-le-Grand became an object of special attention by the Parlement of Paris. This body, though primarily a supreme court of law, was politically very active in the 1760's, having taken a strong initiative in suppressing the Jesuits, and being involved in disputes over the regulation of the bread and grain trades, rights of taxation, and the nature of representative institutions. A few of its members were genuinely concerned with education, notably Rolland d'Erceville. He remained for twenty years the leading figure in the work of the administrative board to which supervision of the new Louis-le-Grand was assigned.

The first step, with the Jesuits gone, was to make Louis-le-Grand one of the regular full-program colleges of the Paris Faculty of Arts. The opportunity was seized for another sweeping reform, of the kind that the eighteenth-century monarchies regularly engaged in, but that in England was delayed for almost another hundred years. This was a reordering of the old medieval foundations called *bourses*. The funds and scholarships of twenty-eight small colleges were combined with those of the former Jesuit college. This consolidation is the subject of the first document in our collection. The former small colleges continued to have a ghostly existence, and their names can be found in documents as late as 1798; but in truth, after 1763, the old names, to use another American parallel, were only the names of scholarship funds, under which financial debts and credits could be entered. All teaching was at Louis-le-Grand, and all students were treated alike. The new consolidated college was a single institution.

In the disposition of the former Jesuit property there was considerable confusion, and perhaps some fraud, but the new administrative board managed to retain most of it, and also to buy back most of the college library. This was a considerable collection of books, for which a catalogue of 1768 still exists. It records works on a wide range of subjects, mainly of the sixteenth and seventeenth centuries, and largely in Latin. It was not a library for the use of students, but might serve the interests of some teachers or of visiting scholars. We cannot know what books were added after 1768, or what else may have been in the library when it was confiscated in 1794, as described in Item 32 below. Estimated to have 35,000 volumes in 1794, it was

in any case a large library for the time. After many vicis-
situdes, it became the nucleus of the present library of the
University of Paris, the Bibliothèque de la Sorbonne.

It was also in these years that the site was being cleared
for the building of what is now the Pantheon, and before
the Revolution was the church of Sainte-Geneviève. Near
the site was one of the old full-program colleges, Lisieux.
The first plan was to merge it into Louis-le-Grand, but
what happened was that Lisieux was moved, and another
full-program college, Beauvais, was dismantled and combined with Louis-le-Grand instead. In fact, almost all the
original professors at the new Louis-le-Grand were simply
transferred from Beauvais. These particulars also explain
why, after the inclusion of Louis-le-Grand, the Paris Faculty of Arts still had only ten full-program colleges, the
same number as before 1763.

Since the old Jesuit school had been more populous than
the new Louis-le-Grand, room was available for other uses.
Hence the rector of the university and the university tribunal, a body in which all colleges and faculties were represented, but which had never had a place of its own,
were given quarters in the college. Official records and archives were also moved there. Louis-le-Grand thus became,
in a sense, the center of the whole universtiy, and remained
so until the Revolution.

The new college was designed from the beginning as
a place for scholarship students. There were, indeed, students on scholarships in the other nine full-program colleges
in Paris, but they were in a minority, totaling about 300
for all nine colleges, or on the average two or three dozen
in each college. The new Louis-le-Grand, by contrast, was
meant to be a scholarship college in principle. Paying students were also admitted at first. By the 1770's, through
successful management of the combined scholarship properties, which were mainly in urban and rural land and buildings, the income was considerably raised, so that at 450
livres apiece the number of scholarships was increased. The

paying students disappeared (or went to other colleges in Paris); their number fell from about a hundred to about thirty between 1770 and 1789. Well before the Revolution Louis-le-Grand consisted of some 500 scholarship students almost exclusively. There were also students of another small category, usually numbering about a dozen, called the *Jeunes des Langues*, maintained by the government to learn the Arabic and Turkish languages. They were usually the sons of French consuls and interpreters in the Near East, to which they were expected to return.

The original idea had been that the scholarship students, coming from homes of small financial resources, should be trained as teachers to be sent throughout the country in place of the departed Jesuits. For this purpose a teacher-training program was introduced in 1766. We have here, in the last years of Louis XV, the germ of the famous and much-disputed French credential, the *agrégation*, which has always been a certificate of qualification for teaching. The later Ecole Normale Supérieure has also traced its ancestry to this point. The decree of 1766 is abridged as our Item No. 4. It provided for sixty new positions in the ten Paris colleges, to be filled by young men who had completed their *maîtrise ès arts*, and who, after selection in an open and rigorous competition, would spend two years as assistants in the Paris colleges. Future professors were to be recruited from their number. Thus, under government auspices, procedures were laid down for selection, preparation, apprenticeship, compensation, and promotion; a career line was mapped out, and a further step was taken toward the recognition of teaching as a lifetime occupation and learned profession.

One other collateral pre-Revolutionary reform deserves mention, the modernization of the College of France. This old institution, dating from the sixteenth century, was composed of nineteen professors. They were almost all laymen in 1770 except the director, the Abbé J. J. Garnier, who was technically in holy orders but actually a professor of

Hebrew. The professors engaged in very advanced studies and gave public lectures, but they registered no students and gave no examinations or degrees. There were some, including Garnier himself, who saw the possibility of combining the College of France with Louis-le-Grand, or other colleges, into a more organized system of higher education. The government, by a decree of 1772, made the College of France an integral part of the University. Nothing much happened, and the College of France has always remained what it was before, a group of separate professors of high prestige, floating in convenient detachment from the more pressing concerns of the Latin Quarter. It was at the same time, however, that it was so "modernized" that Garnier has been called its second founder. Several chairs were converted to more modern subjects, and new appointments were made. The professors at the College of France went through the Revolution without much disturbance, partly because they were almost all laymen, partly because they were identified with modern subjects, and partly because they had no endowments to be confiscated, having always been employees of the state.

It will be observed that in this discussion of educational changes nothing has yet been said of the curriculum. The subject of studies, at Louis-le-Grand as in other colleges, remained what it had been since the Renaissance, that is mainly Latin, with a little Greek, studied mainly for their literary implications. As in the Middle Ages, Latin was valued as a practical and even indispensable tool for the higher studies in theology, law and medicine. Philosophy courses were actually conducted in the Latin language, though we can see from Item 14 that modern thinkers such as Condillac were not unknown in the Philosophy classrooms. For most students, however, after the grammar level, Latin was a medium for the formation of taste, a guide to proper rules of discourse, a training ground for expression in exact French through careful translation, an introduction to an international world of learning, a convenient means

27

of instilling habits of work, and a basis on which the spirit of emulation could be aroused and prizes fairly awarded. In addition, Latin, supplemented with some ancient history, was a vehicle for the teaching of what would nowadays be called civics and political science. It was felt to have strong contemporary significance. From Cicero, Livy, or Tacitus, or from simplified digests and compilations made for students, one learned of the rise and decay of monarchies and republics, the qualities of a self-sacrificing good citizenship, or the proper deportment and accomplishments of a great statesman. The civic attitudes and rhetorical habits derived from such an education became very obvious after 1789 in debates in the Revolutionary assemblies. It must be remembered, of course, that the most pronounced conservatives and counter-revolutionaries had had the same education.

The most evident change in the curriculum was the cautious introduction of mathematics and modern science. As early as 1753 the Abbé Nollet, professor at Navarre College and a member of the Academy of Sciences, gave a famous course of lectures in experimental physics. That the government built for him an auditorium seating six hundred persons indicates that he had far more hearers than the Philosophy students at Navarre College. About 1780, at Louis-le-Grand and elsewhere, the two years of Philosophy were assigned to separate teachers, one for logic and moral philosophy, the other more especially concerned with physics and chemistry. Inventories made during the Revolution at Louis-le-Grand and other colleges, including many in the provinces, often show an array of experimental or laboratory equipment. Essentially, science in the eighteenth century, in France as elsewhere, developed outside the educational system. It is possible, however, that graduates of the best colleges before the Revolution, those completing their Philosophy, had as intelligent a conception of the science of their own time as American college graduates of the later twentieth century, many of whom neither study nor are even influenced by the exact sciences.

What is hardest to trace is the change in the internal atmosphere of the classroom, or in what teachers actually said to their students, even with the continuing and almost exclusive concentration on Latin. Some of the books written by professors before the Revolution make it hard to believe that they were mere pedants or drillmasters. The classics could have a highly radicalizing effect, replete as they were with both talk and examples of "liberty." The ancient world was not without its revolutions, and anyone opposing despotism or priestcraft could draw on it abundantly for examples. It was said of one of the professors at Louis-le-Grand, the Abbé Audrein (admittedly in a piece of counter-revolutionary propaganda written some years later) that he had once cried out in his classroom, *Vive la liberté, mes amis, loin de nous la cagoterie*, which can be rendered as "Here's to liberty, my friends, and away with rubbish!" It is believable enough, in the light of Audrein's book of 1790, of which a few pages are reproduced in Item 17 below.

In any case, in judging the curriculum, it is necessary to remember the objectives of education at the time. Here we run into another problem of meaning, and hence of translation. The French words *éducation* and *instruction* generally mean what they do in English, and are sometimes interchangeable. But sometimes they take on different or complementary meanings, and are used together. In our translations, if the phrase "education and instruction" seems redundant, this distinction should be remembered. "Instruction" meant the conveying of knowledge; "education" meant the formation of character, instillation of motives and attitudes, or development of the whole human being. They referred respectively to the cognitive and the moral. In the latter connection there was a great deal of emphasis on religion, or at least on the religious teachings and practices of the church. Education was supposed to develop and reward *vertu* as well as intelligence. The word *vertu* was exceedingly common in the French of the day, right down to Robespierre's famous pairing of "virtue and terror." But to translate it always as "virtue" would produce an undeservedly ridiculous effect in modern English; it is sometimes translated in our documents as "personal qualities," "good conduct" or "moral behavior." As for education, no one supposed that mere instruction was enough, that the curriculum was decisive, or that the purpose of schooling was to convey a particular body of up-to-date subject matter. Such ideas were more characteristic of the Central Schools which operated under the Directory. In the colleges before 1789 the announced aim was to form mind and character, taste and judgement, incentive and emulation, habits of work and fluency in communication; to teach young people to live with each other, to accept proper discipline and authority, and to recognize duties that were described as duties to oneself, one's family, society, religion, the king, and finally God. It was thought that Latin was a means toward such ends. Probably also, if conservative educators were so steadfast in defense of Latin, it was because it was the one thing that they knew how to teach, in the strict sense of giving "instruction."

The great question is whether, given the strong impetus of reform since the 1760's, the French educational system could have adapted itself constructively to the needs of more modern times if there had been no Revolution. The question cannot be answered, but it is well to ask it in assessing both the old system and the one which followed the Revolution, and which proved to be fairly conservative and fairly rigid. Without the Revolution, the reforming trend might well have continued. Colleges might have made room for more modern subjects, not only in the sciences, but in modern literatures and modern history, as they did in other countries. Increasing numbers of laymen might have gone into teaching, and the church itself, including its teaching clergy, might have been less preponderantly opposed to modern trends if there had been no revolution. On the other hand, we may doubt, as French republican and other liberal writers have done, whether the colleges were really reformable. The reason would not especially be that they were stagnant or backward. Any reform movement generates the question of who is to guide or control the reforms, that is, the question of authority. This is what happened in France in the 1760's and after. The Parlement of Paris and the provincial parlements, which took a strong lead in the reform of education, were in other respects self-interested and privileged bodies, increasingly identified with the maintenance of class distinctions. Their opposition, as much as any other cause, blocked the royal reforming efforts, especially in matters of taxation, by which the old monarchy might have been saved. The bishops contended with the parlements, the royal officials, and the local boards which supervised educational changes; the nineteenth-century conflict between church and state for control of education was already foreshadowed before 1789. Within the colleges themselves many professors obstructed the proposed changes. The very proliferation of interest that the reform movement brought about, the participation of many persons of varying purposes and degrees of competence or incompetence, led to a confusion that offered a standing invitation to royal officials to intervene, as it did also to the prelates of the Catholic Church. We arrive at the conclusion that a desirable gradualism was unlikely in France, in education as in the *ancien régime* as a whole, not because of an unwillingness for reform on the part of the authorities, but because of the power of entrenched opposition, the strength of vested interests, and the confusion of jurisdictions into which the country was divided.

The test of a school lies in the graduates it produces, and we may ask this question also of the pre-Revolutionary colleges and of Louis-le-Grand in particular. The colleges produced the Revolutionary generation, a generation abounding in intelligence, new ideas, and courage; on the other hand, both the utopianism of some and the blind obstinacy of others may be attributed in some measure to inadequacies in their studies. At Louis-le-Grand, the original idea of making it a nursery of teachers, or primarily a teacher-training institute, materialized only in part. Some of its students did become teachers, as did Champagne himself, or Audrein. Three members of the Paris faculties of letters and sciences, as set up by Napoleon, had been educated before 1789 at Louis-le-Grand. One of these was the physicist J. B. Biot. Many others went into careers other than teaching. Unfortunately there are no complete lists of students before the Revolution, so that information is sporadic. The best-remembered of students at Louis-le-Grand in this period was Maximilien Robespierre. Others whose fame is due to the Revolution include Maximilien's brother Augustin, Camille Desmoulins, Lebrun-Tondu, who was foreign minister to the Brissot government of 1792, and François Noël, who was French emissary to the Batavian Republic in 1796. As a scholarship school for needy boys with limited prospects in the old society, Louis-le-Grand naturally produced men who welcomed extensive social changes. The list would also include J. B. Dumouchel, who was rector of the University of Paris from 1786 to 1791, a deputy to the Estates General, and much later, like Noël, a high official in the Napoleonic educational structure. Quatremère de Quincy, though moderately involved in the Revolution, is best remembered for a long career as a historian of art. There were also the refugees. The first Catholic bishop of Boston, Massachusetts, Jean Cheverus, was a graduate of Louis-le-Grand, as was the third Catholic bishop of New York. Such French priests, driven from France in the 1790's, were important in establishing the first Catholic hierarchy in the United States.

As for Jean-François Champagne himself, only a bare outline of his life can be reconstructed. He was born in 1751 at Semur-en-Auxois in Burgundy. He died in 1813 in Paris at his home at 39 rue M. le Prince. As a deceased

member of the Institute of France he was honored by a
eulogy, pronounced by Quatremère de Quincy, who had
known him as a fellow student at Louis-le-Grand, and tells
us that Champagne had spent fifty-five years in the college,
as student, teacher, and head.

His father is described only as a "bourgeois of Semur,"
which is to say a minor notable of a very small town. A
great-uncle, Simon Menassier, had founded three or four
scholarships to send boys to Sainte-Barbe College in Paris.
These were family scholarships to which the Menassier family had the right of nomination, and Jean-François Champagne and his father before him had each held one of them.
The Sainte-Barbe scholarships were among those consolidated into Louis-le-Grand. It would therefore seem that
Champagne, twelve years old in 1763, was among the boys
transferred to Louis-le-Grand in that year, and lived
through the experiences to which all the documents in our
collection refer, beginning with the first. He took his *maîtrise ès arts* in 1774, and was appointed Professor of the
Second in 1778.

He was apparently one of those whose number was increasing before the Revolution, who made a career of teaching but were members of the clergy in hardly more than
a nominal sense. He took only minor orders as sub-deacon,
which however involved celibacy and wearing the cassock.
In the 1780's he belonged to one of the Masonic lodges
in Paris, in which new and progressive ideas were presumably discussed. In 1790, with two other professors, he prepared the plan of educational reform which appears as Item
53 below. In this plan he showed himself open to curricular
changes and to lay control of the schools through the organs
of civil government. He also wanted to break out of the
Latin Quarter by distributing the existing colleges throughout the city, and even to dissolve Louis-le-Grand itself as
a scholarship school, by dividing the scholarships equally
among all the Paris colleges. It had perhaps become apparent
to him, in the new society with new principles of equality,

that there was some disadvantage in segregating the poorer students from their more affluent fellows. Since his plan brought him to the attention of the Revolutionary authorities as a reasonable reformer, and because he took the civil oath required of the clergy, he was made principal of the college in 1791.

Like others, he went along willingly with the Revolution while hoping to check or guide it. In the great radical stirring of the Paris sections in 1793 he played his part. He was active in his own section, called the Panthéon-Français, which was nearly coterminous with the Latin Quarter. We know that on June 2, 1793, the very day on which the armed *sectionnaires* forced the Convention to expel the Girondins, the revolutionary committee of the Panthéon-Français section was meeting daily at Louis-le-Grand itself, and that Champagne was one of its four members. He was still a member in the following September, when in the mounting political frenzy he was himself denounced as a suspect. There is no evidence that he was ever arrested. As the dechristianization movement reached its height late in 1793, he gave up his religious orders, and married. His wife was the widow of P. H. Lebrun-Tondu, whom he had known as a fellow student at Louis-le-Grand, and who was executed as a Girondin in December 1793. Contemporaries believed that he married her in part to protect her and her children, and this would explain why she remarried so soon after her first husband's death; if so, it was hazardous for him, at the height of the Terror, to befriend a woman so closely connected with a discredited party. She outlived him, as we know from a letter of hers after his death, concerning his pension. After the Terror he, like others, deplored the destructive madness that it had entailed.

Champagne was also a scholar, who in 1797 published a translation of the *Politics* of Aristotle, which had not been translated into French since 1568. His reference to Aristotle in a letter of 1795 suggests that he was at work

on the translation even then, when he was desperately strug-
gling to keep his college open. Known as a Greek scholar
and as a good republican, he became a member of the new
Institute of France, in its class of moral and political sciences. He was also elected in 1798 to the lower house of
the national legislature, the Council of Five Hundred, but he
declined to serve. He remained an academic administrator,
director of the college in all its successive phases, and hence
the first head of the Imperial Lycée. In 1800 he published
a small book on the organization of education, which is
abridged as the last item of this present collection. In 1803,
as war resumed between France and Great Britain, and
as his contribution to the war effort, he published a book
on the freedom of the seas, analyzing the conflicting argu-
ments of Grotius and Selden. In 1804 he was made a che-
valier of the Legion of Honor. He retired as head of the
Imperial Lycée in 1810 with a pension equal to his salary
of 5,000 livres, and died three years later. As Quatremère
said in his eulogy, Champagne kept teaching alive at a time
when all teaching was destroyed, he remained at his post
in a storm where no pilot could hold the helm, and his
college was an ark from which, after the flood, the world
of public instruction could be renewed.

A few words may be of interest on the present writer's
philosophy of translation. The first rule has been that everything should be translated, and nothing left in the original
language; hence the following pages are not so marred by
italics denoting foreign words as this Introduction has been.
An exception is made for Louis-le-Grand itself and a few
such words as "monsieur." A second rule is to do justice
to the original; occasionally a word or two is left out if
translation gives an unduly verbose effect, or a word may
be added to sharpen the author's actual meaning. The third
and most important rule has been to translate accurately,
but with enough freedom to produce natural English. This
involves constantly reminding oneself that French is a Latin
language, and English a Germanic language with massive

Latin and French infusions. Certain considerations of word order follow, but above all it must be remembered that the English vocabulary is far larger and more varied than the French. The most common trap is to use the same word when it occurs in both languages. The *grand maître temporel* may not sound any more "grand" to a Frenchman than "business manager." *Eventuel* does not mean "eventual," and *république* before the Revolution is sometimes best rendered as "commonwealth." In some places, especially in academic terminology, a close reader may detect American rather than British usage.

It has been hard to settle upon the right equivalents for two words with which the whole book is concerned, *bourse* and *boursier*. The *bourse*—related etymologically to "bursar" and "purser" and to the Bourse or stock-exchange in Paris—originally meant something like a pouch in which money was kept, and the *boursier* was the person who was entitled to it. In the Paris colleges a distinction was drawn between *petites bourses* and *grandes bourses*, so that we find reference to *petits boursiers* and *grands boursiers*, the latter including students in the three professional faculties, sometimes the "philosophers," and also "masters" as distinct from professors. In English their *bourses* might be called fellowships, and they themselves be known as fellows. In the colleges, however, the great majority of *boursiers* were younger boys, and it has proved impracticable to make any distinction in translation. All *bourses* are called "scholarships," and all *boursiers*, since "scholar" means something else, are called "scholarship students," or occasionally "scholarship holders," and only rarely "scholars" to avoid repetition of these cumbersome phrases.

During the Revolution the whole vocabulary of the old educational system fell into disrepute. Hence we find *bourses* called simply "free places," and *boursiers* referred to as *élèves de la patrie* or *élèves nationaux*. They are here called "national students." The word *patrie*, incidentally, which some seem to think untranslatable, is rendered simply as "country," in the belief that "fatherland" is a Germanism with no real currency in the English language. In the vocabulary of education, the very words *université, faculté* and *collège* were for a time rejected. The twenty-two pre-Revolutionary universities disappeared, the faculties of theology (at Paris, the Sorbonne) were abolished, the faculties of medicine became "schools of health," and no faculties of law existed for ten years. The College of Louis-le-Grand was called the *Collège de l'Egalité* for three years, then the *Institut des Boursiers*, then the *Prytanée français*.

In the attempt to find new names for new institutions, use was made of certain Greek words that were then coming into both French and English. The French gave them a French form, *musée, athénée, lycée*, and *prytanée*. In English they were Latinized as museum, atheneum (or Athenaeum in Boston and elsewhere), lyceum, and prytaneum. The parallel suggests how the unfamiliar "prytaneum" should be pronounced, but the real problem arises with the translation of *lycée*. This word was introduced in the 1780's, like "lyceum" in English, to describe a privately organized series of public lectures. It was also proposed, both by Champagne in 1790 and in the more famous Condorcet report of 1792, as the name for a place of higher education in a new national system. Later, of course, in 1802, it became the word for a kind of advanced secondary school, and as such is used in English to designate such French schools today. In the following translations the Napoleonic creation is called a "lycée," and to avoid confusion the institutions proposed by Champagne or others before 1802 are called "lyceums." The word "prytaneum," in French as in English, relapsed after 1800 into its purely antiquarian meaning, referring to a certain public place in ancient Athens. One other Latinized Greek word occurs in Champagne's plan of 1790—*gymnasium*. It was at this time that the Germans began to call their newly improved secondary schools *gymnasia*. The word had been used in France as well as Germany in the international Latin of the schools, and it meant a place of instruction. It was natural to propose it as a new word for a school in 1790, but it never caught on in French, and it is evident from other documents in this book that *gymnastique* already referred to purely physical exercise.

It has seemed best to arrange the materials in chronological order. They are, however, in two sections. The first section carries the narrative, and most of its items are short. The second section contains two longer pieces, one the manuscript plan written by Champagne and two colleagues, and submitted to the Constituent Assembly in 1790; the other a condensation of his book of 1800, at the time when Bonaparte and others were turning their minds to the construction of a new educational system.

In the translations all matter added by the editor is bracketed. Footnotes that are not bracketed occur in the originals. Words italicized in the translations are italicized in the originals.

Annex I

The successive names of the college synchronized with the names of successive governments:

College of Louis-le-Grand to 1792	Louis XV to 1774 Louis XVI, 1774–1792 National Constituent Assembly, 1789–91 Legislative Assembly, September 1791 to September 1792
Equality College September 1792 to October 1795	National Convention, September 1792 to October 1795
Scholarship Institute October 1795 to July 1798	Directory, October 1795 to November 1799
French Prytaneum July 1798 to March 1800	
College of Paris 1800	Consulate, November 1799 to May 1804
Lycée of Paris 1803	
Imperial Lycée 1804	Empire, 1804–1814
Royal College of Louis-le-Grand 1814–48	Restored Monarchy after 1814

The term "lycée" was again adopted during the Second Empire and retained by the Third and subsequent Republics.

Annex II

The ten full-program colleges of the Faculty of Arts of the University of Paris from 1763 to 1793, with dates of their foundation:

1302	Cardinal Lemoine
1304	Navarre
1312	Harcourt
1314	Montaigu
1316	Plessis
1336	Lisieux
1362	La Marche
1569	Grassins
1661	Mazarin (or Quatre-Nations)
1763	Louis-le-Grand (1564)

Louis-le-Grand, as organized in 1763, had nothing in common with the college of the same name founded by the Jesuits in 1564, except that it occupied the same buildings and received some of the endowed funds, the furnishings and the library. J. F. Champagne, writing during the Revolution, thought of it as about thirty years old.

The more famous Sorbonne, founded in 1257, never belonged to the Faculty of Arts, but was a place of residence and instruction for the Faculty of Theology. Its name came associated with science and letters only in the nineteenth century.

I

THE COLLEGE OF LOUIS-LE-GRAND

1. A new college for scholarship students is established

THE background and meaning of this document, which launched the new College of Louis-le-Grand, are explained in the Introduction. The plan to improve the use of the old endowments was successful; where they produced only 195 scholarships when consolidated in 1764, the number had increased through more efficient management to about 500 in the 1780's.

Letters patent on the consolidation of small-college scholarships and the establishment of a provisional central office of the University of Paris at the college of Louis-le-Grand.

November 21, 1763

Louis, by the grace of God king of France and Navarre. . . .

Our attention to all that concerns the education and instruction of our subjects, especially those whose means do not allow them to enjoy the same advantages as others, has persuaded us that nothing would be more useful than to combine in the same College [Louis-le-Grand] all those scholarship endowments in various colleges of our good city of Paris in which the disappearance of income has long since brought an end to public instruction. By enabling the scholars of the said colleges to profit from the public exercises at Louis-le-Grand, we will restore the original situation in which the scholars had the advantage of instruction in their colleges by the masters of our University;

43

and we will obtain for them a sounder education in morals and discipline, which had been greatly undermined by division among various decayed colleges.

We will charge our University with continuing oversight through a board composed of its principal members, and by so useful an institution we will form a prolific nursery of teachers who are needed by our State, and who will spread the spirit of emulation that is so desirable for the education of our subjects.

We will carefully maintain at the same time the rights and intentions of the founders; and since we have grounds to expect that the administration that we will establish for all properties of the said colleges will increase their income, the use made of this income according to regulations that we will prescribe will even reinforce the rights of the said founders, since a larger number of sons of poor families, whom the founders had principally in mind, will feel the benefit through an increase in the value of their scholarships. . . .

We are the more determined on this arrangement from having observed, on the advice of the most capable persons in our University, to whom our court of Parlement with our good pleasure has entrusted the examination of this important question, that the University regards this consolidation as the only way to reform abuses that have slipped into the said colleges or to render so many scholarship foundations truly useful to our State. . . . In testimony of our affection for the University, we have found no more appropriate use for the surplus buildings of the College of Louis-le-Grand than for the University to house its tribunal, hold its assemblies, and deposit its archives there. . . .

We hope that the example of a wise and sound administration will enable our University, together with our said Court of Parlement, to complete our views for the improvement of education, by proposing the most suitable plans, without delay, for the reform or greater perfection of the full-program colleges of our said University, and even of all our realm. . . .

2. Social origins of the students

THIS item is the only one in the present collection that is not an original document. It is taken from a compendious three-volume history of Louis-le-Grand published in 1921 by one of its professors of history, Gustave Dupont-Ferrier. In this passage he reports his impression of the social and geographical backgrounds of the students, formed in the course of his prolonged and detailed exploration of the records. In the absence of any organized statistics from the period itself, the passage gives an excellent picture of Louis-le-Grand after 1763.

The college drew fewer of its students from the aristocracy than it had in the days of the Jesuits. The thought that it was if anything less "popular" after 1792 is worthy of comment. During the Terror and under the Directory the families willing to have their sons at Louis-le-Grand, or "Equality College," were those most intensely committed to the Revolution and most hostile to the former status of the nobility, the church, and the royal family. The heads of these families were by no means lower-class; they were a "revolutionary bourgeoisie" of men in business and government, science and the professions, reinforced by skilled workers, shopkeepers, and property owners of many descriptions. The sons of such men at Louis-le-Grand, before the Revolution, formed part of a broader social mixture which included the more noble and the more humble at its extremes.

Before the Revolution the scholarship students were generally classified by diocese, rather than by province, civil district, seigneury or town. The ecclesiastical origin of most of the endowments is shown in this way, as in so many others. . . . The part of France most productive of scholarship students was the territory between the Loire, the English Channel and the northeastern frontier; hence, Flanders and Cambrésis, Ponthieu, Artois, Picardy, Normandy, Brittany, Maine, Touraine, Ile de France, Champagne, the county of Rethel, and the two Burgundies. Besides this group, one other region yielded many scholars: the Massif Central and adjoining regions, notably Auvergne, Velay, Vivarais, Limousin, Périgord, and Bourbonnais. The ecclesiastical province of Narbonne was an annex. . . .

The presence of paying students, unlike that of scholarship holders, reflected choices made by their parents. By noting the homes of the parents we can judge the force of attraction of our college on various regions of France and on some foreign countries. It seems certain that more than half the paying students came from families residing in Paris or its immediate environs as far as twenty or thirty leagues away. There were some from Picardy, Champagne and Lorraine, a few from Anjou and Brittany, almost none from Normandy and the South. Colonials and foreigners were even more conspicuously absent. The small group of Language students may be added, which included a few boys born of French parents at Constantinople and in the Levant. Until the end of the Old Regime our college was neither mainly Parisian not yet truly national; too many provinces were not represented. . . .

In a word, by geographical origin, our establishment after 1763 was very different from what it had been in the time of the Jesuit Fathers; boys from the South, the West, the colonies and foreign countries no longer took the road to old Louis-le-Grand.

The same shift occurred in the social composition of both paying and scholarship students. A few nobles continued to come; we find boys in the college from the families of Castlenau, La Morandière, Saint-James, Clermont-Tonnerre, and Rohan-Soubise. But after 1763 they were the exceptions; the higher nobility is hardly represented; the nobility of the robe is, however, less rare. The new Louis-le-Grand received above all the sons of subordinate officers in the households of the king or princes; sons of lawyers, attorneys, notaries, court clerks, and bailiffs; of mathematicians, professors, writers and interpreters; also of postal officials. Even more frequently the college welcomed the sons of drapers, dealers in linens, and cotton and woollen merchants; grocers and grain traders; hosiers and haberdashers; jewelers, gilders, and purveyors of mineral waters; to which may be added the progeny of master tailors, cabinet makers, masons, locksmiths, bakers, and "chandlers"; in short, the offspring of the bourgeois of Paris and other cities, including men in business or in substantial agriculture.

The social milieu from which the scholarship students came was apparently much the same as for the paying students; there was generally little distinction, except for fewer coats of arms. Noble scholarship boys were the exception, but would include the viscounts of Montfort and Ségur, and the families of Vareilles, Guesdon de Beauchesne, Saint-Marseault, La Corgue, du Fresne de Virel, Montpesat and d'Olonne. The lower robe and plain commoners were the rule. Sons of coopers, glaziers, blacksmiths, binders, shop-keepers, etc., were legion. A quarter of a century before the Revolution the college was openly democratized.

Nevertheless, even after the night of the 4th of August, "noble scholarship students" continued to be appointed in 1790. On the whole, indeed, it seems that the social milieu of the scholarship students was slightly higher from 1792 to 1797 than it had been a few years earlier; a third of our youth were now the sons of civil servants; a third had fathers in commerce, agriculture, or industry; and a third of the fathers were army officers, landowners, or simply men who lived on an income. It is very certain that the social classes fraternized at this time. Sons of hat-makers and stocking-merchants, barrel-makers and grocers, wine-growers, innkeepers, and house-porters rubbed elbows with those of generals, representatives of the people, and members of the Institute. Descendants of Alain Chartier, the great Corneille, and de Gressot sat on the same benches.

3. An abortive suggestion for a modern university

WE HAVE here a suggestion that never developed very far, but that reflects the diversity of academic planning in the 1760's.

It was made by J. J. Garnier, director of the College of France and professor of Hebrew, in a little book called *De l'Education Civile* published in 1765. The College of France had never had any actual students. Garnier's idea was to create an actual student body for it by drawing on some of the older scholarship holders at the new Louis-le-Grand. There would thus be something like graduate work in the arts and sciences, corresponding to the professional studies in law, medicine, and theology. Such an arrangement might have resembled the development that was then beginning at Göttingen and other German universities, where the practice of lecturing and publication on a variety of subjects was opening the way to the modern university of the nineteenth and twentieth centuries.

The French government a few years later integrated the College of France into the University of Paris, but conservative opposition in the traditional faculties was such that no consequences of any importance followed.

The Royal College [College of France], founded by Francis I for the reformation and renewal of studies, has been in a position for two centuries to announce to all Europe, as it were, the changes and the expansion that have occurred in public education. It was at the Royal College that we saw the beginning of the study of Greek and Oriental languages, Geometry, Astronomy, Medicine, and sound Eloquence. The Royal Professors, besides the services rendered by their lectures, have from the beginning published a great many works in matters pertaining to their respective subjects. No literary body in Europe can count, in proportion to its size, such a great number of publishing scholars. Hence our kings have always honored this Company with their special protection. Of course the weakening of learning and the frivolous spirit that have overtaken our literature have reduced the number of students in a School that teaches only serious matters, and that seems to exist only to improve the talents of grown men. But despite this kind of desertion the Royal College can still be regarded as the Seminary of Academies. The youth who come to it have finished their schooling and are attracted only by love of the work. That is precisely the kind of students that we want for the new institution that we propose. . . .

The second place suited for the new establishment is the College of Louis-le-Grand or the Scholarship College. The purpose there is to bring together young men from almost all provinces in the kingdom, to whom the State offers a decent subsistence and a distinguished education. These scholars should be considered to be national students. It is appropriate to try on them an experiment that can only be to their own advantage as well as in the general interest of society. To add something to their education is to fulfill the wish of the founders, who brought them to the capital to receive a better education; it is to share the views of the University, which has assembled them in one house in order to give better attention to this portion of youth that is especially entrusted to it; finally, it is to comply with the views of a wise Monarch who has announced, in his Letters Patent on consolidation of the small colleges, that his intention was to use the new College as a nursery of trained teachers, who would then disperse to spread the spirit of emulation in all parts of the kingdom.

These two schools—the Royal College and the College of Louis-le-Grand—will be open to all who desire to profit from them and will suffice for the present, until time and experience will have shown more clearly what may be expected. There will be time to multiply them if the event comes up to our hopes.

4. A program of teacher training is launched

ALTHOUGH it did not adopt Garnier's plan (Item 3), the French government devised a program of practice teaching for the training of future professors in the colleges. As has been ex-

plained in the Introduction, the *agrégation* was introduced in
1766. It disappeared in the Revolution, but was later reintroduced, and has charactered French education ever since. Its
perennial features are already evident in this initial decree:
it is for teaching rather than for original scholarship, it has
a validity throughout the country, it varies by category of
subject (philosophy, rhetoric, grammar), it is highly competitive, and in principle only as many candidates pass as there
may be available positions in which to place them.

A slightly later decree of August 1766 specified the subject
matter of the competition. The candidates, with variations according to the three categories, were to take three kinds of
tests: one a written composition, one an oral argument or an
explanation of the kinds of readings that students would do,
and the third a kind of practice lecture, consisting of a half-hour
of connected discourse and a half-hour of questions and discussion conducted by one of the candidates with the others.
At Louis-le-Grand, to prepare for this competition young men
were allowed to retain their scholarships for another year after
the *maîtrise ès arts*, and to hear lectures by professors at the
College of France. But there were never more than a handful
of such candidates, and the whole development was interrupted
by the Revolution. Probably the candidates are included under
Philosophy in the table in Item 11 below.

The word *agrégation* etymologically means "taking into the
flock," so that an *agrégé* is one so taken in, that is, a fellow
or an associate. The phrase in the following text is *docteurs
agrégés*, and they are here called "associate doctors."

*Letters patent establishing
associate doctors in the Faculty
of Arts of the University of Paris*

May 3, 1766

Louis, by the grace of God king of France and
Navarre. . . .

Article I. There shall be established in perpetuity in the
Faculty of Arts of our University of Paris sixty places for
associate doctors, of which one-third shall be especially attached to the teaching of Philosophy, one-third to the teach-

ing of literature in the Rhetoric classes, and the other third to the teaching of grammar and elements of the humanities in the Fourth, Fifth and Sixth classes. . . .

II. The said associate doctors will be required to reside in Paris, to attend assemblies of the said Faculty, to assist in teaching exercises, in committees, in student compositions for University prizes, in the annual contest and in other activities in which the Faculty may need their services. They will also act as substitutes for professors and teachers who are unable to meet their classes because of illness or other legitimate reasons, and be present at the defense of philosophy theses and other public exercises of the students, in order to engage in disputation against them or to propose questions when required to do so by the person presiding. . . .

III. It is our wish that, beginning next October 1, no one may be chosen as professor or teacher [in the ten colleges] except from among those who are at present professors or teachers in the said colleges, or among the associate doctors attached to the category in which the vacancy occurs, and actually qualified according to conditions as set forth below. . . .

IV. The said associate doctors will have preference in choices made by principals of the said colleges to fill positions as assistant principal, masters of quarters, or others relative to instruction. . . .

V. The said associate doctors may accept appointment as assistant librarians in our University, or even as principal, professor, or teacher in one of the colleges of our realm approved in our edict of February 1763 . . . [and later nevertheless] be chosen to fill chairs in our said University of Paris. . . .

VI. There shall be paid, by the receiver of the Faculty of Arts, a sum of 200 livres as an honorarium to each of the said associate doctors, which may not be reduced because of honorariums they may receive from other positions that they are qualified to hold. . . .

VII. Appointments as associate doctors will be made by competition. We wish that the competition shall first be opened in the next month of October . . . and thereafter annually in the same month, to fill as many places as may then be vacant, or which it may be fitting to add. . . .

VIII. The judges of the said competition will be seven in number, to include the rector of our University and six doctors of the Faculty of Arts. . . .

IX. The said judges will be determined by lot by the tribunal of the Faculty of Arts. . . .

X. Only those will be admitted to the said competition who have given evidence of their Catholicity, good morals and conduct, who are masters of arts of our said University or another university of our realm, and who have attained the age of twenty-two years for associates attached to the chairs of philosophy, or of twenty for those attached to the lower chairs.

XI. The competition will take place in our College of Louis-le-Grand in a hall set aside for this purpose; and it will be announced and published two months in advance in our good city of Paris, with mention of the number and kind of places to be filled. . . .

5. Regulations of the college

THESE regulations, though issued in the name of the king himself, were in fact drawn up by four senior professors of the University of Paris, and then approved by the Parlement. It is noteworthy that these high authorities took such a detailed interest in the internal minutiae of Louis-le-Grand. Endless small matters of daily life are foreseen, and a clear-cut, rational structure and distribution of responsibilities are laid out. The dominant note is one of planning and academic bureaucracy under the authority of the state, for the good of the students and the benefit of society.

Regulations, being normative rather than descriptive, offer better evidence of an ideal than of what actually happened. It is said in the preamble, however, that these regulations are in line with existing practice in the Paris colleges, and it can readily be believed that life at Louis-le-Grand went on very much as the following articles indicate. They suggest a pervading religious atmosphere, an insistence on wholesome moral training, a fear of worldly influence from outside, a close attention to civility and good manners, an enforcement of rules with a minimum of punishment, a lack of privacy for either pupils or teachers, a strict classroom discipline, an exact daily schedule relieved by carefully supervised recreations and excursions—all to be suffused, in principle, by benevolence on the part of the school administration and warm personal association of the younger teachers with their pupils.

The regulations are so detailed that much abridgment is necessary.

Regulations
for the internal exercises
of the
College of Louis-le-Grand

December 4, 1769

Louis, by the grace of God king of France and Navarre:

TITLE I

[8 articles]

On Superiors and Masters in General

1. All superiors and masters being instituted for the same purpose, they should be animated by the same spirit and the same zeal, and live in harmony and peace.

2. Since the value of education consists less in correcting the faults of youth than in preventing them so far as possi-

ble, all masters will be scrupulous in finding a way to help their pupils avoid the mistakes arising from their own negligence.

3. It is very important for them to know the character of the young persons entrusted to them, and to inspire in them by their instruction, and above all by their example, the love of right conduct, and hard work.

4. They will not limit themselves to cultivating the talents of their pupils, but will regard it as a first duty to develop their characters, especially by inspiring them with sentiments of piety and religion.

5. They will use no severity until they have exhausted all other means of making an impression on an honest and sensitive mind.

Title II

[26 articles]

On the Principal

8. The office of principal has two parts. First, its object is the public instruction of which he is the head, and the classes and all class exercises of which he is the supervising inspector. His duties in this connection are regulated by the statutes, decrees, and usages of the University. They consist chiefly in selecting as teachers men who are virtuous, learned, and skilled in the art of teaching. In this selection he follows what is prescribed in Article 10 of the regulation attached to the letters patent of August 10, 1766. It is also his duty to maintain a good understanding and union among the teachers, to see that the classes are regularly and exactly conducted, to distribute the pupils among different classes in a way most appropriate to the success of their studies, to arouse a spirit of emulation, to be present at the defense of theses and other public exercises, etc.

9. The second part of the office of principal has as its object the internal government of the college, that is, of

the teachers to be put in charge of the education of youth, and of the pupils whether paying boarders or scholarship students of whom the college is composed. . . .

14. He will consider it the first and most essential of his duties to give instruction himself in the truths and maxims of religion. . . .

17. He will be present every day at mass. . . .

18. He will take care to remove from the college any book that might in any way be damaging to religion, good morals, or government. He will allow no pictures, prints, or drawings that may be offensive to decency.

Title III

[12 articles]

On the Assistant Principals

Title IV

[12 articles]

On the Prefects

1. There will be two prefects in the college, one for the students in Philosophy, and one for those in rhetoric and the younger classes. . . .

4. The upper prefect will frequently visit the philosophy classes, not only to maintain good order but to arouse and sustain the spirit of emulation and give direction to the studies. He will regularly be present at the examinations which Philosophy students take twice a year, and will ask questions when necessary.

5. The prefect of the humanities and grammar classes will visit in turn the class exercises and the sessions devoted to preparation and the correction of pupils' papers. Sometimes he will only observe how the assistant master gives his instruction. At other times he will take the floor and

offer instruction himself, especially if he thinks it necessary for the pupils' advancement. He will give the advice needed to arouse and sustain emulation, and will always take all possible care not to undermine the authority of the assistant master.

9. In the absence of the principal, the prefects will be charged with replying to parents who inquire about their children.

TITLE V

[24 articles]

On the Assistant Masters

1. The assistant masters are appointed by the principal, who will select them, so far as possible, from among students of the college . . . who have been admitted as associates in the Faculty of Arts.

4. They are charged immediately with all that affects the education of their pupils. They should consider that they are not simply instructors concerned with studies but are men chosen to maintain by example as well as by words the good order of the house, and to encourage religion, piety, and purity of morals along with a love of study.

5. They will make every effort to know their pupils well, to win their confidence by kind and forthright manners, without, however, falling into familiarities that cannot fail to undermine their authority.

6. They will avoid equally both an air of too much gravity or austerity and too much indulgence. Their reprimands and corrections will be given in a way that tempers bitterness, prevents the pupils from falling into discouragement, and makes them desire to do better.

7. Before employing any humiliating mode of correction they will make an effort to recall their pupils to a sense of duty; to win them over they will use demonstrations of friendship, privately given advice, or even threats, and

in short anything that may make an impression on a sensitive being. If, however, it seems necessary to use serious punishments, they will not take it upon themselves to inflict them or order them inflicted, but will have recourse to the authority of the principal, or of the assistant principal or prefect of their division.

16. Each assistant master will often examine the books that his pupils are reading; he will take away those that are dangerous to morals or religion, and not allow even those that are simply useless or might engender a taste for frivolity. He will prevent pupils from lending books to each other without his consent.

17. Though it is natural to give particular attention to pupils whose abilities are most conducive to success in their studies, the assistant masters will remember that they have a duty to all; that those in whom they see lesser abilities have all the more need of their help; and that it often happens that boys of slower mind, cultivated by skillful and patient hands, have become valuable men for the commonwealth.

18. They will endeavor to instill in their students the good manners that are so rare among the young, and yet so likely to win them esteem. It is only gradually that youth acquires such manners, and the best lesson in this matter is example.

19. Neither in the halls of the building nor on the outings from the school will they allow any dangerous or improper game. They will not let permitted games be played for money.

TITLE VI

[19 articles]

On Scholarship Students and Paying Boarders

1. The college being destined by the royal benevolence to lodge the scholarship students formerly scattered among

the small colleges lacking the full program of study, and to enable them to receive a solid and Christian education and so become useful to the State and to religion, the persons named by those having the right of nomination to any scholarship in the combined colleges, and existing in the Faculty of Arts, are required to present themselves to the Faculty in order to enjoy the scholarship to which they have been appointed.

2. On arriving at the college they will proceed to the principal and present him with their letters of appointment, their baptismal extract, and their certificate of good conduct. All these papers will be communicated by the principal to the examiners for certification.

6. If the principal and the examiners find these papers in order, the candidate will be admitted to the examination at a day and hour indicated to him by the principal.

7. If after the examination it is found, in the judgment of the principal and the four examiners, that the young candidate does not have the qualities necessary for his studies to be useful, or that he is not yet ready for any of the classes held in the college, he will not be admitted; but if he gives evidence of suitable qualities and capacity he will be admitted, not yet as a full scholar, but simply as an aspirant, pending the time set for a further examination, that is for one year.

11. During the year of probation the scholar will enjoy the fruits of the scholarship to which he has been named; and if in that interval he fulfills the hopes placed in him he will be admitted definitively in full possession of his scholarship. But if he seems absolutely incapable of instruction, or shows any capital fault, the principal will confer with the examiners; and a plurality of votes will decide whether he shall be sent away from the college. This will however be carried out only with all appropriate precautions which prudence demands.

12. Scholars once definitively admitted in the form pre-

scribed in the preceding article cannot be sent away except for grave causes, and in so far as they may be incorrigible. Decisions on revocation of scholarships will be taken by a two-thirds majority of the principal and four examiners, subject without prejudice to appeal to the tribunal of the rector [of the University], either by the said scholars, or by their parents or recognized correspondents.

13. Scholars may not resign scholarships without the written consent of their parents.

14. On entering the house, and as long as they live in it, the scholars should consider it a refuge prepared for them by Providence, by the bounty and generosity of the king, by the piety of the first founders and by the wisdom of magistrates, to enable them to receive an honest and Christian education. They will let no day pass without giving thanks to God for so great a benefit, and without addressing to him their prayers for the founders and benefactors to whom they are indebted.

15. They will show toward their superiors and teachers the same obedience and respect that a son owes to his father; they will endeavor to profit from their teachers' instruction and to deserve their benevolence and friendship by the regularity of their conduct, and their docility and application in fulfilling their duties.

16. They will avoid all disputes and quarreling among themselves; if they have differences they will rely on the prudence and decision of their teachers. They will consider themselves as brothers and children of one family. Fraternal charity should produce among them peace, good manners, mutual consideration and a praiseworthy emulation in virtue and knowledge.

17. Until the number of scholarship students is sufficient to fill the college it will be allowable to admit paying boarders, who will have the same housing, meals, and instruction as the scholarship students, and be subject to the same teachers, the same regulations and the same exercises.

Title VII

[15 articles]

On the Steward and the Servants

Title VIII

[12 articles]

General Regulations

1. The gates of the college will be opened at 5:30 in the morning and closed at 9:30 at night. The keys will be deposited with the principal, or in his absence with the master who is assuming his functions.

2. No person from outside the house may sleep in the college without permission of the principal.

3. No master, pupil, or servant may sleep outside the college without permission of the principal.

4. Entry to the interior of the college is forbidden to all persons of the female sex, except for the mothers and near relatives of the pupils, who may enter only with the permission of the principal, who will have them conducted, if they wish, to the dormitory of the quarter to which the pupil belongs, and to which the pupil will also be brought. All other women will be received in the parlor.

6. It is likewise forbidden to keep dogs or birds in one's room. Nor may pupils have flower-pots without express permission from the principal.

7. Teachers of dancing, music, and drawing may give their lessons only during hours of recreation. It is at this time also, normally, that tailors, shoemakers, launderers, etc. will be received.

8. Hairdressers may enter only on the days and at the hours set by the principal.

9. All masters will see, in conjunction with the principal, that pupils give no errands to college servants or others, except with permission after due explanation of the purpose.

10. They will most expressly forbid the pupils to sell or give anything to each other, to engage in small trades, or to lend each other money or books or anything else whatever, except by consent of the master of the quarter.

11. They will take care that no one willfully defaces the buildings or furnishings of the house; and if they find that any pupil is doing so, especially if he does so maliciously, they will report to the principal, who will administer punishment according to the degree of defacement and of malicious intent on the part of the pupil.

12. All group exercises will be announced by the sound of the bell, to which all will respond exactly and without delay.

TITLE IX

[34 articles]

On Religious Exercises

1. All persons received in the college, whether teachers, pupils or servants, will make profession of the Catholic religion. Youth will be most carefully formed in the knowledge and practice of this holy religion, and in the respect and obedience due to the Church, to the chief pastors and especially to the sovereign pontiff, and to the sacred person of the king and his authority. For this purpose, the instructions and exercises prescribed in the following articles will be used. [There follow 33 articles on prayers, devotional readings, the mass, the catechism, and the sacraments. There are daily prayers and daily mass, and once a month the students are to make confession to confessors brought from outside the school.]

Title X

[26 articles]

On Studies

1. No moment in the classroom, conferences, preparations or other exercises shall be lost in amusement or in wandering about the house or in anything unrelated to these exercises.

2. Those arriving after a class has begun will drop to their knees and murmur a prayer; if they have not had the teacher's permission they will go to him, before taking their seats, to explain the reason for their tardiness.

3. During the class each will remain in the place assigned to him, and occupy himself exclusively with his classwork. It is expressly forbidden to write on the tables or desks, or to do anything that may damage or deface the furnishings of the college.

4. Complete silence will be kept in the study halls. All will study quietly, and take care to make no noise in opening and shutting the desks. Anyone having to ask permission will do so without disturbing the others.

7. The philosophy students will apply themselves to an understanding of the notes taken from lectures by their professors. They will learn their contents, and be ready to explain them either in class, if questioned, or in the conferences which will be held each day.

9. From All Souls' to vacation there will be held each week, on a day set by the principal, an exercise in philosophy, alternately for the students of physics and of logic. The theology students will be expected to attend and take part in the argument. An invitation will be extended to the philosophy professors to preside, and to as many other persons as possible.

10. Besides these exercises there will be each year two

examinations of the students in each philosophy class, one in Lent and the other at the end of the school year. The examiners and masters will propound questions, and may also have questions asked by some of the theology students and even by visitors.

11. The principal and the examiners will judge the success of the students. They will prepare a list on which students are placed according to degree of capacity. They will assemble the students on an agreed-upon day, read the list aloud, and give each one the praise or the advice that he merits.

12. The humanities students will apply themselves, most especially, to doing the work prescribed by the professor, to preparing their explanation of authors to be taken up in the following class, and to learning the lessons that they will be called upon to recite. The masters will take care that papers are well written, and that lessons are recited distinctly in a way showing that they are understood.

13. When students have done their work badly, or copied from each other, the masters will require it to be done over. If papers show bad handwriting or offenses against spelling, they will also be done over.

14. Every day the last study hour will be devoted to preparation conducted by the masters with their pupils. The masters will assure themselves that the [Latin] authors to be explained in class are not only well-understood but are rendered into our language in an easy and correct way. Teachers of grammar classes will make clear the application of rules that they set forth.

15. Masters will take care to obtain advice of professors of the subject studied by their pupils and will arrange with them on the means to assure and hasten the students' progress. They will allow private reading, with discernment, only for those of their pupils whom they judge capable of using part of their time without loss to their ordinary course of study. They will have the principal or the pro-

fessor prescribe the books which students may read, and they will require the student to submit an extract of what he has read at the end of each month.

26. By the rules and usages of the University it is forbidden to all students without exception to walk in the courtyards during classes. If any one asks to see them at this time, and if the professor judges it appropriate to allow them to leave, they may not remain more than a quarter of an hour with the person who has asked for them, and always only in the parlor.

TITLE XI

[12 articles]

On Good Manners and Cleanliness

1. Since true good manners do not consist in vain formulas or compliments nor in merely outward demonstrations, but derive their principle from the charity that should join all of us together, the masters should make every effort, in encouraging good manners among their pupils, to instill and maintain among them Christian sentiments of brotherly union and accord.

2. They will take care to prevent or stop animosities, disputes, and quarrels. They will tolerate no vulgarity, insults, reproaches, or malicious nicknames. Swearing or other outrageous behavior, for whatever cause, will be rigorously forbidden and severely punished.

3. Destined to live in society after leaving the college, students will acquire from an early age the habit of a mild, easy, and honest intercourse with others. In outward action and speech they will avoid whatever may jar upon well-bred people, such as conceited airs, haughtiness, scorn, sarcasm, ridicule, gesticulation, etc.

4. In recreation and outings they will be considerate of one another. They will not emit confused and piercing cries.

64

nor throw stones or anything that may hurt their school-mates, nor interfere with their games.

5. In conversation they will be more eager to listen than to speak; they will not interrupt when others are speaking nor question their judgment, especially with older or better-educated people. If obliged to speak, they will do so with a candid and modest freedom; they will stop when another begins to talk. They will bear with contradiction without bad feeling, but will not contradict others except when necessary, and then with enough tact to make the contradiction listened to, or indeed useful and sometimes pleasant.

6. At table, they will be attentive to the needs of their neighbors, especially those who are new to the college. They will themselves procure what their neighbor may lack, if they can easily do so, and if not they will ask it of whoever is in charge of the table.

7. On all occasions, if they can be useful, they will be so willingly and without delay. They will gladly praise others, but without affectation or silliness, and they will never speak advantageously of themselves. They will not be tale-bearers on the faults of their fellow students, but will respond truthfully to questions of masters who already have some knowledge or grounds of suspicion.

8. They will show respect, deference, and obedience to all who are charged with their education in any way. They will speak gently and courteously to the servants. It is expressly forbidden to treat them harshly or with condescension.

9. If they see a stranger in the college they will greet him. They will suspend their games to let him pass, and take pleasure in giving him directions if they can, or telling him where to inquire.

10. It is strongly recommended not only to return greetings but to offer them to everyone. They will even greet the servants and the poor, not exactly as a social duty but from motives of religion.

11. Their clothing will be modest, but clean and decent.

They will not wear torn garments; they will comb their hair every day, or oftener if so ordered; the masters, especially of the younger classes, must be especially attentive in this regard. They will wash their hands at least once a day, and change their linen several times a week.

12. If any boy lets himself form dirty habits all possible means will be used to correct him, to the point of punishment if necessary.

Title XII

[14 articles]

On the Dining Halls and Meals

1. Breakfast and the afternoon break will be in the halls; the bread will be served already cut and distributed by each particular master. The student may never, without express permission from the principal himself, have anything brought from outside, such as coffee, chocolate, cool beverages, etc. At breakfast and the afternoon break the students are free, not to play but to talk quietly to each other, without making a noise that would be heard through other parts of the college.

2. When the bell sounds for dinner and supper the students will proceed to the dining halls promptly and noiselessly under supervision of their respective masters, who will accompany them. Once in the dining hall, each will take his assigned place, and remain standing, with his hat off, in silence.

3. The meal will begin with the *Benedicite* and conclude with the *Grace*, after which at both dinner and supper the *De Profundis* will be said for deceased founders and benefactors. The masters will take care that these prayers are offered in a spirit of meditation and piety. After the *Benedicite* each will sit down. The masters will see that each table is complete, especially on days when no classes are held.

66

4. If a student arrives late he will give his reasons to the master in charge of the table, say his *Benedicite* in a low voice, and take his seat.

5. Silence will obtain during the meal; there will be a reading to which all listen attentively; all will sit in a proper position. Students may not leave the dining hall without permission of the master in charge.

6. At each table the presiding master will serve. No student may touch a serving dish; if he wishes something he will ask for it quietly and modestly.

7. Students will take care to cut the bread and meat served to them in such a way that the leftovers are not wasted, since they are to be given to the servants and the poor. Masters will enforce this rule strictly.

8. It is forbidden to make marks on the plates, dishes, or goblets; to pierce or otherwise damage them in any way; to cut bread on the tablecloth, spill wine or water on it or pour anything on the floor, or to throw anything whatsoever.

9. During the meal the steward will make his rounds among the several dining halls to see that the service is properly performed by his staff.

10. The students will form the habit, so far as possible, of eating all that they are served, or at least of refusing nothing from mere caprice. They will not expect delicate foods, and will abstain from all complaint or murmuring on this subject.

Title XIII

[17 articles]

On Recreations, Outings and Leaves

Recreations

1. Recreation will take place in the courtyards, weather permitting. Students will be under the supervision of an assistant principal and two masters of quarters, and may

not leave, even to pass from one courtyard to another, without permission from the assistant principal.

2. Dangerous and unsuitable games are absolutely forbidden. Those that give bodily exercise in proportion to age and strength are preferred. Masters will watch to see that no one plays to excess, even in permitted activities. They will absolutely forbid low familiarities, gesticulation, secret readings, or exchange of notes.

3. If a dispute arises the students will refer it to one of the masters in charge of the courtyard. Those who let themselves go to the point of violence, fighting, throwing on the ground, tearing clothing, etc., or those who allow themselves to be carried away by anger, or use oaths or outrageous language, will be severely punished the first time, and sent away if they repeatedly commit the same offenses.

4. The affectation of talking always to the same persons during recreation is a singularity that shows at least a tacit contempt for others. Connections between students, if they become too close, often give rise to backbiting, calumny, defiance of masters, dissipation, and waste of time. Students will avoid such faults, and masters are expressly charged with careful attention to such matters.

5. When the weather does not permit recreation in the courtyards it will take place in the halls. . . .

Outings

7. There will be an outing on every day free from classes, except for the Saturdays before the first Sunday of each month, and the day preceding days of great solemnity. The place for the outing will be indicated by the prefect to the masters of quarters, who will be required to take the students to that place.

8. In winter, the students will go to their quarters immediately after dinner, to prepare for the outing, from which they will return at five o'clock. In summer, that is, after April 15, they will leave at three o'clock and return at

68

seven. Those who are not ready at the time of departure will remain at the college.

9. Whether going or coming, the students will walk in front of the master of their quarter, in such a way as always to be visible to him. They will walk neither too fast nor too slowly, nor raise their voices, nor offer provocation to anyone. In a word, they will behave themselves with modesty and decency.

The servant of each quarter will walk behind.

10. Students must not stray from the masters for any reason, even to visit their parents. The masters themselves cannot give such permission, without prior notice and consent from the principal.

11. Arrived at the place set for the outing, students will remain together under the master's eye. No one may go away separately, even under the pretense of study, without special permission. They will observe in their games the rules outlined above for recreation. They will avoid anything that may lead to tumult or complaint, such as chasing after game, entering vineyards, trampling in wheatfields, etc.

Leaves in the City

14. Leaves in the city are very rare. Permission will not be given on Sundays or holidays, or on class days, or on days preceding the first Sunday of the month or preceding the great solemnities, or on the half-holidays until the close of the morning study, except for grave and pressing reason of which the principal will be the judge.

15. Students desiring such permission will present to the principal, on the day before, an *exeat* signed by the master of their quarter. The *exeat* will be delivered to them the following morning, countersigned by the principal or by the assistant principal or prefect authorized by him. When the students go out they will deliver the *exeat* to the porter.

16. They cannot go out unless accompanied by reliable and known person, who is responsible for taking them and

bringing them back, or having them brought back by a responsible person.

17. They will return to the college in winter at six o'clock, and in summer before supper. On returning they will report to the principal.

Title XIV

[not divided into articles]

Order of Exercises for the Day

5:30 A.M.	Rising. The half-hour allowed for dressing being more than enough, all will be fully dressed in this half-hour, and no one, after prayers, may return to the dormitory during the day.
6:00	Prayer, followed by devotional readings. For the prayer, all pass from the dormitory into the hall.
6:15	Study hall, beginning with the learning and recitation of verses from Scripture.
7:45	Breakfast, followed by recreation in the halls.
8:15	Classes
10:30	Mass, then study until dinner.
12:00 A.M.	Dinner, followed by recreation.
1:15 P.M.	Study hall.
2:15	Classes
4:30	Afternoon break, followed by recreation.
5:00	Study hall.
6:15	Conference for the philosophers, preparation for the rhetoricians and humanists.
7:15	Supper, followed by recreation.
8:45	Prayers, followed by devotional reading.
9:00	Into the dormitories. While undressing, there will be a reading from the life of the saint whose feast occurs on the following day.
9:15	All in bed. No one may leave the dormitory during the night.

[The Regulations conclude with variations of this daily schedule for Sundays, holidays, solemn days, Christmas, Holy Week, etc.]

6. Rules on admission of new scholarship students

In May 1781 the administrative board published new rules on admission to the college. The first five articles in general only repeated what is said in Title VI of the Regulations of 1769 in Item 5 above. Articles 6 and 7 add a few details. The simple gown in Article 6 may be contrasted with the more elaborate uniform, and other clothing, which the scholarship student was expected to bring with him in 1803, when the lycées were organized under Napoleon Bonaparte. See Item 48 below.

6. The scholar when admitted will bring three pairs of sheets and a dozen small linens for his own use, and will purchase a boarder's gown. The College will furnish a silver table service and a complete bed, meals in sickness and health, wine, heat, candles, and medicine without cost to the parents.

7. As for maintenance to include laundry, hairdressing, body linen, clothing, books, pens, ink, and paper, as well as pocket money, such items will be provided by the parents.

7. A special prize is awarded to Maximilien de Robespierre

ROBESPIERRE, a virtual orphan at the age of six, would probably have had no education except for the scholarship that he received, and would probably, even with the scholarship, have remained a provincial lawyer of only local repute except for the Revolution. "Arras College," mentioned below, was one of the small colleges merged with Louis-le-Grand in 1763. As a native of Arras, in the extreme northern tip of France, Robespierre qualified for one of the four scholarships by which boys were sent to Paris for schooling. He entered Louis-le-Grand in 1769 at the age of eleven, and remained until obtaining his law degree at twenty-three. He held the scholarship for these twelve years and then received a special prize which, consisting of 600 livres, was more than equal to the value of one year of the scholarship.

The Administrative Board of the College of Louis-le-Grand

July 19, 1781

In view of the report of M. the Principal on the outstanding abilities of Sieur de Robespierre, a scholarship student of Arras College, who is about to conclude his studies, and on his good conduct for twelve years and his success in his classes, as shown both in University prizes and in examinations in philosophy and law, the Board has unanimously accorded to Sieur de Robespierre an award in the amount of six hundred livres, which shall be paid to him by the custodian of the funds of Arras College. . . .

8. Regulations for the chief cook

THE administrative board took its mission of supervising Louis-le-Grand very seriously. It watched over a surprisingly complex staff of officers of the college, who included a controller, a cashier, a steward, an infirmarian, a secretary to the bureau itself, and a chief cook. A set of Regulations for each of them was drawn up, and each was printed, presumably for internal circulation, in a leaflet of four to eight pages. The regulations for the chief cook give a ludicrous example of the degree to which planning, anticipation of small details, and organized hierarchy were carried. We know from Item 29 below that in 1792 the chief cook had one assistant cook and three kitchen helpers, reinforced by a baker and wine steward, each with one assistant. Nevertheless, a place is defined for the chief cook in a clearly delineated chain of command, in which he was responsible for subordinates and reported upward through channels.

Presumably the theology students were to get the biggest dishes because they were the oldest, not because of any favoritism to theology.

Regulations for the Chief Cook

January 4, 1782

The Department of the Kitchens being one of the most considerable in the matter of expense, it is important that it be most scrupulously managed. Hence its Chief, his assistant, and those employed in the Department are enjoined to make every effort to perform their duties with fidelity and exactitude, as the only means of preserving their employment or giving satisfaction to the Board. They will conform precisely to the following regulations:

I

The Chief Cook, like chiefs of other departments, and hence those who are subordinate to them, are under the immediate authority of the Steward; they should accept and conform to his orders on all occasions; they should obey in anything that he commands and address themselves

73

to him for any requests to be made to the Board, which will grant them only on recommendation of the Steward.

II

The Chief Cook should understand that in his position he cannot please his superiors or be respected by his subordinates unless he shows himself alert to perform his duties, and gives the example of a prudent and well-regulated conduct.

III

He will most carefully avoid taking too much wine. Besides the disrepute that he would bring on himself by such a fault, he should remember that he would lose his ability to oversee his subordinates, prescribe their duties, fulfill his own, or justly reprimand them for the same failing.

IV

He should give leadership to others employed in the kitchens; he should set an example in his own work; in a word, he is charged with preparing, or having prepared under his eyes, everything to be eaten in the college.

V

The variety of fare cannot be great in a community like the College of Louis-le-Grand. Yet with skill the Chief Cook can avoid the kind of repetition that becomes unpleasant. He will do so, however, with prudence and remembering to avoid too much expense.

XI

Meal service being exactly at noon and at 7:15 P.M., the Chief Cook will make it his law never to be late.

XII

He will hasten to return from his marketing at an hour never later than 9:30 in the morning, so as to have time to judge what has been done in his absence and what still remains to be done in the seasoning and other preparation of food.

XVI

He should know how meat is cut in the butcher shops, how to prepare it for boiling or roasting, and how to use the scraps of veal and mutton to make edible dishes, supplementing the quantity of meat with onions, turnips, and other vegetables.

XVII

He should know how to arrange meats on the platters in a suitable manner and to distribute them with care, giving the largest to the theology students and the others according to ages and classes.

9. Regulations for law students

LAW students having scholarships were supposed to live under the strict conditions outlined in the rules below. But the rules were often disregarded, and many law students roamed about Paris at will. A decree of the Parlement of Paris of March 1788 commended the administration of Louis-le-Grand for its attempts to enforce the regulations, deplored the abuse by which law students lived outside the college without working in law offices at all, and ordered that such young men should lose their scholarships unless they offered proofs of legitimate legal work. But the swarm of idle law graduates and ostensible law students in Paris undoubtedly contributed to the revolutionary outburst of 1789.

Regulations for the law students at Louis-le-Grand

1782

1. MM. the scholarship students who are studying law will be housed in the new rooms on the third floor above the Rhetoric and Second classrooms.

2. Hooks will be placed on the doors of these rooms.

3. The corridor will be closed by a grill to which only the principal and the assistant principal for the philosophers will have the key.

4. Iron bars will be put on the windows along the eaves on the Cholets side.

5. MM. the law students will be present regularly at morning and evening prayers, together with MM. the physics students; immediately thereafter they will retire to their rooms for study.

6. MM. the law students will attend mass with MM. the theology students assiduously every day.

7. They will leave the college at the hour when their law classes begin, and return to the college when the said classes end. Every month, or oftener if M. the principal judges necessary, they will submit certificates of assiduity and application, signed by the professor whose lectures they are hearing.

8. At other times MM. the law students may not go out without express permission of the principal, or in his absence of the assistant principal for the philosophers.

9. The pretext of leaving the college to work in an attorney's office will not be allowed by the principal unless he knows to which office MM. the law students wish to go,

and unless the attorney confirms the assiduity and progress of the students having this permission, which will be revoked instantly if abused.

10. Otherwise MM. the law students may not go out except on days when there are no classes, under the same rules as apply to other scholarship holders.

11. On Sundays and holy days MM. the law students will attend all chapel exercises, sitting on a special bench to be placed near the principal.

12. Arrangements will be made immediately with MM. the professors of the Faculty of Law by which MM. the law students may have regular conferences within the college, to guide them in their work and assure their application to studies leading to their degrees.

13. These conferences will take place in a hall set aside for that purpose, in which the students will assemble only in the presence of the person in charge, or by permission of the principal.

14. It is expressly forbidden to the law students, as to all other students in the college, to saunter aimlessly in the courtyards, staircases, or corridors, or to go into the study halls or dormitories of the other quarters, on any pretext, without the special permission of the principal, or in his absence of one of the assistant principals.

10. A minor *philosophe* shows his scorn for the colleges

LOUIS-SEBASTIEN MERCIER was one of the second generation of writers called *philosophes*, a term used derisively by their enemies, and with satisfaction by themselves. Mainly a playwright and "man of letters," Mercier also composed a huge *Tableau de Paris*, eventually in twelve volumes, shortly before the Revolution. It consisted of over five hundred short chapters on many topics. Two are abbreviated here from the edition of 1782. The rue de la Harpe, which he mentions, was later replaced by the Boulevard Saint-Michel, the main artery of the Latin Quarter today.

Mercier is best remembered for his vision of utopia, *The Year* 2440, published in 1770. It is a picture of a future society freed of the errors of the past. Among its other attractions, which Mercier admires, is that most of the books in the Bibliothèque Nationale have been burned as "frivolous, useless or dangerous," and that the schools teach appreciation of existing society, instead of, as he says in the present selection, instilling republican sentiments under a monarchy.

It will be seen that Mercier had less respect for the "indigent" or for upward social mobility than either the French government or the colleges that he condemns. Yet during the Revolution he sat in the National Convention, and then was for a while professor of history in the Central Schools, in which he eccentrically argued that Locke, Condillac, Copernicus, and Newton had all been mistaken.

Chapter LXXX

Latin Country

The Latin country is what they call the quarter that includes the rue Saint-Jacques, the mount of Sainte-Geveviève, and the rue de la Harpe. There you will find the colleges and the university; and there you will see, forever moving up and down the streets, a swarm of Sorbonnists in their cassocks, private tutors in their clerical bibs, law students, and students of medicine and surgery. Their indigence drives them to their vocation. . . .

Chapter LXXXI

Colleges

The colleges and the free art schools are propagating an abuse, by sending an everlasting flood of young men into the arts of enjoyment for which they are seldom born. This pernicious habit of Paris tradesmen is draining our workshops of mechanical occupations which are far more important to social order. The art schools are mere daubing places; and the full-program colleges, for those who have no fortunes of their own, are filling the world with a crowd of scribblers who have no resources except their pens, and who carry their indigence and ineptitude for any productive work wherever they go.

The present plan of studies is extremely vicious, and the best student after ten years takes away very little knowledge of any kind. It is surprising that we have any men of letters at all; but they educate themselves.

A hundred pedants try to teach Latin to children before they know their own language, whereas in fact it is necessary to know one language thoroughly before learning another. How absurdly misunderstood everything is in these systems of study!

There are ten full-program colleges. Seven or eight years are spent in learning Latin, and out of a hundred pupils ninety come out without knowing it.

All these teachers have a thick layer of pedantry, which is impossible for them to throw off. It can be recognized in them even when they change their trade. Their whole tone is most ridiculous, and insufferable in society.

The name of Rome was the first that struck my ears. No sooner could I hold a primer than I was told of Romulus and the she-wolf, I heard about the Capitol and the Tiber, and the names of Brutus, Cato, and Scipio followed me in my sleep. . . .

It is certain that the study of Latin produces a certain taste for republics, and arouses a desire to revive the one whose grand and sweeping history has been read about. It is certain that, after hearing so much of the Senate, of the liberty and majesty of the Roman people, of its victories, of the justified death of Caesar, and the dagger of Cato who could not bear to outlive the destruction of the laws—

79

that after all this it is a hard lot to leave Rome and find onself again a bourgeois in the rue des Noyers.

Yet it is in a monarchy that youth is perpetually given these strange ideas, which they must soon lose and forget for the sake of their own security, advancement and well-being. And it is an absolute king who pays professors to explain gravely the meaning of these eloquent declamations against the power of kings.

11. Distribution of scholarship students by level of studies

LOUIS-LE-GRAND had students at all levels from the elementary to the professional school, and the proportion of older students was growing in the last years before the Revolution. Instruction within the college went no higher than physics; beyond that, students lived in the college but studied in one of the three professional faculties or with practicing doctors and attorneys. It is known that a few, preparing for the *agrégation*, heard lectures at the College of France; they must be included under Philosophy in the following table. It is not known why medical students were so few at this time, or why the number of theology students was increasing. It may have had to do with career opportunities for young men of limited means under the *ancien régime*. If so, the career plans of theology students were soon upset by the Revolution, and indeed Champagne, writing in 1792, tells us in Item 26 that theology students had caused trouble in the colleges, and that some were shifting to legal or medical studies.

After conversion to the modern lycée in 1803, Louis-le-Grand ceased to have students above the Philosophy level, and so became more purely a "secondary" school. The table suggests that, except for the Revolution, and in line with Garnier's ideas as set forth in Item 3, there might have been a development in the direction of the nineteenth century university, with students at undergraduate, graduate and professional levels combined in one same institution.

NUMBER OF SCHOLARSHIP STUDENTS

Approximate Age	Class Level	1784–1785	1785–1786	1786–1787	1787–1788
20 and over	Theology	83	111	120	120
	Law	29	39	65	64
	Medicine	6	1	2	5
	Total, Higher Faculties	118	151	187	189
19	Physics	55	53	36	31
18	Logic	55	52	42	41
	Total, Philosophy	110	105	78	72
	Total, Senior Scholars	228	256	265	261
17	Rhetoric	61	43	43	40
16	Second	43	48	42	52
15	Third	49	45	56	43
14	Fourth	41	48	38	39
13	Fifth	38	31	33	25
12	Sixth	21	25	18	16
11	Seventh	9	5	4	18
	Total, Junior Scholars	262	245	234	233
	Total, Scholarship Students	490	501	499	494

12. A former professor at Louis-le-Grand defends the University of Paris

THE Abbé L. B. Proyart was a spirited controversialist, conservative before the Revolution and violently reactionary there-

THE COLLEGE OF LOUIS-LE-GRAND

after. He had been assistant principal at Louis-le-Grand from 1772 to 1778, then moved on to be principal of a college in Auvergne. In 1785 he published *De l'Éducation publique*, from which this passage is taken. He ridicules the claims of the new educational theorists and deplores the proliferation of "private" schools as an imposition on credulous parents.

Later he denounced Louis-le-Grand as a hotbed of revolutionaries, claimed to remember Robespierre distinctly, and insisted that the teachers who awarded Robespierre his prize in 1781 did not really know him. It is to be noted, however, that Proyart had left Louis-le-Grand before Robespierre received the prize, and that Proyart, in his book of 1785, made no mention of any subversive influences at Louis-le-Grand. The book is an attack on new private schools, but a strong defense of the established Paris colleges.

A passage from Proyart's book of 1800 appears as Item 42 below. Comparison of what he said at the two dates will suggest the low level of credibility to be assigned to polemics against the French Revolution. In 1785 Proyart praised the sense of equality in the "little republic" of a college. Robespierre likewise once remarked in passing, in 1793, that the colleges had been "nurseries of republicanism, which formed the mind of the Nation and made it worthy of liberty." We have just seen, in Item 10, L. S. Mercier saying much the same thing, though with disapproval.

At the time when the Jesuits departed from their colleges a great cry arose that the moment had come when public education, now directed by enlightened Philosophy, would soon take flight and rise to the highest degree of perfection. This idea fermented in people's heads and turned them into enthusiasts. Soon we saw such an outburst of educational projects as to satisfy the most bizarre tastes, and all kinds of people, including parents who wanted ignorance to be hereditary in their families, now found for their children a plan of education to meet their wishes, and excluding all study of Latin.

Generally speaking, our new theorists seem to have little use for the language of the Romans, those wise and profound men from whom we learn so well to think and reflect.

They only ask that their pupils make a brief and hence useless study of this language; they fail to realize, no doubt, that one learns to speak well in French by reading Latin. . . .

It is not that our modern plans of education are not heavily overloaded; in the intent of their authors they are supposed to produce, and very quickly, men who are prodigies of knowledge, really little Encyclopedists. From the Sixth they will have learned the *history of insects;* in the Fifth, *Pliny the Naturalist* and *Columella;* in this class they will also be introduced to *Political Science;* and if they start early in *Geometry*, says M. d'Alembert, we should see *prodigies and precocious talents* in this line; it is even possible, according to M. the Abbé de Condillac, to make a child of seven or eight *seize by a series of observations the connecting thread of human knowledge.* Why, asks M. the Abbé, should a child, *having the same mental faculties as a grown man, not be able to observe like him?* There is no answer to this argument. Would it not indeed be extraordinary if a man asleep, or confined to a madhouse, having the same mental faculties as a man awake or in possession of reason, could not make the same observations? . . .

. . . The best plan of education would be for wise and virtuous masters, having no exclusive aim in their teaching, and no desire to embrace all fields of knowledge, to bring order and clarity in the minds of their pupils, form their judgment, and introduce them to the fundamental kind of knowledge which is equally useful for all ages, and which prepares for all the functions which an educated man may have to discharge in society.

Now this plan of education is not unknown in France, and according to my observation is precisely the one which the University of Paris sets for itself. It is the one for which I am grateful for having been formerly subjected to it as both student and teacher. It would seem, to hear certain detractors of the University, that this body, today so enlightened, is still the slave to antiquated and truly defective methods of teaching, such as it may have used in former times, and which other schools have followed longer than the University has, and from which not all our provinces are yet free. But it is now long ago that the University of Paris brought order, clarity and greater simplicity into its teaching. It is long ago that it gave up the riduculous practice of putting elementary books written in Latin in the hands of children who hardly understand French. For a long time now, in the humanities classes, it has taught something other than words, and, in philosophy, has replaced the futile questions of the past with questions whose usefulness is generally admitted.

But, to show the injustice and bad faith of those who slander the University, we find on taking the trouble to examine their declamations that the few good ideas they present are taken from the University itself. They publish the ancient practices of the University as fortunate discoveries that give them the right to public gratitude.

. . . . Where, I ask, are the notable products of the schools of our modern mentors? I have looked everywhere for the Emile of Jean-Jacques Rousseau, and I find him nowhere but in his book. But the Emiles formed by the University of Paris I can find at the head of church and state; I can show them to you, standing out from the crowd, in every walk and condition of society.

. . . . If on the moral side the case be supposed equal as between public education and a private education at home, the greatest advantages will still be on the side of public education. The advantage of emulation both in work and in personal qualities in inestimable. Public education is a marvelous instrument for the shaping of character. It gives assurance to the most timid, it softens the wildest, it makes the rigid more amenable and more supple. All inequalities of fortune and condition disappear among classmates. Subject to the same rules, but independent of each other, they know that their only duty is to the truth. They cannot disguise their faults or their more ridiculous characteristics. In the little republic that they form among themselves, it is only the qualities of heart, talent, and virtue that give the right to respect.

Let us continue to examine the educational plan of the University of Paris by evaluating the defects that may still be imputed to it. If keen minds are rare in all ages, we should not be surprised to find in our own time so many frivolous persons who prefer the specious to be solid, so many parents who would rather see their children have the tones and manners of a "good family" than the knowledge and virtues that might estrange them from the parental roof. I remember a lady of Paris, who was speaking for many other mothers, when in a fit of bad humor she said to a man of merit in public education: "In truth, Monsieur, I do not know what anyone learns in your college; I find my son more stupid today than the day he entered; he embarrasses me when he comes home." Yet this lady's son was a good student, sensible, modest, industrious in his work, and very well educated for his age. His mother thought him an ignoramus because he forgot to bow properly in society and did not know how to discourse on inanities. She little suspected that this young man, who already had just notions of what true merit consists in, might feel similarly toward her, and be mortified in the presence of a mother whose whole talent was in knowing how to talk without saying anything, and in being busy while having nothing to do.

It is a good thing to see our public teachers inaccessible to the latest prejudices, resolute in upholding true principles and useful to boys even despite their parents. But this noble courage well befits the University of Paris, an independent body, which will be swayed by no self-interest into cowardly compromises, because it expects nothing from parents, and owes its honorable existence solely to the liberality of our kings.

13. The University salutes
the Revolution

IN June 1789 the Estates General, defying the king, turned themselves into a National Assembly and claimed the power to write a new constitution for France. In July a series of popular uprisings culminated in the fall of the Bastille. The University of Paris sent a delegation on July 29 to pay its respects to the Assembly and express its adherence to the Revolution.

The delegation was headed by the rector of the University, J. B. Dumouchel, who had been a student at Louis-le-Grand. The rectorship was an annually elective office, but Dumouchel was rector from 1786 to 1791, and in effect was the last rector of the old University. He had been elected to the Estates General, and was one of the handful of priests in the First Estate who had joined with the Third Estate in the revolutionary action of June. He was thus himself a member of the new National Constituent Assembly. He later became a constitutional bishop, then gave up his priesthood and married, and ended up as effective head of public instruction under Napoleon's political appointee, Fontanes.

It is the occasion rather than the content of the following document that attracts attention. Dumouchel addressed the Assembly as follows, with four paragraphs of somewhat empty grandiloquence left out.

MESSEIGNEURS:

As faithful bearer of the sentiments of the University of Paris, I come to lay at the feet of this august Assembly its homage of respect and deep veneration, inspired by the union of sublime and patriotic virtues of which you daily give the brilliant spectacle to France and to all of Europe. . . .

Thanks to your noble labors, it is no longer to distant periods of our history, nor to the annals of foreign countries, that we shall henceforth look for grand and magnificent examples of honor and patriotism. . . .

You will thus create, Messeigneurs, by the sole force

of your virtues, that system of truly national education desired for so long. It will become part of the majestic edifice which you are raising on solid foundations at this very moment. It is with joy that the University will receive this precious and sacred deposit from your hands, happy in seconding the zeal by which you are animated, and in preparing faithful subjects for the King, and citizens who resemble you for our country!

14. A student petition requests reform

THIS petition dates from late in the year 1789. The Revolution has begun, and the National Assembly is at work, but the philosophy students who sign the petition are still respectful, addressing the rector as "monseigneur" and the professors as "messieurs," where later they would say "citizens." The rector, who is most particularly addressed in the last two sentences, was J. B. Dumouchel. He is praised for his role in the Assembly, as explained in Item 13. The Faculty of Arts received and discussed the petition, but took no definite action.

The students ask the abolition of the practice of dictated lectures, which a teacher at the University of Paris, writing in Diderot's *Encyclopédie*, had already strongly criticized thirty years before. They also want the philosophy classes to be conducted in French. Their own language reflects the eloquence taught in the schools, with its elaborate sentence structure, rhetorical questions and concluding apostrophe. They share also in the Revolutionary manner of speaking, long prepared by the *philosophes:* the reign of prejudice is at last crumbling before truth and reason. As young men of eighteen to twenty, they look forward with enthusiasm to taking part in the active civil life and public assemblies brought into being by the Revolution.

They expect that the National Assembly will reorganize education very soon. The Assembly recognized the importance of education, and even assigned it to its most important committee, the committee on the constitution, which in turn produced the famous Talleyrand report of 1791. There was no significant legislation, however, given the pressure of other affairs, until 1795.

Petition
Presented to monseigneur the rector and to messieurs the professors of the University of Paris by the students in Philosophy

It is with confidence, monseigneur and messieurs, that the students in Philosophy of the ten colleges come to present their respectful supplications. They are not unaware of how they have been misrepresented in your eyes, or of how their efforts have been subjected to malicious interpretations; but they are reassured by the hope that their conduct will justify them, and they would like to persuade themselves that, far from listening to unfounded charges, you will consult today, as always, your sense of equity and the justice of their requests.

In any other circumstances we would have feared opposing a usage consecrated by long antiquity, but today when the crumbling reign of prejudice gives way to truth and reason it would be an insult to you, messieurs, for us to hesitate to ask the suppression of an abuse simply because it is as old as the university.

The notebooks of the kind we keep, intended at first to receive commentaries on Aristotle, have since been devoted to arbitrary philosophies as presented by each professor by dictation. It is against such dictation that we dare to protest today. We shall say nothing of the ridicule that evil-intentioned people have been able to throw on these great folios that we produce. Written almost always without being understood, preserved without being read, initialled by the professor without being looked at, they serve as a step in our rise to the higher faculties. Nor do we speak

88

of the considerable harm done to the health and development of the body by the need of writing for two hours in a fatiguing position, nor of a disgust brought on unavoidably by such mechanical labor, which leaves none of the agreeable after-effects that are felt at the close of a useful occupation. What we do insist on is that this practice, originating when elementary books were scarce, should be reformed now that our own language provides such books in abundance, now that we have such writers as Bezons, Mably, Condillac, and many others no less esteemed, whose reputation obliges our teachers themselves to recommend that they be read. It is not that we ask to be excused from writing; we know that each professor has his own opinions which are not in elementary books, and we shall be eager to collect them in notebooks for this purpose.

Such a new method, monseigneur and messieurs, would give you assurance of the success of students in Philosophy, and you would no longer hear universal complaint that two years are hardly enough to pursue philosophy imperfectly in its principal branches. Instead of using months in copying insipid dictation, a student delayed by illness would devote these months to catching up with his classmates. Instead of spending two hours a day in writing down what can be found everywhere, we would be occupied in a deeper exploration of questions that the present waste of time allows us only to touch upon, and which the new state of things makes it necessary for every Citizen to understand.

It is thus that we have seen the reforms in Rhetoric extend the scope of that subject and produce results as satisfying for teachers as for students. The lack of printed materials had led to the use of dictated notebooks in Rhetoric, as in Philosophy. They have been abolished; are they regretted? Surely not. Experience thus supports our reasons for opposing an abuse which has only prejudice and antiquity in its favor.

Unfortunately it is not the only one for which we ask

THE COLLEGE OF LOUIS-LE-GRAND

reform. The use of the Latin language in philosophy arose from a love of vain erudition and from the ignorance of barbarous ages, in which the lack of good works in French made necessary the recourse to works in Latin. But today, when philosophy seems to have become the distinctive attribute of our nation, when French is the adoptive language of Europe and its clarity seems to have made it the proper idiom for the exact and philosophical sciences, what motive can deter you, monseigneur and messieurs, from the suppression of a practice that is condemned by reasons? Would it be the need of speaking Latin in the law schools? But do we not know that the wisdom of our new lawmakers, in simplifying the legal code, will put the laws made for all citizens in a language that all citizens can understand? Would it be that spoken Latin is the rule in the schools of theology? But is it necessary, for the small number for whom the speaking of Latin in our classes might be useful, and who even so could do without it, that the greatest number should be deprived of advantages? If some now acquire the facility in Latin that they need, how many others are there who would draw solid advantages from speaking French? Habituated to using French in the study of reasoning, moral questions, and nature, with what ease will we not employ it in society, to which we now ordinarily bring only rude and scholastic expressions? How much better will we not discuss laws that are a thousand times less abstract than a syllogism or the solution to a logical problem? And especially, with what advantage will we not appear in those august assemblies which henceforth will arouse the ambition of all citizens, and to which each of us would be unworthy to be called if he had not had, beginning today, the noble ambition to prepare himself?

Would you object that the National Assembly is soon to turn its attention to education? No, messieurs, you are too wise to desire, while awaiting the decree of the Assembly, that we should any longer be the victims of a practice obviously contrary to our own advancement. Condemned as we are not to benefit from future reforms in education, we have a right to demand some kind of compensation, and you are not so indifferent to the success of your pupils as to postpone the suppression of an abuse, on the pretext of coming changes from which none of us will have the happiness to profit.

We dare therefore to hope, monseigneur and messieurs, that you will soon take action on our just complaints, that you will hasten to overcome the obstacles that stand in our way, and that you will make it evident to France that the university is not the last to perceive the great truths that are at the base of our constitution. What a presumption it will be in your favor when the National Assembly, looking for wise men worthy of the trust of national education, shall find such men in you, who, while attached by duty to the ancient ways, have known of your own accord to yield to just petitions! And we urge you, my lord rector, charged by your status with the care of the young citizens who address you, and deserving by free election your role in the preparation of our new laws, to make it clear to the illustrious companions of those labors that the spirit that animates you in the Assembly presides also over your activities in a lesser sphere. Confident of the gratitude of the present generation, earn also the favor of those who are moving along to succeed it.

Signed by all the students in Philosophy

15. A deputation of students appears before the National Assembly

In the enthusiasm of the first months of the Revolution, and in the financial crisis caused by the breakdown of the old tax revenues, all sorts of groups and organizations appeared before the National Assembly to offer patriotic gifts. One of these was the Logic class of Louis-le-Grand, that is, the students, generally eighteen years old, who were in their first year of Philosophy. The same individuals must have signed the petition in Item 14 above. In the following address, presented at the bar of the Assembly on January 26, 1790, they excuse themselves for not being the first group of students to come, and regret that as young men in modest circumstances they cannot give as much as some others.

Aroused, messieurs, by the inspiration of your decrees and by the needs of the State, twenty-seven scholarship students composing the Logic class at the College of Louis-le-Grand wish also to come before you and offer their modest tribute. As sons supported by our country, we should have been in the forefront of the young citizenry; we would be happy if we had not been anticipated in so noble an action or if our offering could have been richer.

But you will no doubt excuse us, messieurs, for not setting before you more than a sum of two hundred livres. Slight as it is, it will have value in your eyes, for those who present it have no resources except what their country provides, and for them it is as much a sacrifice, or a privation, as a larger sum would be for many others.

May you then accept this gift as a sign of the efforts we shall make in the future to repay our debt! May you, by the warmth of your reception, encourage our fellow students who are in the same refuge, who enjoy the same benefits, and who will surely some day bring offerings more worthy of you. While our hearts form so many other wishes, this is the one that we beg to express.

16. Signs of student radicalism

PRINTED as a leaflet, this proposal must have been intended to circulate among the Paris colleges, in the hope that their students would elect delegates to the meeting announced in the last paragraph. No such meeting is known to have ever occurred.

The language and content are more radical than those of Item 14. The dating "second year of liberty" signifies the year 1790, and the first footnote implies a time later than July. There is a violent attack on the clergy as teachers, with bold quotations from Holbach and Helvetius. It is hard to tell whether the footnote in Latin is meant to be serious, amusing, or merely pompous. The corporal punishment complained of may have been more severe in other colleges than at Louis-le-Grand, if we judge by the Louis-le-Grand regulations of 1769. Champagne's plan as submitted to the Assembly in October 1790 also called for the abolition of corporal punishment, which was in fact permanently suppressed by the Revolution. For comparative purposes, it may be observed that the headmaster of Eton College, some years later, once flogged eighty boys for one collective act of indiscipline.

Note that these radical students expect everything from the government. The identity of the signer, Desramser, is not known.

THE DEATH AGONY OF THE UNIVERSITY

OR

PROPOSAL

For the immediate reform of education,
For no longer entrusting it to ecclesiastics,
And for the abolition of corporal punishments.

Letter
Of a young student at the University of Paris
to his fellow students.

MY FELLOW STUDENTS:

You know as well as I do the infinite abuses that infect our present system of education. We groan together at having so long been its unfortunate victims. Let us unite in our efforts to escape them and to hasten their complete destruction. Here is a plan that has seemed to me suitable

93

for the purpose. I have communicated it to several other students; they have reached the same judgment, and approved it with all the greater satisfaction in that, having only one or two years left for their education, they would like to share with you the advantages to be found in a plan for education emanating from the National Assembly, the center for the enlightenment of France.

The marks of benevolence with which the Assembly has already designed to honor us[a] should be a sure guarantee that it will not refuse so just a request, even if it were not firmly persuaded that the regeneration, the glory, and the fate of the Nation depend on the reform of education; and that without this precaution the laws dictated by its wisdom will become useless and even harmful to the state. The Assembly, without doubt, convinced that the University is the mother and nurse of the errors and prejudices that have so much obstructed the reorganization of the country, will not allow it any longer to mislead us in the realm of darkness over which it rules. The Assembly will not expose itself to the reproaches that Plutarch made against Numa, the lawgiver of the Romans, for not having begun his legislation by considering the education of youth.

Let us avow openly and sincerely our esteem for worthy ministers of the Catholic religion, to which we shall always be faithful, but let us not be afraid to declare that public opinion, supported by our own experience, makes us believe that the task of national education should not be entrusted to them, that they are in no way capable of being at its head. Such has always been the judgment of those Philosophers who have had sound views in politics. "Everything proves," says the author of the *Social System*,[b] "that priests are of all men the least suited to form fathers of families, statesmen, magistrates, citizens, or reasonable and enlightened beings."

---

[a] Twelve members of the National Assembly were present at the last distribution of prizes of the University.

[b] Vol. 3, p. 106 [Holbach, *ed. note*].

"Woe to the nations," says Helvetius,[c] "which entrust the education of their citizens to priests! They teach only false ideas of justice; it would be better to teach none at all." Many convincing proofs confirm these assertions[d] and present themselves to any enlightened mind; it is for this reason, my fellow students, that I refrain from developing them in detail which the brevity of this letter would not allow.

Let the priests then confine themselves to the already extensive obligations of the priesthood. Let them charge themselves with the choice and instruction of worthy successors. Let them preach the gospel to us, more by the integrity of their conduct than in the sanctity of their pulpits. In a word, let them form us for God and our heavenly home, but leave it to others to form us for our home here below and for our fellow citizens.

This duty, the most important and honorable of all, should be given to men distinguished for their moral life, their probity, their common sense, their sound knowledge, their virtues in the various occupations of society for which we are destined. Their principles will be founded on reason enlightened by long experience, and not on abstract reasonings and capricious and absurd ideas. They will instil their lessons by example and gentleness, and not by authority and by punishments.

Let them educate us under the supervision of government, to which they will give an accounting for their conduct toward us. Let them respect the dispositions, qualities, and talents that nature has given each of us. Let them make our bodies robust and agile, while adorning our minds with useful and agreeable knowledge, and our hearts with all

[c] On Man, sect. 10, Chap. 7.

[d] Ego adolescentulos existimo in scholis fieri stultissimos, quia nihil ex iis quae in usu habemus, aut audiunt aut vident. Petronii Satyricon. [I think young men are made very stupid in schools, since in them they hear nothing, and see nothing, that we find of any use, *The Satyricon* of Petronius.]

social virtues. Let them arouse us more and more to cherish our country, to shed our blood courageously in its defense. . . .

Though this letter is already too long I cannot bring myself, my fellow students, to finish it without another striking observation. The unnatural men, the cruel tyrants hitherto charged with our education, have felt no horror in using punishments as unseemly as they are humiliating, to correct the faults not of mere children but of young men from fifteen to eighteen years old. They have been cruel enough to be eye-witnesses to these punishments, worthy of their inventors.[e] and even to administer them themselves. What shall I say? By a perverted taste, they have inflicted these punishments or watched while they were inflicted, with the eyes of complacency, not to say concupiscence, and always to the great resentment and outrage of the classmates of the unfortunate who endured them. Nature, my fellow students, calls for its rights, too long ignored. Let us drive from our colleges those degraded beings called *correcteurs*. . . .

To summarize in a few words. I propose, fellow students, to name deputies in each college who will assemble on a day of your choosing to deliberate, with a view to presenting a petition to the National Assembly, asking it to draw up a new plan of education before the opening of the next academic year, to order that positions as professor or other teacher, merit being equal, should be given to laymen rather than to ecclesiastics, and that positions as head or principal of a college should always be given only to laymen. . . .

> *Your very humble and obedient servant,*
> DESRAMSER, student at the
> University of Paris

Paris,
second year
of liberty

[e] The monks.

17. A professor writes a radical book on education

THE Abbé Yves-Marie Audrein, like Proyart in Item 12 above, had been an assistant principal at Louis-le-Grand in the 1770's. His development was opposite to Proyart's, for he enthusiastically accepted the Revolution, and was elected to the Legislative Assembly and to the National Convention, in which he served on the Committee on Public Instruction. He then became constitutional bishop of Finistère in Brittany, where he worked to reconcile Catholicism with republicanism. But feeling against the Revolution was very strong in Brittany, and in 1800 he was assassinated by rightist guerillas, who dragged him from a public stage-coach and shot him on the road from Quimper to Vannes.

In 1790, being then an administrative officer at Grassins College, one of the ten full-program colleges of the University of Paris, he presented to the National Assembly a plan of education which he published the next year as a small book. It may be compared to the plan drawn up at the same time by Champagne and the two Guéroults, and printed as Item 53 below. Audrein's plan is typical of many other such proposals and writings, many of them by professors in the colleges, but in some ways it is more radical. It calls for the suppression and expropriation of all existing colleges without delay. It places its whole faith in the "nation," and in a public interest which is seen as wholly embodied in public officials elected under the new constitution. No "private" school, apart from the state system, is even to be allowed to exist. Independence means freedom from private, selfish, corporate, or professional interest; there is as yet no fear that independence may be threatened by the state. Unlike many Revolutionaries, Audrein sees women's education as important; he makes a place for non-Catholics; he wants the heir to the throne to attend public schools from the elementary to the highest level; and in the democratic enthusiasm of the first years of the Revolution he lays out a plan for a kind of student self-government.

This radicalism goes along with a strong sense of order, and a firm insistence on duty and discipline. There is also a stern note of social utility: young men are educated to be useful to society, and not for their own pleasure or status

97

or self-fulfillment. The insistence on equality is very pronounced, and it always means that in a world of unequal talents those with equal ability should receive equal treatment regardless of differences of social background. The stress on equality leads to a demand for national uniformity and standardization; no part of the country should be deprived. Fraternity is also an ideal, and this in turn makes an ideal of what would later be called assimilation; all are to participate in a common culture, without disabling peculiarities or sense of inferiority. Authority should be in the hands of the competent, and persons should be recruited, not by favoritism or social connection, but by education and training and demonstrated abilities; hence a peculiarly French emphasis on severe competition, in which some are admitted and others eliminated.

Audrein, though highly revolutionary, continued to think of himself as a Catholic. He worked to establish the constitutional church, and issued blasts against the "so called philosophy" of the *philosophes* until shortly before his death.

Proposal
on
French National Education

National education includes, besides physical exercise and personal accomplishments, two kinds of teaching, one of which is devoted to the instruction of the mind, and the other to the development of the heart and feelings. The first has knowledge for its object; the second is for the direction of actions. . . .

To look among foreign peoples for the idea or model of such an education would only be to deceive ourselves and mislead our lawmakers. There is no national education anywhere. There are indeed many great schools, whose usefulness is shown by their fame, but they are of limited influence. Even England, whose constitution fits it for national education, hardly has any except in its universities. Let us then not look abroad; it is in the genius that has created the French constitution that we must find the means to preserve it. . . .

98

General order, which is the life of empires, requires that education be divided according to the kinds and classes of individuals for whom it should exist.

Not all have an equal need for the same extent of knowledge. If great positions demand eminent qualities and trained abilities, for ordinary functions a more modest merit will suffice. . . .

Nor should that part of the human race, the most loving and beloved, be forgotten. The female sex, destined especially for domestic occupations but capable of greater things, will in time receive the attentions of our lawmakers. If the whole destiny and ornament of some girls must be work on the farm followed by maternal cares, there are others who are obliged to take more part in the life of society, and who are in need of more knowledge for this purpose. Some are born to renew the moving image of those Roman women who, by their sacred quality as mothers and their use of acquired talents, were deservedly both the glory of their sex and the admiration of their time. To all of them the nation owes its support, and it will find the principles to guide the education of girls in the same foundations as are decreed for boys and men. Though in different degree, it is still the same public spirit and the same national interest that must be created. The goal being the same, the means should be analogous.

The same principle of general order makes for an even more evident distinction. It requires that those for whom elementary knowledge is enough for their own interest and the public interest should be sent without undue delay into agriculture and the trades; that those for whom the study of languages and elementary sciences has made it possible to exercise useful functions should also go into civil life after a few years; and finally that those endowed by nature with a finer intelligence and deeper judgment should be reserved for the sciences and the fine arts.

Hence we have three orders of education naturally established: the little schools, the small colleges or language colleges, and the great or senior colleges.

[There follow several pages on the lower schools, leading into a discussion of the senior colleges, which are to be few in number so that high quality can be preserved, and located in five principal cities. Audrein's most original thought at this point is the idea of practical employment to follow completion of work at the senior college. He envisages a system by which each young man from twenty to twenty-five has a "patron," who initiates him into a career in law, medicine, the church, government, engineering, commerce, etc.]

It is not enough for an ordinary course of national education, prolonged to the age of twenty, to enrich the student's mind and shape his early youth. Since they are to be men of more influence, they need more education. Since others will depend on them, they must know how to be of service. Four years of practical application should enlighten and consolidate the six years of principles.

. . . . The constitution should set the age of twenty-five as the time at which their education is considered complete, so far as having the right to occupy important positions in the state is concerned. I say the "right," because, unless the social system is bad, those who have undergone a long and laborious education should be preferred, if indeed they add good conduct to the merit of ability; for to pretend that, in an examination for public functions, it should be only a question of ability, without regard to other conditions, is an infinitely dangerous political error. A government which would admit the ignorant as well as the educated to demanding positions would of course be as absurd as one which made good and bad men equally the judges of morals. The National Assembly will continue in its wisdom to require credentials and titles for important places. . . .

He who would raise his son for himself in his own way

THE COLLEGE OF LOUIS-LE-GRAND

is a *bad citizen enjoying freedom;* but the man for whom the public good and the national glory are the highest law will submit willingly to conditions which the nation prescribes, and in which he will see the safeguard of his own liberty. Liberty is never better saved than when its abuse is prevented.

For varying studies to be guided by the same spirit and made truly national, they must be subjected to a single universal pattern. . . .

. . . . All schools in the realm must be placed on a ground that belongs to no one, that is made absolutely independent of any private society or particular profession, solely under the direct inspection of the nation, or, what is the same thing, of the different administrative bodies created by decree of the nation's representatives. . . .

Associations of men of letters, men of learning, and artists are undoubtedly useful in a great empire. They would be more so if combined and identified as a French National Academy, with its common center in Paris. While their self-regarding spirit isolates everything, it is important that by a civic spirit everything should be nationalized. . . .

[There follows a discussion of subjects to be taught and professional chairs to be set up, then of the need of boarding establishments for a full and rounded education. These must be public, and operated by the state; in such schools no private tutors for individual students will be permitted.]

Since any system of national education must rest upon equality, the admission of a single private master or preceptor would be a crime. All resources, all zeal should be put in common when one aims at the public good. . . .

If asked in the name of the nation what I think of private rooming arrangements in a public school, I would say that, with very few exceptions, they are for the discipline of colleges what public prostitution is for the morals of the capital.

By the same principles of equality the food in a college,

while always healthful and adequate, should be the same for all. Dress should be national, and whatever distinguishes the students out of doors should make them known as the nation's youth. There should be three ways of admission to the boarding establishments. Some parents are well-to-do and can pay a reasonable fee. . . . Some parents are less fortunate, and some have nothing at all. Help must be given to the former, and everything must be done for the latter, always supposing that we are speaking of boys of unusual talent. . . .

To remove imprudent discussion of the great subject of religion, which would be raised by the indiscreet curiosity of boys of different faiths living together, private boarding establishments should be set up in towns having a certain number of non-Catholics. Their organization should be the same as for the others, and they should be under the same public supervision. The private teaching of religion would be the only difference.

[There follow a few pages on the administration of the colleges, to be in the hands of an administrative board, under which there is to be a disciplinary board, which in turn, by one of the most unusual features of Audrein's plan, is to act in conjunction with a "private board" elected by the students themselves.]

We have wished a thousand times that young people would learn to be their own judges early in life; that they should come to know the basic conflict between sensibility and justice, which will be of such importance for them to understand in the future. Hence there should be a sort of private board, composed of one student elected from each hall, with a few younger teachers; this institution, as salutary as it is national, will be a most important adjunct to the disciplinary boards.

The reader may wish to see a sketch of the duties of youth, the transgression of which should be submitted to the judgment of the private board, and then if necessary to the judgment of the disciplinary board.

[The ensuing list of "essential duties of students" is far from being permissive or anarchical; it describes duties to the Deity, to parents, to teachers, to fellow students, to domestic servants, to the public, and to oneself.]

Such is the chain of duties and the order established to punish transgressors. It gives confidence to the students, for they are judged by their peers; satisfaction to the teachers, for it is the law which decrees penalties; an equal resource to all, for all may appeal to the disciplinary board, or finally to the administrative board itself.

The disciplinary boards will not only deal with the particular conduct or duties of individual students; they will also attend to the general order of college exercises. Everything relating to regulation of the classes, the enforcement of rules in the boarding facilities, which should be the same throughout the country, will be within their jurisdiction. It is under their auspices that wise laws will produce good citizens for the nation, giving them the habit of doing each thing on time; those harmonizing rules that combine continuity with variety in the students' work; that natural justice which attaches each individual to his duty, by making him feel that *one is free in obeying when it is the rule that commands.* The boards will prevent slackness and stop license; it will be to their glory when, by their inquiries or remonstrances, they have persuaded both teachers and students that order comes before all else, and that to reject one's duty cannot be a virtue.

The powers of the disciplinary boards will be supplemented by two levels of exchange of correspondence. If it is important that those who preside over the general destiny of education should know each other and lend mutual aid, so as produce the same spirit everywhere, it is no less important that the students should follow this example in laying the foundations of their future society. The sons as well as the fathers should know how to fraternize. Nothing, then, is more useful than to establish relationships in instruction and subjects of rivalry among educational houses in the same town. Students should share in the feelings of those who inhabit the same country. Wherever they find brothers they should feel affection; their young souls should be stretched for the common good. Such an extension of knowledge, and of a sympathy full of national spirit and civic dedication, cannot fail to have a beneficial effect on both morals and studies.

[Details on how students in different colleges can correspond and associate with each other, and with the public, are then spelled out.]

From what has preceded, it is evident that our old system of education is no longer admissible. New methods are needed for the support and glory of new principles. . . .

The Assembly wishes that throughout the country there should be only one system of weights and measures. Why? Because it is not enough, if all parts of a large people are to hold together, to have only general connections between them. Their particular usages and day-to-day habits must also unite them, reminding them that they are destined to act in the same direction, and to be always themselves.

In a word, the Assembly tells us that the same customs should produce the same sentiments, and that uniformity must always go with fraternity.

[Audrein's little book concludes, as did many others at this time of general enthusiasms for renewing society by legislation, with the text of a bill proposed for enactment by the Assembly. Its twelve articles add details to the discussion above. The final Title XII is very sweeping.]

Title XII

On the Suppression of the Colleges

1. All universities, colleges, boarding institutions, and houses of public instruction are and will remain suppressed, beginning on the day of publication of the present decree, but they will continue their exercises until the next vacation.

2. All property belonging to the said educational establishments, of whatever kind or under whatever name, will be administered according to the principles stated in Title VI above [i.e., by the new civil powers set up by the Revolution], and the income will be paid into the educational funds.

3. Principals, professors, and other officers formerly paid by the colleges or by the government, and who will not be employed in the newly created institutions, will be retired, on such terms as existed in the various colleges before the present re-organization. . . .

18. The ten professors at the College in 1790–91 and 1794–95

IN one of the most drastic measures of the Revolution, the Constituent Assembly reorganized the Catholic Church in France, confiscating all its property late in 1789, and setting up a new constitutional church under the Civil Constitution of the Clergy in 1790–91. Oaths to the new constitution were required of public servants and ecclesiastics, including teachers. When some took the oath and some refused, the colleges were split between "jurors" and "non-jurors."

At Louis-le-Grand the oath was refused by the principal, Romet, by one of the two Philosophy professors—Royou (who was at the same time a flaming counter-revolutionary journalist editing the *Ami du Roi*)—and by the Professor of the Fourth, Germain; in addition, the Professor of the Seventh, Gosset, voluntarily retired with his pension in October, 1790. Romet left in January 1791, and on May 3, 1791, Champagne became principal in his place. Noël, Professor of the Third, went into politics in 1792, but later returned to teaching and became a councillor of the Imperial University under Napoleon. Note that the two Germains are not the same person; more is heard later of Germain (2).

The following table shows two things clearly. More than half the professors at Louis-le-Grand took the civil oath. After the crisis and readjustment of the spring of 1791, the teaching body remained surprisingly stable in the even more turbulent years that followed. In 1794–95, the first academic year after the death of Robespierre, the same men were still holding professorships as had been in June 1791, except for Noël who was serving the Revolution elsewhere, and La Garde, a young man of twenty-three of whom nothing is known and who may have been in the army.

The Ten Professors in 1790–91 and 1794–95

Level	Late 1790	Changes to June 1791	1794–95
Principal	Romet	Champagne	Champagne
Physics	Duport	Duport	Duport
Logic	Royou	Labitte	Labitte
Rhetoric	Selis	Selis	Selis
Second	Champagne	Noël	La Place
Third	Noël	La Place	Marcandier
Fourth	Germain (1)	Marcandier	?
Fifth	Le Provost	Le Provost	Le Provost
Sixth	La Place	La Garde	Bérard
Seventh	Gosset	Germain (2)	Germain (2)

19. Champagne's first problem
as principal

THIS and the two following letters, as well as Item 23, are all in J. F. Champagne's own handwriting. The originals do not show to whom they are addressed. On the face of the letter of

May 19 is written in another hand, "M. the Abbé Sieyès begs MM. the commissioners of education to examine this letter and report their observations to him." Sieyès, one of the more prominent Revolutionaries, was at this time a member both of the constitutional Committee of the National Assembly and of the directory of the Department of Paris. It seems likely that this and the following three letters were all addressed to the directory of the Department of Paris, which Items 20 and 21, addressed to "Monsieur" in the singular, being sent to Sieyès himself as a member of that body.

Some explanation is now necessary of the political organization created in the early phase of the Revolution. Though the new constitution was not proclaimed until September 1791, many of its provisions went into effect during the two preceding years. The old provinces were dissolved, with their various special features, and the country was uniformly divided into 83 departments, all structurally alike, which have existed ever since. Each department was divided into districts, and each district into cantons. Cities and villages received a new municipal organization, each being called a commune.

The Department of Paris (later called the Department of the Seine) included the city and its environs. Beneath it was the "commune" or municipality of Paris, which was divided into 48 "sections," each comprising a few square blocks of the city. Each section had an assembly open to all citizens entitled to vote. The commune and the department each had a council, elected indirectly by the section assemblies. Each section had its committees to do its work, and the commune and department had their boards of administrators who reported to their respective councils. The Directory of the Department of Paris was the executive board of its council. The "revolutionary" and "civil" committees of the sections were very active from 1792 to 1794; these neighborhood militants were the famous *sans-culottes*.

The colleges came under the supervision of the departments. The right of nomination to scholarships, formerly in the hands of town councils, bishops, abbots, private families, or others, was also transferred to the departments. Though administered at the department level, the scholarships were thus in a sense nationalized. The endowments were also nationalized, being equated with the property of the Church, which was nationalized late in 1789 (that is, confiscated, called *biens nationaux* or *domaine national*, and sold off to private persons); but the sale of college and hospital property was deferred, and the colleges continued to receive the income until 1793. Scholarship students therefore continued for a time to be supported, though late in 1791 the Department of Paris ordered that no new appointments to scholarships in the Paris colleges should be made. It is now evident why Champagne, as principal of the college, had so much business with the Department of Paris.

The Constituent Assembly, unlike its successors, never had a committee on public instruction. Instead, as noted above, it assigned educational reform to its committee on the constitution. It is therefore unclear who the "commissioners" mentioned in the letters of May 12 and 19 were. The word *commissaire* then also meant a committee member, and they may have been a kind of sub-committee of the national committee on the constitution, or members of a committee of the Department of Paris.

The following letter of May 9 was written a few days after Champagne became principal. The Department of Paris had ordered him to eliminate non-jurors from the college. Since two of the non-jurors, Romet and Royou, had already gone, his reply is in conformity with the table that appears above as Item 18. It is clear that the college is in disarray, having not only had a turn-over among the professors, but also lost its assistant principals and several masters. Chapel services in the Paris colleges had also just been suppressed, late in April. Champagne uses the Revolutionary language in referring to the religious scruples of some of his students as "the malady of fanaticism." We see also that, having tenure as scholarship holders, various young chaplains and masters who had refused the oath, and so were relieved of their duties, nevertheless continued to live in the college. The resulting acrimony can be imagined.

May 9, 1791

MESSIEURS:

By your letter of May 5 you instructed me to expel from the college all persons who have been replaced for failure to take the civil oath. Allow me the liberty to set before you the state of the College of Louis-le-Grand in this respect. I beg you to indicate to me the course which I should follow. I only wish to act according to your orders.

1. Only one professor has refused the oath. He is M.

Germain, professor of the Fourth. When he came to the College of Louis-le-Grand the room intended for him was occupied by a former professor, M. Poquette, who is still there. M. Germain was placed in the building occupied by retired professors of the University. The principal of this College has never had any power of inspection over this building, which is entirely separate from the interior of the school. Living in it are M. Camyer, who has not taken the oath, and M. Turquet, whose case is the same and who is also in a state of most extreme senility.

2. The professor of the Seventh, M. Gosset, turned in his resignation last October, and the Board granted him a small pension of 300 livres. Since he had been in the house for eighteen years he claims that at the suggestion of the Board he remained here by agreement until Easter. He has just left. He maintains that he had to leave at this time. When he was replaced he went to the city officials to protest against his removal as a non-juror. But it is true that the oath had something to do with his giving up his class.

The four assistant principals and the head of the infirmary have left.

Nine confessors have broken relations with us. I was obliged to let the Easter season pass without changing them, since I saw that many of the students were infected by the malady of fanaticism, and I preferred to let these confessors withdraw gradually at their own choosing, as almost all have now done.

Several masters have left. Seven remain in the college. But they hold scholarships, and two have gone into law studies, with the rest in theology.

The chaplains were replaced from the first. But they remain in the college since they hold scholarships.

I beg you, Messieurs, to be so kind as to indicate the course I should follow, and I will comply exactly.

In the actual operations of the College, there is no person with even the least educational function who has not accepted the law, or who will not take the oath on whatever day the municipality may specify.

I have the honor to be with profound respect,

Your very humble and obedient servant,
CHAMPAGNE, principal

20. Champagne reports agitation among the students

THOUGH Item 16 might suggest the contrary, the French Revolution saw no student radicalism of the kind that appeared in the revolutions of 1830 and 1848 in France and other European countries, and in many parts of the world in the twentieth-century. Various explanations may be suggested for its absence. For one thing, there was a real and massive revolution actually in progress, in which persons of all ages, both sexes, and various classes were taking part. For another, the number of students of age eighteen or over was very small, in proportion to the whole population; they were distributed in handfuls among colleges which had little connection with one another. A third reason might be that youth and adulthood were less distinct than they became later, so that young adults could attend revolutionary clubs along with their elders if they wished. After April 1792 young men of eighteen volunteered for the army, and were later conscripted, along with older men, in support of a war and an ongoing revolution in which they believed. There was no issue of youth versus age; there was no youth culture; there was no literary romanticism; and no outside forces—political, ideological, literary, commercial, or journalistic—sought to recruit followers among the young.

But if there was no student radicalism, as known later, there was much student unrest. This and other letters of Champagne offer evidence of it. It seems to have had no particular political direction. It would appear to reflect a general excitement, or eagerness to become engaged in the great events going on outside the college walls. Perhaps it arose also, as he says, from a sense of futility or irrelevance in their studies, especially when degree requirements were abolished, and it was momentarily expected that a new system of education, new codes of law, and a whole new kind of society would make everything that one was asked to learn obsolete. In the circumstances, Champagne's hope that a few clearly announced regulations would calm the disorders seems optimistic.

May 12, 1791

MONSIEUR:

Yesterday the peace of the College of Louis-le-Grand was broken by a serious incident, of which I wish to inform you in view of the consequences which may follow. At half past ten our students received a letter from Montaigu College urging them to take the afternoon off. This letter circulated through the whole house and produced a kind of effervescence. At one o'clock, during recreation in the courtyard, six young men arrived saying they were deputies from Montaigu. Groups of students soon gathered around them. I arrived without delay and ordered them positively to depart. I myself escorted them out the door. Arrived in the street, I explained to two of them the dangers in their conduct, but they seemed unimpressed. The scene began to attract the attention of passers-by. I went back into the college and was immediately surrounded by two hundred students who seemed more surprised than persuaded. Some protested, though without going beyond the bounds of propriety. But I saw that the general feeling was for the six so-called deputies. For that reason I thought it best not to have the gates of the College closed. The rest of the day there was a general fermentation. This kind of coalition of students, and sending of letters, could have dangerous consequences for education. The students will have time off today, but many of them hope that on Saturday they will be given the free time that they claim to have lost yesterday. You will take on this subject whatever line of action your wisdom may indicate. But I think that it would be useful if, on Saturday morning, MM. the commissioners of education would send a circular on this matter which could be read in the classes.

I am with profound respect,

Your very humble and obedient servant,
CHAMPAGNE, principal

21. Champagne reports more student unrest

The comments in Item 20 apply here also.

May 19, 1791

MONSIEUR:

An opinion is spreading through the colleges that the students should have vacation for July 14, the great celebration of our French unity. Several young men are proposing to address a petition on this subject to the Directory of the Department. Once written, such a petition will not fail to be received and signed with applause in all the colleges. This premature vacation would however be harmful to the students, who have already done little work this year, disagreeable to parents who would not know what to do with their children, and bad for the city of Paris in that parents would object to sending their children to study in a city where vacations were so long.

For the same reason, moreover, since the suppression of the university tribunal which used to preside over the annual prize awards, the young men are persuaded that there will be no awards this year.

It would perhaps be useful for these young men to know immediately that the awards will be made. Such knowledge will restore life to their studies and arouse emulation for a few months, and emulation will be good for the students and for the colleges, by directing the students' ideas to useful ends.

The young men now studying Philosophy are almost all scholarship students. Before going on to higher studies they used to be required to take the degree of master of arts, which today has become very useless. Most of them, having no fixed objective, are giving up their classes from boredom, especially at a time when they are looking forward to vacation. To hold them to their duties it would perhaps be advantageous to require, if they are to retain their scholarships, that they present statements from their professors, not to be delivered until the first of August.

You will judge in your wisdom, Monsieur, together with MM. the Commissioners, whether you would not think it useful to send a circular to all the classes of the university, settling the opinion of our youth on these matters and avoiding further fermentation. It might be enough to announce such intentions to the rector of the university, who could issue a printed order in which the ruling of the Directory or of the commissioners could be inserted.

I have the honor to be with profound respect,

Your very humble and obedient servant,
CHAMPAGNE, principal

22. The Department of Paris takes a dim view of the colleges

THIS document shows the dangerously low esteem in which the colleges were held by the Department of Paris, even in the early and supposedly moderate phase of the Revolution. It is a statement made by the Paris directory to the elected departmental council. Its hostile tenor should not be attributed to the anti-intellectualism of ignorant persons. The Paris council in 1791 included Sieyès, Talleyrand, the philanthropic duke of La Rochefoucauld, the scientists Lacépède and Jussieu, and various lawyers and men of affairs. It was the fatal weakness of the old educational system that the educated themselves did not believe in it.

It should be remembered, in reading this item, that "gothic" before the Gothic Revival was an ordinary term of reproach. The "nations" referred to were shadowy organizations within the University of Paris, which had once been important, but in the eighteenth century were more like large faculty clubs, in which professors could get together, talk, view with alarm, and pass resolutions.

The "single day of scandal" probably refers to the violence at Sainte-Barbe College on April 25, 1791. The incident is also mentioned in Item 26 below in Champagne's letter of September 30, 1792. As one of the few occasions during the French Revolution when students became wantonly destructive, it deserves a few words of explanation. Sainte-Barbe was an old college, founded in 1460; its few scholarships were consolidated into Louis-le-Grand in 1763; but unlike most of the consolidated colleges it continued to exist separately, and in the last years before 1789 had become a small and select institution for paying students, some of whom used it as a residence hall from which they went out for studies in the higher faculties. Many were theology students working for degrees at the Sorbonne. In 1791 the principal and all the teachers at Sainte-Barbe refused the civil oath. They were supported by their students. An officer of the Paris municipality, J.A.J. Cousin, who happened also to be a professor at the College of France, appeared at the college to enforce the law. Meeting solid resistance, he peaceably withdrew, probably with intimations of further action against the college. The students then broke loose, tore the wood paneling from the walls, smashed the tables and chairs, and broke the windows. The old Sainte-Barbe College disappeared during the Revolution. The modern college of the same name is actually an offshoot of Louis-le-Grand, which developed when Lanneau, assistant to Champagne, left to set up his own "private" school about the year 1800.

A Statement by the Directory of the Department of Paris

November 16, 1791

While from one moment to the next, like the rest of the country, we impatiently await the organization of national education, it is not clear what the Directory can do with all those gothic institutions called *colleges* that are piled up together in one quarter of the capital, with those *Nations* and *Faculties* of law and of arts which are so alien to the names they bear, or with that abstract body called the *University* which can never be seen to exist or to act, except in a few ridiculous ceremonies and useless processions of the rector, questors, apparitors, and other salaried drones who share a considerable revenue among themselves. The council will learn with surprise that all this teaching apparatus consumes 1,336,175 livres of annual income from funded revenues, farms, and house rentals, and that after all ordinary expenses are paid there remains an annual surplus of 135,632 livres for extraordinary outlays.

Useless as they are, these schools have sometimes attracted the attention of the departmental Directory. Adversaries of the Constitution, to make their venom more dangerous, have been trying to corrupt our youth, like cowardly enemies who poison springs in their rage. The vigilance of the Directory has stopped these disorders. We have removed some boys who were misled and fell into excesses against their classmates, so that these atrocious schemes of fanatics have produced only a single day of scandal. Professors and other employees subject to the civil oath have been replaced for failure to take it. The Directory has decided out of prudence to close the theology schools of the Sorbonne and Navarre College. In the colleges a few chairs in logic, which had too few students, have not been filled. But all the efforts of the Directory have not been enough to overcome the stubborn resistance of officers of the University removed for not taking the oath, who are still arguing their cases in the law courts.

23. Champagne again on student disorders

WE SEEM TO have here the case of a troublesome philosophy student who had appealed to the administrators of the Department of Paris. Champagne writes to justify his own course of action, which seems to have been very moderate.

Paris, January 2, 1792

MESSIEURS:

The petition from M. Tanqueray that you have sent on to me assumes two matters to be facts. First, that the departmental directory intended to punish the Philosophy students simply for their disorders in sounding the bell, summoning the other students, and striking the principal in the dark. Second, that M. Tanqueray was not present at this scene, as he tries to prove by M. Rosen's declaration. These two facts are not correct.

The directory intended to repress student insubordination, and in particular the insurrection on the whole day of Sunday, November 27. This insurrection was marked by three circumstances of which the evening scene was merely the conclusion. At morning mass the Philosophy students broke out in an uproar especially during the credo. They let out all sorts of cries, and I distinctly heard the song *Vive le Vin* ["Here's to Wine!"]. M. Tanqueray was singing himself. But I was at the other end of the chapel trying to control the Humanities students. I do not know whether the bounds of decency were exceeded, and I do not insist on this point. At dinner all the masters, professors, principal, etc. as they came in were hissed or applauded ironically. I observed M. Tanqueray and called him to order, but he went on doing the same with the next master who appeared.

That evening at supper, a quarter of an hour before the final scene, the hissing and applause began again. I observed M. Tanqueray starting up on two occasions. He added a mocking word that was a nickname given by the boys to one of the masters. I again called him to order. He replied that the word was in the language and repeated it, shouting as before. I do not know whether this evening scene had been prepared in advance. But one of the students who has been sent away told me, on the day he left, that I had done well to stop it because there were still three or four "scenes" to be played. But what happened at dinner and supper indicated M. Tanqueray to me as one of the authors of the trouble. It is on these grounds that I reported him as one of the guilty ones.

As for M. Rosen's declaration, it is not accurate. Before the bell rang I had already been hit several times in the darkness. Just as it stopped ringing the grill opened and the boys poured out. I felt a stone or hard object strike me on the arm. They shouted to the other students to come down while running into the second court. I ran after them at my risk and peril, taking another way, so as to reach the door of another building and hold back the younger boys for fear of some accident. Passing by the refectory, where the lamps were still lit because the servants were still there, I clearly saw M. Tanqueray close to a lamp. He passed in front of me and went into the first court to join a group of his companions. The scene was not yet over, for in a second court when I saw the humanists quietly at their windows I followed the philosophers to get them back inside, or to identify them, and it was then that I was struck by a violent blow on the head.

I spoke to M. Rosen about all these incidents, in the presence of M. Coatpont, the master of the Oriental Language students, who had also seen M. Tanqueray after supper. Both declared that M. Tanqueray had remained with them, but that when he heard the bell he had left them, saying that he was going to see what was happening, and that he had returned some time later.

These particulars, while they refute M. Rosen's statement, do not implicate M. Tanqueray in what affected me personally. I may say that I have made no inquiry as to the blows I received. Good order had been troubled for a long time. I had already warned MM. Gallois and Dupré. The total insubordination of the philosophy students was already spreading to the humanists, and by the admission of one of those sent away it was fomented by influences from outside the school. In the difficult position in which I find myself I consulted all the masters. Nevertheless, to avoid mistakes, I have made no charges against any student without having evidence myself of his insubordination. It is from M. Tanqueray's conduct at dinner, and especially at supper, that I have reported him as one of the authors of the trouble.

I am with deep respect

Your most humble and obedient servant,
CHAMPAGNE
Principal, College of Louis-le-Grand

24. Students volunteering for the army are assured of keeping their scholarships

ON APRIL 20, 1792, after several months of agitation, propaganda, and legitimate fear of foreign intervention against the Revolution, France declared war on Austria. The Austrians were soon joined by Prussia and Sardinia-Piedmont, and by the following February by Great Britain, the Dutch Netherlands and Spain. An unprecedented Coalition against France was thus formed, with various French royalists, noblemen, prelates, and émigrés taking its side, and with Louis XVI and Marie Antoinette secretly hoping for an Austrian victory.

The French army, from which many regular officers had defected, and somewhat disorganized by their new ideas of liberty, at first suffered a series of defeats and humiliations. With the Austrian and Prussian armies poised for the invasion of France, the Legislative Assembly proclaimed a national emergency. Young men including students volunteered with enthusiasm. This was called "flying to the frontiers," and for several years to be "at the frontiers" was synonymous with being in the army.

The present item is from the proceedings of the Assembly on July 30, 1792. It heard a delegation from Louis-le-Grand in the morning, and responded that evening.

A few days later Paris received the Brunswick Manifesto, signed by the Prussian commander, which threatened the city with destruction and all revolutionaries with punishment unless Louis XVI was obeyed as king. Thereupon, on August 10, several thousand armed militants attacked the Tuileries, forced the dethronement of Louis XVI, put an end to the constitution of 1789–91, and brought about the election of a new assembly called the National Convention.

(I)

July 30, 1792

Morning Session

A delegation of students from the College of Louis-le-Grand is admitted to the bar:

Its spokesman states that the oldest among the students, those in Logic, in Rhetoric, and even in Theology, eager to share at the frontiers in the dangers of several of their comrades who have already been honorably wounded in defense of the country, are resolved to go off to fight against the barbarians of the North who are coming to attack us. But, since their intention is to resume their studies after the foreigner is defeated, he informs the Assembly of the concern of those who have scholarships, and who fear that they may not find them still available on their return. He asks on their behalf the just favor that these scholarships be preserved.

(II)

July 30, 1792

Evening Session

The National Assembly, having heard the petition of several students of the College of Louis-le-Grand, who state that their philosophy course being finished they have the right to retain their scholarships for three more years, and who ask to serve at the frontiers while retaining this right, considering that in fighting for all they should not lose an advantage that they would enjoy if working for themselves only;

Considering that it is in the country's interest that at this moment of danger the greatest possible number of citizens should fly to its defense, and having heard the report of its Committee on Public Instruction;

Declares as a matter of public emergency that:

Sieurs Charpentier, Creuset, Courtois, Vinot, Monvoisin, Loques, Croissy, Maugras, Lestamand, Flosen, and Lamare, students at the College of Louis-le-Grand, and all others in the same case who may in the future wish to follow their generous example, shall preserve their scholarships while serving at the frontiers, for as long a time as they would have enjoyed them had they preferred to remain in Paris.

25. The College is disrupted by the quartering of soldiers

The National Convention first met on September 21, 1792, and proclaimed the Republic. A name recalling Louis XIV now became highly unsuitable, so that the College of Louis-le-Grand was renamed Equality College. The uprising of August which dethroned the king also "revolutionized" both the commune and the department of Paris. The executive officer of the department of Paris was now called the attorney general syndic, and it is to him that the following communication is addressed.

Volunteers continued to rush forward. So many came from Louis-le-Grand that the Convention passed a resolution in its honor—that it had "deserved well of the country." On September 20 the ragged French army turned back the Prussians at Valmy, and a few weeks later defeated the Austrians in a pitched battle at Jemappes.

Volunteers were quartered at Equality College, and Champagne's message tells what happened.

September 27, first year
of the French Republic
[1792]

To Citizen the Attorney General Syndic:

Next Monday is the day of reopening of the school year. But at this time our establishment is occupied by four hundred Volunteers quartered in it by the municipality and the section. Twenty have just arrived at this moment. I beg you to believe that they have been welcomed with all the fraternity that is possible. We were short of sheets, but have managed to find some by our own efforts and by the zeal of good citizens of our section. We spare ourselves no hardship or pains when the public need so demands. Twelve of the Volunteers are sick and are in our infirmary. We shall keep these Volunteers with pleasure as long as is necessary, and I am glad to do justice to their good behavior and honesty towards us.

But the great number of troops occupies almost all our space. Two of our classrooms are serving as guardhouses. Our courtyards are occupied by ammunition chests and four pieces of cannon. Moreover, they are used every day for drills.

The dormitories and study halls are used for sleeping or stacking arms, or for the soldiers' cooking.

I have put in a separate place those students who happen to be here now, and who number about eighty, so that while the Volunteers may have whatever they need the order necessary in an educational establishment can be maintained so far as possible. Yet I foresee that in the midst of arms, drums, and the drilling of 400 Volunteers, and the considerable number of outsiders who come to see them, it will be hard for us to attend to our peaceable schoolwork.

On the other hand, the bulk of our students will not arrive until the 12th or 15th of the month, and it is a hundred times better not to begin classes than to begin them in such unavoidable tumult.

I request the Directory, in the circumstances, to authorize me to postpone the reopening of classes for a week or ten days.

If the Volunteers must remain here for a certain length of time, we will do everything possible to reconcile what we owe the country, in the persons of our brave Volunteers, with the duties we owe our students.

CHAMPAGNE, principal of
Equality College, formerly
Louis-le-Grand

26. Champagne describes the senior scholarships at Equality College

THE Department of Paris, whose officials were of course located in the city, was hard pressed by the revolt of the sections and the radicalization of the commune. It seems likely that many of these popular revolutionaries, who might be roughly literate but without much education, had little patience with what went on in the colleges. The Department of Paris began inquiries into the scholarships held by students from ages eighteen up into the twenties. Such young men were needed in the army, and in any case, at this point in the Revolution, the study of theology would be considered useless if not positively harmful, lawyers were out of favor, and medical doctors could be the victims of popular skepticism also.

Champagne's reply gives a good picture of how scholarships were used to support professional education. He is sufficiently revolutionary himself to propose that the theology scholarships be simply abolished. He still hopes for early legislation from the new Convention, which, however, was delayed for another three years.

September 30, first year
of the French Republic [1792]

To Citizen the Attorney General Syndic:

I hasten to give you the information you desire on what are called the "senior scholarships" existing in Equality College, formerly Louis-le-Grand.

Formerly, when young men had finished their philosophy course they had the right to study in what were called the three higher faculties, namely medicine, law, and theology.

The medical course lasts about six years. Those going into this kind of study enjoyed, by law, the right to retain their scholarships while outside the College. They received 550 livres a year.

Forty scholars are studying medicine today. They are paid every three months on receipt of certificates of study or registration. After three years they must pass examinations and defend theses; otherwise their scholarships are declared vacant.

A great number of our young men devote themselves seriously to this study. Yet some are content merely to register, so as to be in order for receipt of their payment.

The law course lasts three years. Students can either live in the College while taking this course, or, alternatively, the law allows them to live outside with a scholarship payment of 500 livres a year. In that case they are required to reside with a lawyer, and to be registered at the law school. The number of these students is about 50.

Since 1789 most of them have neglected to register, because they counted on the early reorganization of public instruction at any moment.

The schools of medicine and law still exist. Several decrees have ordered that their courses should continue as in the past, until the definitive reorganization.

Despite the abuses existing in these studies, and the decay of the schools, it is well to consider that five-sixths of the scholarships belong to Departments in all parts of the Republic. The Departments are very attached to their rights of nomination. If their present scholars were suppressed, and if they were not permitted to nominate new ones, I believe that there would be loud complaints, as there were when the Department of Paris suspended the nominations to junior scholarships in 1791.

The theology course used to last ten years. This was the time, the most precious in life, that was thought necessary to produce what was called a "doctor." The Departments of the Oise and the Somme each had 12 scholarships for this kind of study. The number of such students rose to about 50.

The law allowed them to enjoy their scholarships outside the College while preparing to take holy orders.

So long as the theology classes continued to exist, these students claimed the right to enjoy their scholarships by a decree of the Constituent Assembly ordering institutions of public instruction to be maintained as in the past until the definitive reorganization.

As soon as the theology classes were closed I took strong steps with the Directory to obtain a decision on this category of students. From one delay to another, things have remained just the same.

Meanwhile these students were without occupation or aim. They were lodged and fed. That was all.

Many of them, attached to all the usual theological prejudices, showed a revolting lack of civic spirit. It was students of this kind that destroyed Sainte-Barbe college in an insurrection. The same causes might produce the same result here. I have found no other way of protecting the younger generation confided to me than by letting the theology students use their permission to board outside, while forbidding them so far as possible any communication with the younger boys.

The existence of such students can only be harmful in every way in a college. Since the enjoyment of their scholarships no longer has any purpose, I think it would be appropriate for all scholarships in theology to be declared vacant.

I note that there are two other colleges, Harcourt and Cardinal Le Moine, that have respectively 24 and 36 or 40 theology scholarships.

All these students are now on vacation. If they present themselves I shall not have the right to refuse them admittance, by virtue of their tenure as scholarship holders.

One other observation suggests itself. It is that several of these students, after doing six months or a year of theology, have left this study to take up medicine or law. It would perhaps be fair to let these students finish their studies, crediting them in their new courses with the time they have already used. In any case any provisional ruling will not be for long, since we are assured that public instruction will be one of the first concerns of the new National Convention.

I note the letter you sent me authorizing postponement of reopening of the college for a few days.

May you long live free, Citizen Attorney General Syndic,

> CHAMPAGNE, principal of
> Equality College, formerly
> Louis-le-Grand

27. The National Convention orders the sale of all college endowments

AT THIS point a brief view of the general background for Items 27 through 34 is in order. The year 1793 saw the convulsive climax of the Revolution, with popular and insurrectionary pressures exploding repeatedly from below. By the following year the revolutionary government under the Committee of Public Safety, of which Robespierre was a member, won a degree of control over this spontaneous revolutionism; and after Robespierre's death, in July 1794, those remaining in power, while generally republican, were chiefly concerned with holding the gains of 1789-91 against the hostility of both left and right.

The year 1793 began with the execution of Louis XVI. This was followed by the final formation of the First Coalition, military reverses, the defection of the trusted revolutionary General Dumouriez, and the outbreak of civil war. To a rural insurgency in Western France was added the revolt of the great provincial cities against the radicalism of Paris. As the Revolution seemed about to dissolve into anarchy within, and to be undone by military intervention from outside, the most active and determined of the Paris militants, in their sections and in the commune, demanded various kinds of emergency action from the National Convention. The inflation of prices and shortage of bread, brought on largely by the Revolution itself, made such demands intense and uncompromising. An air of appalling suspicion and hatred spread everywhere; to call it paranoiac would be misleading, because the grounds for it were very real. On May 31 an armed crowd of tens of thousands besieged the Convention. The party in the Convention called the Mountain, carrying a more moderate majority with it, as it did for another year, expelled the group known as Girondins, whom the popular activists especially detested. The Mountain dominated the Convention until July 1794.

In July 1793 the popular hero Marat was assassinated, the civil struggles continued through the summer, and the foreign invaders seemed on the threshhold of victory. Another insurrection on September 5 pushed the Convention into further "revolutionary" measures. It decreed a *levée en masse*, or mass rising, to provide troops and stimulate war production. A national or citizen army now confronted the more sluggish aristocratic officers and professional soldiers of the other powers. The Convention also introduced price controls and a kind of state-managed economic system, which was understood to be temporary, and was allowed to lapse when the military crisis was over. It enlarged the Revolutionary Tribunal, passed a more rigorous Law of Suspects, instituted the Terror, and set up the revolutionary dictatorship of the Committee of Public

Safety. What followed was in effect the first example in history, in a country as large and populous as France, of an enforced national mobilization of manpower, resources, opinion, and fanatical enthusiasm in a total war.

The impact of all this on the colleges was ruinous and final. The ten Paris colleges managed to hold their annual distribution of prizes in August 1793, and awards were made to eighty-four students whose names are known, and who came from all the ten colleges. For some unknown reason Louis-le-Grand was poorly represented in these honors, but it was the only one to survive the general liquidation. It did so, in all probability, because Champagne himself was a good revolutionary, and because he stuck to his post, but also because the college had been a scholarship institution for thirty years, and could rightly be said to have long embodied the principles of equality.

The universities, to whose faculties of arts many of the best colleges belonged, were never formally abolished during the French Revolution. As their historian Liard put it, they simply vanished. It is true that the Convention, under strong pressure, decreed their abolition on September 15, 1793. The decree was repealed, however, on the following day. The legal situation therefore remained ambiguous, but in fact the universities and colleges ceased to function. They did so because of the hostility of local revolutionary authorities, because their teachers were demoralized and dispersed, because even those who wished to remain were paid very irregularly or not at all, because older students went off to the army and younger ones were kept at home by their parents, and—last but not least—because they lost their endowed income.

Item 27 is the action by which the Convention ordered the college endowments to be sold. Consisting mainly of pieces of real estate, these endowments, along with the property of the Church, had been confiscated in 1789, and so were in the hands of administrators of the national domain, who according to the law transmitted the income to the colleges until a final decision on their disposition should be made. This decree of March 8, 1793, represents that final decision.

It is difficult to assess the forces or purposes which the decree reflects. There was undoubtedly, at this time of rising anger among working-class militants, a good deal of scorn and contempt for the colleges with their classical education. There were also high-level pressures within the government itself; especially in time of military emergency the finance committee of the Convention wanted to produce revenue by selling as much of the confiscated property as possible. But it seems also that those who voted to liquidate the college endowments did so with the best interests of education in mind. It was probably true that the endowments were "wasting away," to quote the speech below, in the hands of temporary official administrators who had little incentive to collect rents, which in any case under revolutionary conditions a great many tenants were refusing to pay, and which if paid were losing their value through inflation.

The idea of disendowing the colleges was not altogether shocking. The Abbé Audrein and others, who were genuinely concerned for education, had proposed since 1790 that the endowments be transferred to the state. There was a respectable body of opinion which held that all perpetual foundations were bad; Turgot had said so in Diderot's *Encyclopédie*, and had wished they might be suppressed. It was a belief of liberal thinkers at the time, expressed by Thomas Jefferson among others, that the past should have no binding force upon the present, that the living generation must always be free. It was felt to be unfair, or contrary to the principle of equality, that some colleges should be wealthy from their own resources, while others were poor; that some parts of the country should be well provided for, while others suffered from lack of schools.

The reader will observe in Article 2 that the decree was by no means aimed at former ecclasiastical property alone. It expressly included college and scholarship funds of which lay bodies or private persons were the trustees. The educational endowments were ordered sold not because they were church property, but because they were educational property, and because it was believed that education itself would be the better if no longer dependent on ancient foundations with their archaic provisions. Some in the convention, at least, intended that schools and colleges should henceforth be paid for by the "nation." If succeeding governments—and their taxpayers—had been willing and able to realize this intention, a system of state universities and schools of a modern kind might have developed. This did not happen for many years, and the loss of their endowments was a blow by which large segments of French education were permanently crippled. The question of the endowments, or of what might be done to replace them, remained a subject of discussion for some time, and was one of the main themes of Champagne's book of 1800, of which extracts appear as the final item in this book.

It is a curious fact that the spokesman for this action of

March 1793 was the famous Fouché, later Napoleon's chief of police. He had been a professor and head of a college himself until the preceding summer, when he was elected to the Convention from Nantes. In 1793 he was an advanced revolutionary, soon to be known for his ruthlessness in repressing rebellion at Lyon. In his speech, he is reporting for the committees on finance and on public instruction, who jointly recommended the decree. It was immediately enacted.

CITIZENS:

It is only gradually that the lawmaker can bring about the good of his country, either because he is afraid to overthrow the foundations of past errors at one blow, or because he becomes aware of them only in stages.

The Constituent and Legislative Assemblies ordered the sale of various properties in the national domain, but to avoid alarming public opinion they respected the endowments of colleges, scholarships, and other establishments of public instruction, while wishing also to do homage to science and letters.

The National Convention has the advantage of a more enlightened public opinion. It can show, in no less solemn a manner, its love for the sciences by devoting special funds to their support, and it can be sure of general assent in ordering the sale of all the public domain, which is wasting away day by day in the hands of the administrators who are in charge of it. Three years of experience have convinced those who may have any doubts of the usefulness and urgency of such a measure.

Yet we must admit that if opinion is formed on this matter, it still needs to be reassured, and we ourselves must be free of any suspicion of indifference to whatever concerns public instruction. Surely, any regime might be stigmatized by the spectacle which France now presents. Misguided or ignorant persons, left to themselves, run the risk of falling into false and dangerous ideas. The houses of education in our departments offer nothing but ruins to our eyes; the colleges are almost entirely abandoned; professors and students depending on scholarships ask vainly for the basic elements of subsistence, which are stagnating in the offices of those who administer the public domain.

It might be said that we are falling back into the barbarism of early times. It might be said that what we want is the liberty of savages, who see in revolution only the pleasure of overturning the world, and not the means to order it, to improve it, to render it more free and happy. It might be said that, like tyrants, we purposely leave man in darkness and degradation, the better to transform him, in our interest and for our own passions, into a ferocious beast.

Citizens, slander seizes avidly on such observations, to turn them against the real friends of liberty and public order. Let us make haste to refute them. Let us devote all our time to the serious work of education. It is necessary to the establishment of the Republic. And, to cite even a more favorable augury, it has become a necessity of the French people, who demand it insistently, because they feel profoundly that they cannot be free without it, that liberty and education are inseparable, and that they must be joined together for the improvement of human nature, and to fulfill our double hope of becoming the example and model for all peoples of the earth.

Here is the projected law which I am charged with presenting to you in the name of your committees of public instruction and of finance:

ARTICLE I

The properties forming the endowments of colleges, scholarships and other establishments of public instruction, under whatever name they may exist, will from the present moment be sold in the same way and under the same conditions as all other domains of the Republic, subject to exceptions as specified below.

ARTICLE 2

These same properties, whether their administration was formerly entrusted to regular or secular religious congregations, or to lay bodies or private persons, will be administered from January 1, 1793, until the date of their sale by the officials in charge of the national domains, under supervision of the administrative bodies. . . .

ARTICLE 3

The said colleges and establishments will cease, beginning today, to receive the income and the arrears that may be due to them from the public treasury.

ARTICLE 5

Excepted from the provisions of Articles 1 and 2 are the buildings which are or may be in actual use by the colleges, and by all other educational establishments for both sexes; the lodgings of teachers, professors, and students; also the gardens and enclosures adjoining them, and others which though separate are for the use of educational establishments, such as botanical gardens and sites used for natural history.

The administrative bodies are required to proceed with the urgent repairs needed to prevent the ruin or deterioration of buildings reserved above, but must not, on the pretext of this authorization, allow themselves to undertake any works of enlargement or aesthetic improvement.

ARTICLE 8

Beginning as of last January 1, 1793, the pay of professors and teachers, both in the colleges and in other French establishments of public instruction, shall be at the expense of the nation. . . .

28. Champagne reports that the Equality College must close unless aided financially

THIS letter is a cry for help, made necessary by the loss of college endowments. The Convention responded by sporadic grants to keep Equality College open, but the funds authorized were paid irregularly, tardily, and sometimes not at all, and the three school years 1793–96 were the most difficult of the whole revolutionary decade. By 1795 there were only fifty students left in the college.

Champagne's remark that in thirty years the college had educated "over 15,000 young men" must have been written in haste. If it enrolled about 500 students a year for thirty years, the number of young men educated would depend on the number of years they stayed. Probably two or three thousand would be a more accurate figure for students actually produced since 1763.

Paris, May 29, 1793

To the Committee of Public Instruction of the Convention:

The law of March 8 orders that the properties forming the endowments for colleges and scholarships shall be sold, and that the colleges shall cease to receive both their income from such property and their arrears of income, which henceforth are to be collected by the receivers of the national domain.

The property of Equality College will be sold in consequence of this decree; the income will be collected by the receivers, and nothing has been done to replace it.

This house, the greatest educational establishment in France, is therefore today in the greatest distress, and if the Convention does not come to its aid it will be closed in a few days.

This establishment belongs to the whole Republic. It consists of five hundred scholarships assigned to more than forty departments.

By the law of May 5 [1793] it is decreed that vacant

scholarships shall be given to sons of citizens who have taken arms in defense of the country. Already a great number of local governments are preparing to execute this decree, and in a short time a great number of scholarship-holders will arrive from different departments at the college. However, no funds remain, and nothing replaces them.

It is not only a question of indemnity for the scholarships, but also of arranging for the expenses of organization, if only provisionally, for example of the infirmary which no one wishes to suppress, etc. Agreement must also be reached with the departments as to the number and distribution of the scholarships. These arrangements will require considerable time on the part of local governments. Meanwhile it is impossible to meet expenses, for our suppliers refuse to provide except for cash, not wishing to be caught in the liquidation.

Moreover in this house, which for thirty years has educated over fifteen thousand young men, there are a number of persons attached to the administration since its beginning, and several masters who have grown old in the difficult work of education, and who will be turned out of doors without the slightest indemnity.

The law of August 18 [1792] provides for indemnities to various monks operating colleges, such as the Mulotins, the Bonics, the Trouillardistes. It makes no mention of colleges operated by citizens. Subsequent laws are equally silent, assuming such indemnities to be already accorded. They are indeed a matter of strict justice.

Note that over a hundred young scholarship-holders of Equality College are now serving in the armies of the Republic and that they retain their scholarships by decree. It has been thought a sacred duty to pay them in April before any other expenditure, but today their payment must fail.

Surely there is a difference, so far as their property is concerned, between this college and those maintained by monks and orders which are harmful to the public cause.

The property of this college has been administered under supervision of the municipality and the department, which receive and verify its accounts exactly. All objects of value, which reach a considerable total sum, are today kept under lock and key, and the constituted authorities will see with what scrupulous fidelity they have been preserved for the Republic.

It cannot be the will of the Convention to dissolve this college, which it declared under the difficult circumstances of September 17, 1792 to have deserved well of the country, at the time when all our young men capable of bearing arms flew to the defense of the Republic. Yet this establishment will be destroyed in fact, unless aid is immediately received. . . .

I think that, since this establishment is charitable in nature and belongs to the whole Republic, it would be right to include it under the decree concerning hospitals, and so to keep it in operation until the definitive organization of public instruction.

If this is not possible, it is at least only a matter of justice that Equality College, composed uniquely of scholarship-holders, should be authorized provisionally to receive its revenues, until the constituted authorities shall have provided definitively for their replacement. Otherwise in a few days this house will be destroyed. . . .

CHAMPAGNE
Principal of Equality College
LESIEUR, steward

29. Champagne reports statistics on College income and expenses

THE Department of Paris, following the decree of March 8 which deprived the colleges of their endowed income, and upon orders from the Minister of the Interior, made inquiries of the ten full-program Paris colleges to ascertain the amount of this income, and also of their expenses. Its purpose was to learn the value of the college properties when and if sold, and how much it would cost if they were to be supported from public funds.

All the colleges replied, and this is Champagne's report for Equality College. It gives a good picture of internal arrangements and operations. It may be noted that only one-eighth of the college's endowed income (66,030 out of 528,114 livres) came from the kinds of property rights that the French Revolution abolished—tithes and feudal, manorial and seigneurial dues. Seven-eighths of its lost income came from property in the modern sense, which the Revolution in principle, and usually in practice, respected.

Equality College

July 6, 1793

Statement on Scholarships actually in effect in the different colleges and endowments composing Equality College, on vacant scholarships, and on the income and ordinary expenses of the College.

[There follows an itemized list of the endowed income and number of scholarships for each of the twenty-eight former colleges merged into Louis-le-Grand in 1763. Totals are as follows:]

Endowed income:	410,216 livres
Scholarship students:	
Present at the College	293
At the frontiers	58
Absent	71
	422
Vacant scholarships	23
Total scholarships in effect	455

The income of this college [Louis-le-Grand proper, without the twenty-eight former small colleges merged with it] is today about 59,115 livres. To wit: 23,865 l. in funded income [*rentes*], 31,100 l. in rural farms and 5,150 l. in house rentals.

In addition this college receives 30,000 l. a year from the income of the University, which raises its income to 89,115 l. [This sum of 30,000 was actually provided by the government, by the agreement going back to 1719, and was used to pay salaries to the principal and the professors, and apparently some overhead costs. Hence the professors' salaries and most of the principal's income do not appear in the tables below. The Department of Paris had asked for information only on the "private" or endowed income of the Paris colleges.]

In 1777 the amount of income permitted the establishment of 24 new scholarships, but income having since diminished by about 12,000 livres through abolition of the tithe and feudal dues, it was ordered that the 24 new scholarships should be suppressed, and that the number of endowed scholarships should be in proportion to net income that remained.

Statement on Masters and Their Honoraria

Principal—honorarium and annual supplement	2,400	l.
postal service, carriages, and other expenses	600	l.
	3,000	l.
Five scholarship examiners at 300 l. each	1,500	
Two assistant principals at 800 l. each	1,600	
Doctor of Laws, associate	600	
Conference master for law students	500	
Four philosophy masters at 400 l. each	1,600	
Two rhetoric masters at 500 l. each	1,000	

One Second master	450
One Third master	450
One Fourth master	450
One Fifth master	400
One Sixth master	400
One Seventh master	400
One Seventh regent	400
Three supplementary masters at 150 l. each	450
One master for students kept in college on days of leave	72
One chaplain	150
	13,422

[It is likely that these sums, down through the "doctor of laws," are in the nature of supplements for extra work, beyond professorial salary, and for the masters are cash payments in addition to board and room.]

All masters receive lodging, meals, heat, light, etc.; service at the cost of the College, and care in event of illness.

The eight professors of the College receive meals. Those who do not eat in the dining halls receive 500 l. a year in lieu thereof. Four professors at present are receiving this indemnity, which adds 4,000 l. to the above figure, for a total of

17,422

[There is no explanation of the discrepancy by which four professors at 500 l. are made to total 4,000. It must be simply an error.]

The principal having no boarders on his own account, as in the other colleges of Paris, can draw no profit from their fees.

The number of masters is in proportion to the number of students residing in the college. It is carried here at its present level. But if the number of resident students were to increase, it would be necessary to increase the number of masters.

THE COLLEGE OF LOUIS-LE-GRAND

STATEMENT ON THE SERVANTS

Three porters	650 l.
Wine-waiter and assistant	360
Baker and assistant	500
Chief Cook, assistant and three kitchen helpers	790
Servant to the Steward	150
Twenty quarter-boys at 150 l. each	3,000
Two watchmen, in charge of lamps	400
Three visitors	350
Servant to the Principal	150
Servant to Grand Master, 150 l., plus his meals, at 500 l.	650
	7,000

In addition, from income from the sale of fats, a distribution is made every year to employees of the kitchen, bakery, and wine cellar of about	500 l.
To an old kitchen servant almost blind	120
To a very aged former quarter-boy	75
These two also receive meals, and render the College such services as may be asked of them	
	7,695

EXPENSES FOR THE INFIRMARY

At the time of the consolidation of the small colleges with Louis-le-Grand in 1763 it was recognized as absolutely necessary to establish an infirmary in the College to care for students who might be ill. The scholarship students being of small means, and coming from all parts of France, most of them having neither relatives nor even acquaintances in Paris, it was impossible to return them to their homes when sick, or to have them cared for at their own expense outside the college, as is done in the other colleges of Paris. An infirmary was therefore indispensable. The expense of this establishment is considerable, and almost entirely at the expense of the College of Louis-le-Grand in the narrow sense, considering that the sums received from scholarship endowments of the consolidated colleges are hardly sufficient to pay for the food, heat, light, and instruction of the scholars.

The following is an indication of the expenses of the infirmary:

Physician	1,000 l.
he is lodged in the college	
Surgeon	800
Infirmarian	400
Three assistants at 150 l. each	450
Oculist	300
Medicines, about	1,500
	4,450

All scholars, professors, masters, and servants are cared for in this infirmary. When one of them is attacked by a contagious illness, such as malignant fever, smallpox, etc., he is cared for in a separate room, with special attendants who do not enter the rooms of the other patients; and this often occasions considerable expense. Sometimes, according to the gravity of the illness, we call upon doctors and surgeons other than those of the College for consultation or operations together.

No exact estimate can be given for the cost of supplying meat, wine, fuel, candles, washing, upkeep of linen, furniture, and utensils in the infirmary and for its servants, since all these items are included and mixed in with similar items provided for the college as a whole. They vary according to the number and nature of illnesses, but one would not be far from a reasonable estimate in carrying these items at about 10,000 livres a year.

Hence one can count on all expenses of the infirmary, in an average year, reaching a sum of about 15,000 l.

Oriental Language Students

Since 1763 there have always been in the College a certain number of students learning the principles of oriental languages, and who are then sent to various stations in the Levant. They are usually the sons of French consuls and interpreters employed in these places. Their number has never gone beyond ten. There are only four at present. They have their own master, an assistant master chosen from among the senior scholars of the College, and a servant.

The College receives, from the treasurer of the Navy, 500 l. for the board of each student present; 540 l. for the maintenance of the master, and 590 l. for his honorarium; 300 l. for the honorarium of the assistant master; and 560 l. for the wages and maintenance of the servant. The College pays their honoraria or wages to the master, assistant master, and servant, but since the rate for their board has not been raised since 1763 it is clear that these students represent a net cost to the College. This question has been raised several times, but hitherto always without result.

For this purpose in the year 1792 the College received only 5,253 l.

Statement of Expense for Food, Heat and Light for Masters, Scholars and Servants for the Year Ending October 1, 1972

Bread	46,456 l.
Wine	22,342
Butcher's meat	74,279

Preserved meat and sausage	2,849
Salted products	260
Groceries	10,052
Butter and eggs	20,942
Fats	2,330
Vinegar and mustard	903
Candles	7,713
Wood fuel	7,029
Out-of-pocket expenses of the Steward	28,200
	223,359

In addition, payments to scholars enjoying their scholarships outside the college, i.e., those at the frontiers, medical students, and absentees for reasons of health, reach a sum of

	59,091
Hence total expense is	282,450

SUMMARY

The sum of income of the various colleges and endowments forming Equality College is at present 462,084, viz.:

Annuities (*rentes*)	214,056
Rural farms	58,778
House rentals in Paris	189,249
	462,084

But it is to be noted that the College has lost by abolition of tithes, feudal dues, manorial dues paid in kind, etc., an income of

	66,030
Hence in 1789 and 1790 the income was	528,114

141

THE COLLEGE OF LOUIS-LE-GRAND

Statement of Expenses

Honoraria of masters at present are 17.422 l., but this expense should be estimated at

	20,000 l.
Servants' wages	7,695
Infirmary	15,000
Administrative and general expense	36,130
Repair and upkeep of buildings	25,000
Life annuities paid by the College	26,116
Arrears of life and perpetual annuities	20,076
Food, etc.	223,359
Payments to absent scholars	59,091
Prizes, etc., to scholars	6,000
	438,467

Certified as correct at Paris, June 20, 1793, second year of the Republic

CHAMPAGNE, principal of
Equality College

Seen and noted by us, administrators composing the Directory of the Department of Paris, July 6, 1793.

DUBOIS   E.J.B. MAILLARD
HOUZEAU   BOURGAIN

30. Equality College and its director are denounced as aristocrats

THE Law of Suspects of September 17, 1793, was one of the measures that initiated the Terror. No one, whatever his record, could be sure of escaping denunciation, and the following are two revealing pieces of paper, almost illegible, and hastily jotted down in incomplete sentences. Their author, Rolin, was a regular observer, or spy, in the service of the police. He apparently stood around in the street outside the college, and found Germain, the teacher of the Seventh, willing to talk.

Germain, as can be seen from Item 18 above, had come to the College in 1791 and was still there in 1795. We can imagine the atmosphere among the teachers, a small group of men living closely together, when one of their number was secretly reporting their conversation at dinner, accusing the principal, and maligning the students. There is no evidence that any member of the teaching staff at Equality College was ever arrested. There is little reason to believe anything that Rolin said about them, and his reports were probably discounted by the higher revolutionary authorities.

Observations of Citizen Rolin
on September 19 and 20, second year
of the Republic [1793]

Equality College (formerly Louis-le-Grand)

Most of the professors in this establishment are as much aristocrats as they could possibly be. It was said yesterday at dinner in the dining hall—that the prisoners were in danger of their lives—and that the prisons were mined and might be blown up.

Rue Saint-Jacques—across the street from the door used by the professors of Equality College—is a perfume dealer—with a wooden leg—this man is a pronounced aristocrat—there is no term he will not use to ridicule the Republic—he goes to impossible lengths to propagate his detestable sentiments—to have reliable information on these two matters you can turn to Citizen Germain, a teacher of the Seventh in the said college.

Section of the French Pantheon

General Assembly

It was announced in the assembly that a coal hoarder was going to have his head sliced off by judgment of the revolutionary tribunal.

Some washerwomen in this section stopped five sacks of coal coming by water from Choisi. The owner said he had brought twelve sacks—of which he still has seven, and the other five will be sold by order of the section. . . .

A volunteer with no leave papers was arrested by the general assembly and taken to the revolutionary committee of the section.

Observations of Citizen Rolin
on September 21, second year
of the Republic [1793]

The paper called the *Observateur* continues to print details that even moderates would find revolting, if you read this month's number—the enemy has all the advantages—the French are dying wherever they go into battle—in a word I will not cease to repeat my astonishment that such stuff still soils the hearts of Frenchmen.

Citizen Tillaud, head of Lisieux College, domiciled at Rue de Saint-Jean de Beauvais above the carriage gate of the said college—since 1789 has never stopped giving evidence of the most revolting lack of civic spirit, almost never going to his section assemblies, and cursing the Revolution in private; he is giving private instruction to a young man who lives with him.

Citizen Champagne, principal of Equality College, has now been forced to give up his place on the revolutionary committee [of the Pantheon section]. (He is really a Sainte-Chapelle clubbist.) This Citizen has always seemed outwardly a good patriot, but as such he should never have so abandoned the pupils entrusted to him, so much that they have not only been doing nothing in their classes—but they have been so corrupted that a teacher in the said house assures me that they had almost all corrupted each other—going into Paris at every hour of the day and night—and moreover he added that they shut themselves up in their rooms for their depravities, and that some of them had been surprised—even in bed together. This same teacher has told me that a year ago, when a great many

144

of these students left "for the frontiers," they were publicly boasting, all over the house, that they were going to join their parents and friends who were émigrés. Which is what most of them did. How is it that Champagne did not inform the authorities?

31. The College's cash and silver are confiscated

THE school year 1793–94, running from the first of October to late July, coincided almost exactly with the period of the Terror, "revolutionary government" under the Committee of Public Safety, the predominance of Robespierre, and the famous Year Two of the French Republic. At this height of heroic revolutionary and military exertion all kinds of individuals and institutions found their hard money and objects of gold or silver appropriated by the state.

The Republican calendar was adopted in September 1793, but dated its beginning from the proclamation of the Republic a year sooner. Hence contemporary documents never refer to a Year I. The Year II ended in September 1794. For a quick understanding of republican dates, which were in use until 1804, it is enough to add the numeral for the republican year to 1792, always remembering that the early months of the republican year, corresponding to October, November, and December, fell in the year preceding. That is, the Year VI in 1798, except that its early months fall in late 1797. The months, in order were Vendémiaire, Brumaire, Frimaire, Nivôse, Pluviôse, Ventôse, Germinal, Floréal, Prairial, Messidor, Thermidor, Fructidor.

Department of Paris

September 26, 1793
second year of the
French Republic

The Directory of the Department, informed that there exists at Equality College a sum of approximately 50,000 livres in coin, which the College administration believes it cannot use without authorization; that there also exist about 500 silver table settings, including drinking mugs, which were formerly used by the scholarship students and which the administration has thought it proper to replace with tin; and finally that there exists in the sacristy of the College a great quantity of silver objects which no longer serve any purpose;

Considering that the objects in question are of no use to Equality College, and that in the present circumstances it is important not to leave in private hands such national properties as may be valuable to the Republic in repelling the last efforts of the enemies of liberty,

Orders, on the advice of the Attorney General Syndic,

That the sum in coin now at the College shall be transported to the National Treasury and converted into paper money, which will be returned to the Temporal Grand Master of the College to be employed for the daily needs of that establishment and accounted for in the manner prescribed by law;

That the silver table service and mugs, together with the silver objects in the chapel, shall be likewise transported and that a receipt shall be given for them to the Grand Master;

That Citizen Dubois, Department Administrator, shall proceed to Equality College, to oversee the execution of the present order.

32. The College library is confiscated

It was estimated by a contemporary that twelve million books were confiscated during the French Revolution. Mostly they came from monasteries and religious houses, many came from the private collections of wealthy émigrés, some from persons condemned to death, and some from educational institutions. The Temporary Commission on the Arts tried to preserve them from vandalism or neglect, as it did with objects of art; but many were lost, sold to booksellers, or quietly appropriated by revolutionary connoisseurs. Many wound up in the Bibliothèque Nationale and other public libraries. The books confiscated from Equality College were returned a few years later, and then found their way into the library of the University of Paris.

The library of Louis-le-Grand, which had originated in the Jesuit period, was a sizeable collection for its time, over twice as large as that of Harvard College in the 1790's. It occupied an impressive room, which we know had twenty-five large windows. The present document refers to the paintings that adorned it. "Coronelli globes" refers to pairs of globes, one showing the earth, the other the celestial bodies, made by the Italian cartographer Coronelli for Louis XIV. A pair of the "ordinary size," each over three feet in diameter, may still be seen in the Museum of the History of Science in Florence.

The author of the present report, H. P. Ameilhon, was a professional librarian.

15 Floréal An II
[May 4, 1794]

Account of recent operations
by Citizen Ameilhon of the Temporary Commission
on the Arts

The library of Equality College, rue Saint-Jacques, has been transported to the Cultural Depot. I estimate that this library, on which I will give further details when the necessary work can be done, may contain at least 35,000 volumes, printed and in manuscript. The latter are few in number, and I have noted none of any great interest. It is otherwise with the printed books. They offer an assortment of the best works in all fields. It is evident that the library was brought together by men of learning.

Four Coronelli globes that adorned the library, two of ordinary size and well preserved, and two smaller ones, have been taken to the Depot of the Petits Augustins, along with a relief model of the building that was once planned as a central office of the University, to be erected at the former Place Sainte-Geneviève. All paintings have been taken to the same place. No medals were found, but in one dark corner I discovered two old microscopes with various pieces used in optical operations, among which I noticed some lenses whose special qualities showed their merit; also a magnet that seemed strong enough to lift ten pounds or more, a glass cage for objects in natural history, and finally some animal horns or claws, and some seals or stamps. I have had all these articles most carefully transported to the Cultural Depot, and I am ready to turn them over to whichever members of the Commission are in charge of such matters.

33. Champagne reports on the difficulties of the preceding years and the present state of the College

THIS item and the following one were written by Champagne about two months apart, a year after the death of Robespierre. They are drafts in his own hand, with various corrections, and somewhat disjointed as if he was putting down thoughts as they occurred to him. No final copies have been located, but both seem to be addressed to the Commission on Public Instruction. This body was different from the Committee of the same name. The Committee was a committee of an elected assembly, the National Convention; the Commission was an appointive branch of the executive government under a reorganization effected in the spring of 1794. When the new constitution of the Year III went into effect in October 1795, and the regime of the Directory was set up, the Commission was carried over as a bureau of public instruction in the Ministry of the Interior.

148

This letter shows what had happened to Equality College during the climax of the Revolution. Only fifty students were left in residence in the summer of 1795, and the old program of studies, with its emphasis on Latin, its set curriculum, and its sequence of graded classes from the Seventh to Philosophy, had completely disintegrated. The fifty students were a miscellaneous lot, ranging from young men studying medicine to boys who had to be taught elementary reading and writing. The buildings were in a chaotic state. They had been used as barracks in 1792–93. In the following year a part of Equality College was combined with its next-door neighbor, Plessis College, to form the famous Plessis prison of the Terror. Like many other places in Paris, the college was also used as a temporary workshop for the production of small arms and other military necessities. Doors and windows, walls and partitions, had all been altered. The result may be glimpsed in Item 40 below, which incidentally shows that little was done to restore the physical accommodations during the four years of the Directory.

In 1795 the staff of the College was still on the ground, along with the fifty students; for although the endowed income was gone, the Convention granted 380,940 livres from the public funds to support Equality College during Year III, which was substantially the school year 1794–95. Teachers, employees, and pupils in 1794 and 1795 suffered from inflation, administrative confusion, food shortage, and winter cold, but only because the whole population suffered likewise.

Paris, 25 Thermidor An III
[August 12, 1795]

Equality College, like all establishments of public instruction, has suffered from the decay which all peaceable arts undergo in the midst of revolution.

In 1789 this house was made up of 550 scholarship students. For the thirty years that it existed, it produced a host of men of distinguished talent who have served the country and the Revolution in all kinds of positions.

It maintained itself until 1792, resisting by the strength of its own constitution the various events that had shaken or already destroyed other educational houses. At that time an order of the Department of Paris forbade it to receive new scholars. Young men successively left on completion of their studies and were not replaced by a new generation. The crop was harvested but the field of education was no longer sown.

France has been similarly afflicted for four years, and may she not serve too cruel a penance for this political starvation!

The first assault on the discipline of this great establishment goes back to October 1792. At that time almost a hundred of our students had just taken to arms with cries of "the country in danger!" They departed after requesting the Convention to assure them of retaining their scholarships. The request was granted, and in addition a solemn decree proclaimed that the College had deserved well of the country. The students have been faithful to their oaths. Their conduct has been such that almost all now hold honorable rank, the just recompense of their good behavior and their courage.

But this decree became fatal to education by another development that could not be foreseen. The young men departed, and we saw them off with all the feelings of anxiety and pleasure inspired by their devotion and by the dangers they would run.

On the same day the municipality, whether from ignorance, or from indifference to our school program which was already very unjustly attacked, or from the pressure of a real problem, ordered a whole demi-battalion to be quartered in the College. Repeated protests and observations proved fruitless. Every government body, even sections of Paris outside our own, obtained orders to lodge armed men in our midst. Some 3,000 were quartered from September 18, 1792, until August 1793. Student discipline and studies suffered seriously during this time. Efforts were made to separate the soldiers from the students. General Berruyer himself ordered and obtained such a separation. But the soldiers broke through the barriers under his very eyes. We knew the dangers, and simply had to accept and suffer the evils.

In October 1793 our youngsters reassembled for the new school year. We were about to resume our exercises and follow a plan of study approved by the Committee on the Constitution in 1791 and ordered by the Department of Paris for the year 1792. The difficulties of the stormy year 1792 had prevented us from making more than an imperfect trial of the new program. Suddenly arrived an order from the Department suspending all teaching in the colleges. We asked in vain for a provisional resumption. We were obliged to keep silent and obey.

We had in secret, so to speak, carried on instructional exercises so far as circumstances would permit, when a new incident came to complete the disorganization already begun. A prison was set up next to the College, and largely at its expense. With part of our premises taken over, the fatal blow came with the establishment of a general work-shop in what remained to the College. As if it were not enough for all our doors to be flung open, even more entrances and exits were constructed, and 500 workmen were masters of the house from the month of Pluviôse to Thermidor of 1794. With all these disadvantages and misfortunes we had to do what we could for the numerous youth still entrusted to our care.

At this truly painful moment, far from keeping the youngsters in a place where the complete breakdown of teaching, and the disorder and the confusion of the workshop interfered with any educational purpose, we had to make contact with parents to invite them to keep their children at home.

The presence of the soldiers, before this, had already induced several families to keep their children, and the severity of the winter and bread shortage in the spring made other students return home.

The number now absent for these compelling
reasons is   101
The courage of students going voluntarily to the
frontiers, and then the requisition of troops, has
taken to the armies and to hospitals as surgeons'
assistants   138
I consider it certain that the number of those
vacating their scholarships, including those who
have died at the frontiers, rises to   38
There remain at the College   50

Among the absentees some would be disposed to return
in the event of a stable and definitive organization. Such
is the wish of the parents.

Some are reaching the age when their education will
be finished, and for four years no appointments to scholarships have been made. Others have taken to various occupations or professions. It is impossible to calculate accurately
the number who will return to continue their studies.

The disfavor into which the old system of education had
fallen, the scorn that seemed to be poured on the educational
process and on those noble languages [Latin and Greek]
to which France owes most of its literary successes, obliged
us if not to abandon them at least to speak of them almost
surreptitiously, and replace them with more ordinary forms
of knowledge.

We hastened to turn our youngsters' minds to the elements of mathematics.

We gave them writing masters.

Most were in their adolescence, and were encouraged
to take lessons outside the school that would be useful for
some occupation.

Some studied medicine.

Others surgery. Some, botany.

Some, sufficiently instructed in writing and arithmetic,
succeeded in getting office jobs.

Others went into legal studies under lawyers or notaries.

The younger boys were mostly given mathematics and writing, with a few lessons in grammar and literature. This state of affairs is still going on.

It is evident that such circumstances were bound to destroy the internal discipline of the college. The decree suppressing all the colleges was the last blow. Our pupils thought themselves thereby freed from any kind of subordination except the ordinary decencies among men who will soon see no more of each other. Yet it must be admitted, in fairness, that they did not interrupt their mathematics and writing lessons.

Today the commission desires to revive this old establishment, to bring together the few scattered sparks, to reanimate according to the wish of the Convention the sacred fire of education which is almost extinct among us.

Let me offer a few reflections.

Before the Revolution not everything that ought to be taught was taught in the colleges. Undoubtedly there was need of reform both in curriculum and in method. But there was order and discipline, and the result was an education.

Today there are fine theories setting forth all that ought to be known, and all kinds of teaching methods. But subordination and discipline have been allowed to perish, and education has disappeared.

Let us apply this truth to Equality College. What shall be taught? Let us leave this question aside for a moment and consider another, more important. How can a wise and regular discipline be restored? With this problem solved, there remains the easier one of applying a theory of education.

The fifty students now in the College fall into various categories:

1. Volunteers returned because of wounds or on leave from the frontiers. Various solemn decrees assure their reinstatement. The college will be their second home. It is

difficult to impose a college discipline upon young men who have often issued orders that put our enemies to flight on the battlefield.

2. Students in medicine and surgery. They must take courses at the Hotel-Dieu or elsewhere.
3. Some have become supernumerary in office jobs, or have none at all, or are working under lawyers or notaries.
4. Others take courses at the Central School or the former Palais Bourbon.
5. The rest are of two kinds.
6. Some young men of seventeen or eighteen who are taking courses in mathematics, geography, and writing.
7. A few younger boys with separate studies of their own.

The absentees who may return will divide in the same proportion among these categories.

It must be said that for some time, and especially since the suppression of the colleges, not only order but the mere suggestion of a teacher arouses little more than laughter. The spirit of rectitude in the younger generation inclines them to some deference for men who have helped to bring them up, but such deference hardly goes beyond respect, without reaching the point of compliance. Order can be restored only by the authority of the Commission. I submit to your consideration the following proposed regulations, whose further development will help you to understand the nature of the problem.

It must be realized that the extreme difference between students and their kinds of studies presents great difficulties for bringing about any uniform order. The Citizen Supervisors will take whatever measures that their wisdom and experience may indicate to remedy these serious inconveniences.

CHAMPAGNE

[The proposed regulations are omitted, since they are repeated in the next item.]

34. Champagne offers a plan for the Scholarship Institute

WITH the impending final adjournment of the National Convention, and general cooling-off of political ardors, Equality College received a less revolutionary name, becoming the *Institut des Boursiers* or Scholarship Institute. By the very name, the republican authorities recognized the continuing existence of scholarships derived from the Old Regime. As Champagne said, the Convention had abolished their funds, but had never abolished the scholarships. They continued to be financed by annual grants until the further reorganization under Bonaparte.

In this letter, after repeating some of the preceding one, Champagne goes beyond it to consider not only the 500 scholarships of the former Equality College but about 300 others which had formerly been distributed among the other nine full-program Paris colleges of the Old Regime. These nine colleges had been closed since 1793, but their scholarships still enjoyed an uncertain existence in principle. Champagne's proposal that they all be combined under one roof was gradually realized, producing what was called, by another slight change of name, the "Central" Scholarship Institute.

The letter also contains his rough plan for instruction and internal arrangements at the Institute. The problem was complex. On the one hand, there were many scholarship holders who had the right to resume their studies at unknown future dates, and students of an extreme diversity of ages had to be considered. Among them were boys and even teen-aged youths, who, with the breakdown of schools during the Revolution, had had only the sketchiest elementary education. On the other hand, the outgoing Convention created an array of other schools to which the relationship of the Scholarship Institute was unclear. Most famous and permanently successful were certain advanced institutions, such as the school of science and engineering called the Polytechnic, and the refurbished medical faculty of the former University of Paris, called the School of Health.

In addition, on the very day before its final adjournment, the Convention passed the legislation always referred to as the law of 3 Brumaire of the Year IV (October 25, 1795). This remained the code of education until 1802. It made a wholly ineffectual provision for primary instruction, and it created a system of Central Schools.

The Central Schools would be the main theme in a balanced

history of education under the Directory; it can only be said here that, as an attempt to institutionalize various modern ideas on education they were a subject of hot dispute by contemporaries, and have remained so for historians. They were much favored by the group of thinkers known as *idéologues,* and consequently held in suspicion by others. Designed for boys from twelve to twenty years of age, they were meant to replace the colleges of the Old Regime. They were called "central" because one was located in the central town of each department; that is, they were not really central at all, but represented an effort to spread high-quality schooling uniformly throughout the country. The Central Schools were day schools, having no boarding facilities; hence there was no charge for board, and although a small fee was charged for tuition, the law provided for its remission in a certain proportion of cases, so that talented boys might receive a free education at public expense.

Three such Central Schools were established in Paris in 1795, called the Panthéon, Quatre-Nations, and Rue Antoine. The Panthéon school was near the old Louis-le-Grand, located in the former abbey of Sainte-Geneviève (the later Lycée Henri IV). The Quatre-Nations school was located where Mazarin College had formerly been, and where the Institute of France has been installed since 1802. Rue Antoine (or Saint-Antoine when saints' names returned to use) represented the definite break-out from the geographical constraints of the Latin Quarter; it was on the right bank of the Seine, in buildings later assigned to the Lycée Charlemagne. These three, like all Central Schools, were day schools only, but they were supposed to replace the ten full-program colleges of the old University, which had been preponderantly residential.

The question was how the Scholarship Institute, which consisted essentially of several hundred free places giving the right to board, room, and instruction over a period of years, would fit in with these new and more modern arrangements. Champagne's ideas, as outlined in this letter of 14 Vendémiaire of the Year IV, were gradually put into effect. By it, the Institute taught within its own walls only the more elementary subjects, both to younger boys and to older ones whose education had suffered from the troubles of the preceding years. Others, if qualified, would live in the Institute but take courses in one of the Central Schools; as it turned out, most of these went to the Panthéon. Others, whose ages might rise into the upper twenties, would also live at the Institute, but study at the Polytechnic, the School of Health, "or others established by decree of the Convention." The pattern was somewhat as it had been before 1789, except that there were no theology students, and law students learned their trade by working with attorneys or taking the course in Legislation at the Central School. The existence of the Scholarship Institute, with its boarding facilities, also made it possible, as before 1789, for boys and young men of limited means from the rest of the country to study in Paris. Finally, as a residential establishment the Institute could do what the Central Schools as day schools could not do so well, that is, give what the French called *éducation* as distinct from *instruction*. The difference is explained in the Introduction. *Education* at this time meant producing good replican citizens by instilling republican attitudes and republican virtues. The Institute was thus heartily disliked by the more zealous royalists and articulate Catholics, who survived the Revolution in embarrassingly large numbers.

How it worked out is suggested in Item 41 below, where we can see both the attempt to educate the whole person, and the numbers of students in the several levels of studies.

Paris, 14 Vendémiaire, An IV
[October 6, 1795]

[To the Commission on Public Instruction]

The Commission at last desires to make use of the scholarships founded in the former colleges of Paris. The funds of these scholarships were declared in recent years to be a part of the national domain. But it was contrary to all justice to deprive the scholarship-holders of their advantages. These scholarships had been founded for the most part by families for their own members, by towns for their fellow townsmen, or by good citizens for the advancement of science and letters. Establishments having so generous an origin deserved to be maintained.

Hence, when the Convention, pressed by the imperious needs of public interest, declared these properties to belong to the national domain, it ordered at the same time that they should be replaced for the benefit of the scholarship holders.

The actual law concerning scholarships is limited to this. Other rulings emanated from secondary authorities which, in rivalry with the Convention, believed themselves empowered to make laws concerning education. These laws were death-warrants for the colleges—forbidding masters to teach, forbidding pupils to attend their classes, forbidding new appointments to vacated scholarships. Such was the whole educational code as it came from the secondary authorities. All was torn down, nothing rebuilt. Even worse, the teachers were insulted, vilified, and hunted down. Most colleges, the ancient dwelling places of youth and the Muses, were transformed into appalling prisons. So the teaching of the young in Paris came to an end.

It is time to remedy this political plague which threatens France with vandalism and the new constitution with approaching ruin. No state can last, says Plutarch in his treatise on education, unless its children are brought up in the principles of its government.

Aristotle in his *Politics* discusses the causes of the greatness and decline of the republics of his day. He observes that the constitutions of the most famous peoples went into great detail on the instruction of children. He assigns as the first cause of the collapse of the constitution of Sparta a strange oversight on the part of Lycurgus. This law-giver, he says, had established the wisest laws for the formation of men from their childhood. He neglected the education of women. That was why Sparta fell.

What would this profound political thinker have said, if he had seen a people among whom not only the education of women, but that of men also, was entirely neglected?

Today the Commission seeks to reassemble the scattered debris of education. It is turning its attention to this scholarship establishment which is now on the verge of ruin. It wants to reshape this useful institution in the public interest. To reach reliable results let us examine the state of scholarships at the present moment, and secondly see how they may be made as useful as possible in the light of the present time and circumstances.

In October 1791 there were 800 scholarship-holders in

the ten colleges of Paris. These scholars were divided into four classes according to the plan of study then existing. These classes were humanities-philosophy, law, medicine, and theology.

Five hundred boys up to the ages of seventeen or eighteen studied the elementary courses in humanities and philosophy in the colleges.

About 150 studied theology, and about the same number were divided between law and medicine.

Toward the end of 1791, the appointment to scholarships was suspended. Since that time the scholars in the higher studies have finished their courses, and their scholarships are vacant.

There remain 500 younger scholarsip-holders who were then studying in the colleges. Let us see what has happened to them in the torrent of revolution by which everything has been swept away or displaced.

The greatest number of them remained in the colleges until October 1, 1793, when instruction was prohibited by the Department of Paris, on pretext of establishing new institutions which have not in fact been set up.

At that moment most of the colleges were closed. Others were not so much preserved as forgotten. Teachers dared no more than to teach secretly. Many parents called their children home.

Other students went home because of the food shortages.

Then came the requisition which took many into the armies. The oldest of those remaining, that is boys of sixteen to eighteen, whose education was well advanced, took to studies of medicine and surgery. The need for such students led to their employment in the armies, at a time when they had hardly completed their preliminary studies in the healing arts.

Finally, a great many parents, annoyed at seeing their sons' youth pass without education, put them into careers in commerce or the useful arts.

Hence the 500 scholarship holders whose names are still

on the college registers may be divided by an estimate not far from the truth into the following categories: 250 are at the frontiers. They retain their scholarships and their return to the colleges is assured by several solemn decrees. In age they are from 20 to 23.

One hundred are engaged in the study of medicine or mathematics, or occupy various administrative posts. These are from 16 to 23 years old.

About 80 are living with their families and are employed in various occupations. It seems clear that these have renounced the advantages of their scholarships.

Finally the rest of the scholarshipholders, numbering about 80, are living either in the colleges or with their parents, where they are only waiting for instruction to be renewed to resume their course of study. Appointed to their scholarships in 1790 or 1791, the youngest of these are now at least 15 years old. Some are already 18.

Hence there remain in the hands of the Commission, at the present moment, 150 scholarship-holders who are no longer children but are in the age of adolescence, independently of those who are with the armies and may return at any moment. The problem is to bring them together in a residential establishment affording instruction, order, and discipline, so that these young men may do their work usefully, and the country not lose the fruit of its expenditures on them.

I shall propose a few ideas, not to serve as the basis of a perfectly constituted educational institution, but to show what seems to me best suited to the circumstances, the age of these young men, and the public advantage.

My observations do not seem to me to require any preliminaries. They have two objects—instruction and discipline.

Instruction

1. All scholarship-holders over 18 years old, even those returning from the frontiers or who may return on

leave, will be required to declare which part of the sciences, such as mathematics, medicine, or architecture, they intend to study.

2. Their declarations will be entered in a special register, to remain in the hands of the college supervisors.

3. The Commission on Public Instruction will then transmit the names of these scholarship-holders to the Central Schools, the School of Health, or others established by decree of the Convention. The Commission will have their names entered in the registers of these schools. They will be supervised by the teachers in these schools, and be subject to the same educational exercises as other students.

4. The scholarship-holders will be required, every two months, to show evidence of their assiduity and their progress by obtaining certificates from the professors with whom they are studying. These certificates will be deposited with the Commission on Public Instruction. Those unable to present such certificates will be obliged to resign their scholarships.

5. Scholarship-holders registered for a course which they have chosen will not be able to change courses without approval by their supervisors and the express wishes of their parents.

6. All scholarship-holders under 18 years old will take a preliminary examination. According to the knowledge they show, they will be allowed to enter upon higher studies, or they will be put into the various courses inside the Institute.

These courses are:
Mathematics including algebra and geometry.
Arithmetic and elementary geometry.
Literature
Grammar and Latin
Practical writing

7. These students may change courses only after an examination showing their capacity and their progress.

8. Every six months the Commission will appoint examiners to ascertain the progress of the scholarship-holders, each in the course of study that he has been pursuing. A report will also be made by the school directors on the personal conduct of the students.

9. All scholarship-holders working in office jobs, or studying in schools other than those established by the government, will be obliged to give up their living quarters at the Institute.

10. Scholarship-holders returned or who will be returned on leave from the army will be required, unless sick, to declare within one month after their arrival the kind of study in which they mean to engage.

Discipline

1. Students taking external courses will be required to return to the Institute immediately after their classes, without prolonging their absence, unless they have received permission in advance.

2. The Commission will arrange with the professors to assign to the students the number of courses that they must take.

3. The entrance and exit of students will be recorded every day at the Institute.

4. Students taking courses inside the Institute may not leave the premises without express permission of the directors.

5. On the *décadi* and *demi-décadi* they will go out on group walks after dinner, or leave individually with permission.

6. They may not on any pretext be exempted from attendance at their assigned courses, or from other study hours of the day.

7. Mealtimes will be set in a manner most convenient for all students. No one on any pretext may be served elsewhere than in the common dining hall.

8. No student may go out after supper.

9. Directors will distribute the students in the various sleeping rooms or dormitories according to their levels of study. They are enjoined to execute the present order exactly.

10. Students are required to observe provisionally whatever may be prescribed by directors, subject to complaint made to the supervisors, who will then determine what seems most useful to them for general order, and for the advantage of the students.

CHAMPAGNE
Director of the Institute

35. Two scholarship students return
from the wars

The following are two examples of cases discussed by Champagne in his reports of 1795, that is of absentee scholarship holders who had the right to return. Both were reinstated, and are known to have been studying medicine in 1799.

(1)

Paris, 24 Messidor An V
[July 12, 1797]

To the Citizen Minister of the Interior

CITIZEN MINISTER:

Citizen Pierre Jean Baptiste Daniel, aged 21, native of Beauvais, Department of the Oise, and scholar of Equality College on the foundation called the Cholets, states that he departed for the frontiers and remained there until the present moment in the capacity of a medical officer, as is proved by certificates of which he is the bearer. Today, desiring to return to his studies, which were unavoidably

163

somewhat ill-digested, he wishes to take the course at the School of Health and enjoy the benefit of the law which authorizes scholarship students at the frontiers to resume their education. He therefore begs you, Citizen Minister, to authorize for him the advantages you have accorded to the scholarship students in surgery now admitted to Equality College as external students. Citizen Daniel will comply with all regulations and try to make himself worthy of this favor by severe and sustained application to his work. His only aim is to obtain an education and fit himself for an honest profession.

DANIEL

[Below Daniel's signature is a note in Champagne's hand:]

I affirm that Citizen Daniel is in fact a scholar on the foundation called the Cholets, that he was three years at Equality College, which he left at the end of his Third, and that he constantly distinguished himself by his gentle demeanor, good conduct and industrious application.

24 MESSIDOR AN V   CHAMPAGNE

(II)

Paris, 6 Messidor An VI
[June 24, 1798]

CITIZEN MINISTER:

I have the honor to inform you that as a scholarship student at the College of Louis-le-Grand, today Equality College, I had the benefit of the law of August 3, 1792 (old style) by which students at the said college were to preserve their scholarships while serving at the frontiers, for as long a time as they might have enjoyed them if they had preferred to remain in Paris.

Wounded dangerously in the army, detained by the need of recovery, and hardly able to stand up, I found it difficult for some time to obtain the proceeds of this scholarship. To this real obstacle was joined another, namely the dissolu-

164

tion of the college by the confiscation of its property which proved to be temporary. Coming to Paris to obtain the aid provided for the wounded, I presented myself to the administrator of my college, who informed me that he could not assist me in the object of the request I now address to you, since there has been an opposing decision on your part; but informing me also that your decision should not be retroactive for four years, and that since my comrades in the service had been paid I should be paid also, or that they should reimburse what they have received. I flatter myself, Citizen Minister, that you will accord me the four years arrears that are due.

Respectful greetings,
LACROIX

[Two documents accompany this letter, one a certificate from the College attesting that Lacroix is entitled to a sum of 500 francs a year since July 1, 1793; the other a certificate from his regiment attesting to his wound, as follows:]

We the Administrative Council of the 14th Regiment of Infantry certify to all concerned that Citizen Jean Anne Eulalie Lacroix, lieutenant in our regiment, was gravely wounded by a bullet in the left leg at the battle of Jemappes, and that he distinguished himself on the battlefield by an energetic action, worthy of being reported.

As he fell from the wound several soldiers left their ranks to assist him, and as some of them expressed sympathy he said in a firm voice, "Courage, friends, it is nothing. When fighting for liberty one should not feel the pain. Courage!" We attest further that Citizen Jean Anne Eulalie Lacroix, lieutenant in our regiment, showed the most regular conduct and performed his service with the greatest distinction and most exact probity from May 16, 1792, when he joined our unit, until November 6, 1792, the date of his wound. In faith whereof we have delivered the present certificate to him for his use as may be needed. Done in camp near

Cassel, June 8, 1793, second year of the Republic. Signed: Vassard, captain; Laval, captain; Hérault, captain; Guinet, battalion leader; Beaulieu, brigadier general.

36. The further sale of college endowments is halted

THE law of March 8, 1793 (see Item 27 above) had initiated a process by which properties forming the endowment of college scholarships were sold off to private buyers bit by bit. In 1797 the Central Scholarship Institute petitioned the national legislature to halt this process. In particular, it urged that the former college endowments be treated like former hospital endowments, whose sale had been halted by a law of 2 Brumaire of the Year IV, on the ground that they were philanthropic foundations.

The following is a speech by Portiez, called Portiez de l'Oise, delivered on 20 Messidor of the Year V (July 8, 1797) to the Council of Five Hundred, the lower house of the legislature. Portiez had been a member of the Convention and its Committee of Public Instruction, he took an active interest in education under the Directory, and when law schools were revived under Napoleon he became head of the Faculty of Law in Paris.

The result of the petition and of his speech was the law of 25 Messidor of the Year V. Since it is referred to in later documents of the present collection, it is important that its provisions be understood. The law of 25 Messidor stopped the sale of the old endowments. It did not, however, re-endow any individual colleges. The properties remained in the hands of the government as a kind of endowment for education in general, from which the allocation of income was still determined by the state. Much of the property was already sold before 25 Messidor, and some of it leaked away thereafter—so much so that Portiez, in a later speech of 1799, estimated that where endowed annual income for scholarships in Paris had been 844,010 livres in 1789, it was only 256,666 ten years later.

As a consequence of the law of 25 Messidor the endowed funds of the other nine full-program colleges of the Old Regime were combined with those of Louis-le-Grand in the Central Scholarship Institute, which was renamed the French Prytaneum. The Prytaneum had been a kind of guest-house for distinguished visitors in ancient Athens, and the implication was that Paris was an Athens to which the whole country sent young men for an education.

It thus also happened that Louis-le-Grand, having absorbed twenty-eight "small" colleges in 1763, now also absorbed the other nine functioning colleges which had operated until 1793. It was the heir, in a sense, to all Paris colleges founded since the Middle Ages. It became, at the college level, the one continuing tie between the old and the new regimes, a funnel or channel through which funds, spirit, and personnel flowed from the older into the more modern educational system. It also became much larger, for the union with the other nine colleges brought in 357 more scholarships. Where Louis-le-Grand had had about 500 students in 1789, and Equality College was reduced to 50 in residence in 1795, the French Prytaneum in 1797–98 could boast, at least on paper, of having 790.

But while thus enlarged and unique, it ceased to be a college at all, in the sense of a "college" either before or after the Revolution. With the Central Schools taking boys above the age of twelve, and with older ones also attending various institutions of higher learning, the former Louis-le-Grand, now the Prytaneum, taught only introductory subjects and was more in the nature of a residence hall. Such an ambiguous institution proved to be short-lived. It was cut down in size in 1800, and converted into the Lycée of Paris in 1803.

Portiez addressed the Five Hundred as follows on July 8, 1797:

You have referred to a special commission, of which I am the spokesman, a petition from the Central Scholarship Institute, or from students at Equality College and a few other former colleges, asking that the advantages of the law of 2 Brumaire be applied to them. Your commission thinks that the question raises no difficulty if, as it hopes to show, the scholarship foundations are regarded as philanthropic foundations. . . .

We are going to tell you what these scholarships were. . . . They were founded to provide education for poor boys. The intention of the founders is literally set forth in the titles of the foundations. Such is the sole purpose of the properties given for the endowments of these posi-

167

tions, and such has always been the use made of them.

It is hard to understand by what title the Nation appropriated these college properties. The national domain to which one might at first glance compare them would be the ecclesiastical property. But a form of wealth which really belongs to scholarship holders could not in any way be considered to be ecclesiastical property.

In fact, the scholarships were never thought of as benefices, even temporary ones. Whenever enterprising and inconsiderate prelates tried to assimilate them to church benefices, they were overruled by solemn judgments of the courts.

College properties were never subject to the internal taxation system of the church. They always paid public taxes like the property of private persons.

To reasons of justice and humanity there is added a greater reason, the need of restoring public instruction in France. . . .

Since the organization of the Central Schools it has been realized that they cannot exist without associated boarding establishments for their students. Such establishments have already been proposed in this house. But the fact is that this idea can be realized in Paris at once, for if the scholarships are restored to their original purpose they will form a boarding establishment, from which the scholars will go to the Central Schools for instruction.

Citizen Representatives, the history of the City of Paris tells us that, in the time of storm and trouble, its educational institutions were dispersed and public teaching entirely suspended; but the principles and elements of instruction were preserved, like a sacred flame, in the colleges whose funds are now in question; and when the return of peace and calm allowed these studies to be reorganized, it was in these houses that were found the materials for reorganization. But if these establishments resisted the ravages of the time, they owed this advantage to their being endowed. For a time they felt the shock of revolution, but a few years of order and economy have brought back their earlier splendor.

Representatives, it depends only on you to obtain the same results. The time of trouble and revolution is over. You will give life to these establishments, and bring about the rebirth of education in France. . . .

The commission has demonstrated to you that these college properties, here in question, have truly and only arisen from acts of philanthropy.

37. A Catholic journalist denounces a "college of atheists"

During most of the Directory the press was comparatively free, with the result that both pro- and anti-republican journals abounded. The present item is from the *Annales Catholiques*. The exact date is uncertain, but it apparently follows shortly after the law of 25 Messidor of the Year V, described above. It shows the depth of hostility felt by the most intense Catholics toward all works of the Revolution and the enlightened philosophy which preceded it. We can see also how debates over the schools, which racked France for generations, began as soon as the end of the Terror allowed more freedom of expression.

It is to be noted, too, from the author's footnote, how private schools were arising to compete with the state-sponsored educational system. While it was unusual to spell Rolin with only one "l," and while the same individual might indeed reverse his opinions in these years, it is hard to believe that the Rolin so warmly recommended by the *Annales Catholiques* in 1797 could have been the same Rolin that denounced Equality College as a nest of aristocrats in 1793.

A College of Atheists

It is important at this time, with a commission appointed by the Legislative Body to consider restitution of the scholarship endowments in the various colleges of Paris, for someone to denounce to right-thinking people one of the greatest scandals in the history of public instruction—the scandal of a college of atheists. Whether there are many such in the republic we do not know; we speak only of one that we see every day in the capital, the College of Louis-le-Grand, that famous and illustrious nursery which once produced so many talents and virtues.[a]

This college, like all the others, fell under the axe of the revolution, and now begins to emerge from beneath the ruins. But by a fatality that attaches to everything attempted by modern philosophy, whether it builds or destroys, the re-establishment of this college has become a new calamity. It now has more than three hundred students, in place of the former scholarship holders, but now named by the Minister of the Interior. Not only is any religious exercise forbidden to them, but the name of God is not even pronounced, and these unfortunate children get up and go to bed like mere animals. . . .

How is it possible to find men who will conduct such a system of education? We know of some who regret the atrocious necessity in which they find themselves, and who feel as much shame for themselves as fear of the consequences for their pupils. We know that they have tried to propose changes, but have been told that by virtue of the rights of man the students are free to make their own choice of religion or God, that it is beneath the dignity of the French people to speak of such foolishness to students maintained at its expense, and that since the nation, as a nation, knows nothing of God it is out of order for the children to be more religious than their mothers. So an

---

[a] Now called Equality College. A bizarre and contradictory name. It should rather be called the college of the *privileged*, for nothing more resembles a privilege than a scholarship obtained by favor and influence. The scholarship endowments may indeed be restored in the name of justice, but it will be hard to distribute them in the name of equality.

atheism of fact follows from an atheism by right, and the very doctrine that the nation abhors becomes, by such a fiction, the national doctrine. No government servant can *officially* mention God, and every individual brought up in the name of the sovereign people is considered thereby to be politically atheistic. Who ever heard of such a policy? What country or century ever saw a college of atheists?

Good heaven! What can a college of athesists be but a den of little monsters or an infected sewer from which nothing will come except barbarism, perversity, and corruption? Unfortunate children! Unfortunate parents! Which are the more to be pitied? Ah! if our former houses of education were subject to so many disorders, if the most austere control was hardly enough to restrain an indocile and fiery youth, despite the powerful check of religion, despite the respect felt for masters who were obliged to give moral teaching by instruction and by example, what horrible depravity and execrable licence threaten our national colleges from which God has been driven out, which are conducted by freethinkers and apostate priests, where the growing passions are only restrained by a few lines of mathematics, and little philosophers who will soon be big reasoners become their own highest judges of their basic duties. . .

How long shall we suffer such an order of things, such an overturn of all order, civilization, and morals? O you who now demand, in the name of justice, the return of these honorable college endowments, do not forget that they are doubly sacred by right of property and by the intent of the donors, and that to prostitute them for schools of impiety, when they were given for schools of virtue, would be an outrageous abuse of their purpose. . . .

Banish from our schools that reasoned morality which is good for nothing. . . . Give us pupils who study their duties without knowing their rights. . . . Get rid of those professors of analysis who know only how to analyze their own interests, and those paltry professors of the human

understanding by whom all human understanding is overturned. Bring us back our old principles and our old education,[b] the only good one despite some abuses, as the new
is bad despite its reforms. Come back to it soon, unless
you wish the social body to disintegrate and end by burying
you in its own ruins.

38. Champagne publishes his *Politics* of Aristotle

SOMEHOW during all the troubles that afflicted his college Champagne managed to make a translation of Aristotle's *Politics*
and publish it in 1797. Though Aristotle was known in the
eighteenth century, favorably or unfavorably, for his general
philosophical writings and his poetics, the *Politics* had not been
translated into French since 1568, and was seldom read. His
political theory was hardly congenial to liberal thinkers of
the Enlightenment. Not only did he believe in natural slavery,
which the anonymous memorandum in Item 39 indignantly
rejects, but he held to a cyclical conception in which each
form of government is subject to peculiar stresses which tend
to turn it into something else, which may be either more free
or less free, more desirable or less so. Such an idea was far
from the thought of a progressive improvement to come with
increase of knowledge, the spread of science and the growing
emancipation of the mind from past errors.

Champagne in his preface to the translation recognizes his
debt to modern French thinkers, or at least to Montesquieu
and Rousseau, and most of all to the experience of the French
people in their then recent past. He has had the advantage,

[b] Most parents who do not dare to send their children to the new
schools, which the republic pays for at such expense, and which
we see fortunately deserted, are having difficulty in finding suitable
places of education. We think to do them a favor in informing them
that a number of private boarding establishments are being organized
in Paris, whose aim is to make not philosophers but Christians, and
which follow the plan of study of our old colleges. We know among
others of one run by M. Rolin, in the rue de Vaugirard near the
barrier. . . .

he says, of three great commentaries which previous translators of the *Politics*, had been unable to consult: "They are the *Spirit of Laws*, the *Social Contract*, and our revolution, the most instructive and extensive commentary of all."

It is a curious exercise to compare a few passages of Champagne's translation with the one into French by Loys le Roy more than two centuries before, and with Ernest Barker's into English a century and a half later. For example, where Champagne often uses the word "revolution," and Barker hardly less often, Loys le Roy does not know the word in a political sense, and speaks of *sédition, mutation, mutinerie* or *mouvement*.

Here are three other examples in which it is interesting to see how Champagne stresses "republic" and "public", which Barker avoids, probably as misleading anachronisms.

Loys le Roy 1568	Champagne 1797	Barker 1946
Hence sedition comes about every where because of inequality . .	Inequality—that is the apple of discord in all governments.	It is the passion for equality which is at the root of sedition. . . .
Nevertheless democracy is more secure and less subject to mutiny than oligarchy s. . . . Moreover a republic made up of people of mediocre condition, which makes the most secure of all such republics, comes loser to democracy than oligarchy does.	Moreover the true republic based on the middle class comes closer to democracy than oligarchy does, and is the most stable of all governments.	Democracy too has the advantage that it comes nearer than oligarchy does to the form of government—the "polity" based on the middle classes—which is the most stable of all the forms with which we are concerned.
n this the Lacedemonians are to be praised or the great care they ake in bringing up their children. Hence is necessary to provide for such an institution, and it should e done in public.	The Lacedemonians from this point of view deserve our praise. They have neglected nothing for the education of their children, and this education is always public.	Here, as in some other respects, the Spartans are to be praised. They pay the greatest attention to the training of the young; and they pay that attention collectively, and not in their private capacity.

39. Champagne's *Aristotle* is noted in the Ministry of the Interior

THE following is the draft of a memorandum by one of his subordinates to the Minister of the Interior. It is not known who wrote it, or even whether it was actually submitted, but in any case it offers evidence on Champagne and his work.

Memorandum to the Minister

The *Politics* of Aristotle has just been published, translated by Citizen Champagne, Director of the Scholarship Institute of Equality College. It is an important service that this skillful Hellenist has rendered to his country and to the world of letters, by making generally available a work in which one of the finest geniuses of all time brought together all the ideas of which the political science of his day was composed, and enriched them with the new ideas of his own sagacious and elevated mind. His thorough examination of each form of government, his advice on how each form can be maintained, prove how deeply he had reflected on these important matters, and make believable the prodigious work that he did on 158 constitutions of different peoples. This work has unfortunately not come down to us, but the translator has compensated us for its loss, so far as he could, by assembling everything that may be enlightening for this purpose from ancient and modern authors, which he presents in notes that are as pleasing to read as they are instructive. . . .

Aristotle's doctrine of *natural slavery* has been so long and so fully refuted that no warning against it is needed. The syllogistic method has also been recognized as more likely to confuse the mind than to be a guide to truth. But the errors for which Aristotle has been reproached are as nothing compared to the vast and luminous views that he gives to those who study him. The *Politics* is the richest possible mine of materials for the building of societies. It will be extremely useful to professors of Legislation in the Central Schools, and with this in mind, as well as education in general, it is proposed to the Minister to order 120 copies of Citizen Champagne's translation of Aristotle's *Politics* for distribution in the libraries of the republic.

The Minister will learn with interest that Citizen Champagne joins the merit of being an excellent citizen and true friend to that of a skillful translator. When the widow of the unfortunate minister, Lebrun, was left without resources and responsible for a numerous family, it was Citizen Champagne who married her, because she had been the wife of his old schoolmate. The Institute of which he is now the head also shows his talents for the administration of this kind of establishment.

40. Request for repair of buildings damaged by war and revolution

FIVE years after the emergency of 1793-94 the number of students and teachers was rapidly rising, but the physical plant was still very much disarrayed, and various departments of government were trying to pass the expense of rehabilitation to each other.

The following is a letter from the administrative board of the Prytaneum to the Minister of the Interior:

Paris, 23 Nivôse An VII
[January 12, 1799]

To the Citizen Minister of the Interior
CITIZEN MINISTER:

The greatest part of the buildings forming the French Prytaneum and all those of the former Plessis College which adjoins it were converted into a prison in 1793 (old style).

At that time all the arrangements and distribution of space, made at great expense to lodge the students, were demolished. These buildings have now been returned to their previous use, but in a state of dilapidation difficult to describe.

It seems to us, Citizen Minister, that you will doubtless agree that it is only just that all expenses for rendering these buildings weatherproof and habitable should be borne by the Department of Public Works, and not in any way charged against the subsidy granted by the Treasury to the Prytaneum for the maintenance and instruction of the students, nor against the modest income that remains to that establishment. This will hardly suffice for two or three years to provide revenue from the houses owned by the Prytaneum in Paris, considering the ruinous state in which we have found them.

The architects of the Public Works in fact drew up, more than eighteen months ago, on the orders of your predecessor, a plan for restoring the buildings of the Prytaneum and of Plessis College, which had served as prisons, to a condition of habitability, but this preliminary operation has remained without effect. Meanwhile the increase in the number of students, the preservation of their health, and the progress of their studies imperatively require that some of the students be located in these buildings, and no longer be piled up, so to speak, in a few study halls and dormitories that must become highly unhealthy for them. . . .

> *Respectful greetings*
> [The Administrators of the Prytaneum]

41. The Prytaneum assembles at its new country place at Vanvres

VANVES, then called Vanvres, is now an inner suburb at the city limits of Paris. Before the Revolution it was a large open park belonging to the princely house of Condé. The prince of Condé, distantly related to the Bourbons, was one of the most famous émigrés of the Revolution, since he commanded a small force of French noblemen, called "Condé's army," which fought on the Austrian side in the war against the French Republic. Vanvres, like all other émigré properties, was confiscated and put up for sale, but was acquired in 1799 by the Prytaneum, to be used as a place for exercise and recreation for its students.

The present item is from a brochure printed in 1799, describing the event by which the Prytaneum took possession of its new grounds. More than a thousand persons were probably present, for the names of 422 students are listed, and many of the parents also took part, as well as teachers, officials, and spectators.

Planting
of a
Tree of Liberty
by students of the French Prytaneum
at Vanvres House

16 Ventôse An VII
[March 9, 1799]

The Administration of the French Prytaneum, by agreement with the Minister of the Interior, has acquired the house and park of Vanvres, situated six kilometers from Paris, for use by the students of the Prytaneum. It has sought as far as it could to fulfill the views of the Government in the education of youth, by forming not only the minds but also the bodies of students through exercises that are suitable for young Republicans. This house with its pure air used to belong to the family of Condé, which for a century brought up its children here.

Gymnastics and bodily exercise have become essential parts of education in a Republic, which all, and especially the young, are called upon to defend. Here, on the days indicated, students of the Prytaneum will engage in their games and contests, and by developing strength and skill will prepare themselves to serve the Republic to which they owe the benefit of their education. The park offers also considerable space for cultivation. It has been ordered that several hectares of land be divided among the students for practice in agricultural labors. The Constitution prescribes that all young citizens should learn a trade; of all trades agriculture is the first and most useful. So the useful and the agreeable will be combined, and this house will gradually become both a playing field and a primary school of agriculture and botany.

The Minister of the Interior has made available 400 young trees, to replace the fine avenues that were cut down a few years ago. This fact has been seized upon by the Administration and the Director to give the students a little civic and agricultural ceremony. It was ordered that on 16 Ventôse a Tree of Liberty would be planted at Vanvres, and the students thereupon asked the favor of individually planting the other trees, with each student promising to defend and care for the tree that he himself planted.

[The brochure then prints the following address by Citizen Champagne, "Member of the National Institute and Director of the French Prytaneum":]

YOUNG CITIZENS:

We are about to plant a few trees. Why such a celebration? Why do we observe such a simple and daily action as a solemnity? It is, young citizens, because nature gives us a secret pleasure when the hand of man embellishes his dwelling place. And the finest adornment is given by these superb plants that seem to animate the earth, beautifying man's domain, growing with him, and being so to speak his companions and his friends. . . .

The occasion should remind you forever of this Prytaneum which will have seen the development of your own youth and virtues and talents. These trees that you are to plant are of about the same age as you are. They will grow by your care, as you are growing by the care of your country. If you are upright and honor your masters, your parents, and the Republic by your talents and services, you will some day return with pleasure to view these trees again, which will have grown as you have, and become ornaments to the earth that bore them. If not, you will stay far away, and they will reproach your ingratitude.

Nor is this all. You see this great expanse that the country has given you and that now lies sterile and dead. It must regain life from your hands. It must again become verdant, covered with flowers, enriched by precious plants for your instruction and pleasure. . . .

Youth of the Prytaneum, it is by your varied labors that you will worthily succeed to the children of those haughty princes who once inhabited this spot, where they idly exhibited their tedium and their pride. This chateau saw the childhood of that sneering despot, Condé, who said that men were only made to obey their masters, who took flight at the mere word "equality," and who has declared himself to be the bitterest enemy of France. Adoptive children of our country, you will purify this place in making it echo with the cherished words of equality and liberty, proclaiming your love and your gratitude toward the Republic. . . .

As this Condé and his band fled six years ago before your fathers and brothers, so must the children of those traitors flee from your very glance and from your republican arms. And here, in this very place, with all its memories of despotism, may the tree cherished by all free Frenchmen rise by your hands, recalling to your descendants the glory of your fathers and all that you will yourselves do to imitate them. You will be careful of this tree especially, without neglecting the others. You will love them all, for all are your pupils. You will defend them from every enemy and every attack. You will be persuaded above all that whoever preserves a useful tree performs an act of justice and almost of humanity, and that whoever injures the life and beauty of such a tree is a malevolent and almost inhuman being.

[Another address was delivered by Citizen Cambry, Administrator of the Department of Paris and Chairman of the Administrative Board of the Prytaneum. Afterwards, during the planting of the liberty tree, the students sang civic hymns. Individual students from fourteen to sixteen years old then read pieces of their own composition in poetry or prose. A banquet followed for students, parents, and others, concluding with a skit in which the returned Prince of Condé, much surprised, is mortified and put to flight by a student in a dialogue set to the music of a popular tune. The names of 422 students are recorded as present, grouped by their classes as follows:]

   17 in Medicine
   12 at the Polytechnic School
   12 in Oriental Languages
   36 in Mathematics and Physics at the Central School
   63 in Ancient Languages, Literature, History and
       Natural History at the Central School
  104 in middle-level studies within the Prytaneum itself,
       in Ancient Languages, History, Geography, Ethics,
       and Drawing
  178 in the lower level within the Prytaneum, in Grammar, History, Geography, Drawing, and Writing

42. A former professor, changing his mind, recalls the College as a hotbed of revolution

THE Abbé L. B. Proyart, whose book of 1785 is noted in Item 12 above, left France during the Revolution and became one of the most prolific and vehement counter-revolutionary writers. Before the Revolution he had spoken favorably of the Paris colleges. In 1795, in a book on "the life and crimes of Robespierre," he recalled unflattering details of Robespierre's character and behavior at Louis-le-Grand. Since Proyart had in fact been at Louis-le-Grand in the 1770's, his statements have passed into some of Robespierre's biographies, though his tone inspires no confidence in the accuracy of his alleged recollections. In 1800 he published another book, in London, from which is taken the following passage, called "Louis XVI dethroned before being king." Here he joined with other polemicists of various nationalities who attributed the French Revolution to a conspiracy, engineered by intentional subversives over a long period of years before 1789. He added the thought that a vicious and godless education, notably at Louis-le-Grand, was one of the causes of the Revolution. It should be evident from Items 5 and 9 above that Louis-le-Grand before 1789 was hardly irreligious.

In the following paragraphs Proyart imagines a scene in the royal council of ministers in 1762. The council has just decided to go along with the Parlement of Paris and expel the Jesuits from France. Proyart pretends that the Dauphin, Louis XV's middle-aged son who died in 1765, is the only member of the council who defends the Jesuits. A prophetic speech to the ministers is put into his mouth; he predicts a horrible revolution to come in twenty-five years. "Philosophism" was a derogatory word for the ideas of the *philosophes*, especially their free-thinking speculations on moral, religious and political questions. Choiseul, addressed here by name, was the chief minister at the time.

The Dauphin is speaking, as of the year 1762:

You are yielding to the demands of philosophism transmitted to you by the Parlement of Paris. You are consummating the destruction of the Jesuits; as ministers, you are blind to the future, if indeed you are not something worse! Are you not afraid to leave the whole youth of a vast empire suddenly without teachers? . . .

No, the children of this state, and your own children, will no longer be the pupils of religion. Philosophism awaits them, and will be their doctor. Wait then, yourselves, until they have learned in its school that virtues, like vices, are no more than prejudices; that the science of morals is only a science of pleasures; that conscience and remorse, hell and its punishments are only phantoms, empty bugbears of a superstitious schooling. Wait until your children have learned to doubt that they have a soul, or to think, supposing they have one, that it only dies with the body, or at least that the God who reigns in heaven is too exalted to cast down his eyes on the weak mortal creeping on the earth. Wait until philosophism, after freeing the young from all feeling of indebtedness to the authors of their being, has also revealed to them its great secrets on the authority of the powers that govern the world. Wait, I say, until the rising generation, formed by the new principles of a new moral philosophy, becomes the active and directing part of the French nation. You will wait twenty-five years. . . .

From these peaceful sanctuaries of morality and instruction, which you now propose to turn into arenas of gladiators, you will see arise a licentious, unchecked, and untamed generation of youth breathing disorder and combat, sometimes running to arms without command, sometimes pushing the government into an immoral war, then embroiling themselves in foreign countries, and returning to set fire to their own by their anarchical frenzies.

If this is not enough of a prophecy, do you wish me to be more precise? Then Choiseul, write it down on your tablets: among these degenerate schools that will hatch the evils that I announce, there is one that you know well, and that all France knows; one more celebrated than others as the nursery of great men, long famous by the name and favor of the great Louis—Louis-le-Grand. I will speak only of it; it will be my only example. Refuse if you dare to recognize your work, or to see the avenging product of your present decision, in the monstrous contingent which that one house will furnish in the catastrophe that I predict. Yes, remember that it is from the house called Louis-le-Grand, from which you are today expelling the Jesuits, that will come in twenty-five years two seditious madmen sounding the tocsin of revolt against kings and their ministers. One will be called Desmoulins, the other, Chénier.[a] It is from this same house that will come other heralds of blood and sedition, too well known to be named.[b] From the same house will come an apostate priest, whose sacrilegious hand will violate the secret portfolio of his king, to draw from it regicide charges of capital crimes; his name will be Audrein.[c] And it is from this house that will come, in human form, a more atrocious being than any known to the barbarism of antiquity, who, after deciding on the murder of his king, will himself rule over you and yours by daggers and assassinations, and will drink the blood of a million men, most notably of magistrates of the Parlement, condemned in mass without being heard, as the Parlement has condemned the Jesuits—his execrable name will be Robespierre.[d]

[a] Camille Desmoulins, author of several atrocious and bloody libels, contributed very effectively to the uprising of the provinces by his *France libre;* and the plagiarist Marie-Joseph Chénier, by his rhapsody on Charles IX, inoculated the habitués of the theater with his rage against kings. Yet he had been a student at Louis-le-Grand, supported by Louis XVI. [A more reliable source states that M. J. Chénier attended Mazarin College.]

[b] Robespierre and Tallien were rivals in provoking anarchy and regicide by their journals, along with a crowd of others who had studied at Louis-le-Grand. Tallien was the one who spent the shortest time there.

[c] Audrein had lived at Louis-le-Grand as a prefect. He had a vile mind, and his heart was corrupted by ambition. He was charged with making an inventory of the king's papers, after the pillage of the Tuileries, and his accomplices rewarded him by making him the intruder bishop of Quimper. Other intruder bishops, such as Porion at Arras, Dumouchel at Nîmes, Desbois at Amiens, also came out of Louis-le-Grand after the destruction of the Jesuits. [An "intruder bishop" was what counter-revolutionaries called bishops set up originally under the Civil Constitution of the Clergy of 1791. On Audrein see Item 17 above, and on Dumouchel Item 13.]

[d] Without the destruction of the Jesuits France would not have had its Robespierres. Most of those who are in question here were poor scholarship students, like these monsters, and would never have received their schooling, at least in the capital, if the Jesuits had preserved their existence.

. . . In this violent crisis of education, as one sees in epidemics, the eager troop of empirics will press forward to multiply their services, and will be welcomed by credulous parents in the vain hope of something better. Bizarre plans of instruction, conceived by philosophism or suggested by greed, will take the place of wise rules matured by experience and justified by success. Impertinence and stupidity, launching with impunity into so grave a matter, will propose an array of systems that rival each other in absurdity or impiety, but will nevertheless attract their dupes. On such a basis we shall see charlatanism organizing schools and academies, and youth running from all directions to buy the gift of universal knowledge for gold. The young man is promised that on finishing school he will know how to sing, dance, ride horseback, swim a river, and botanize. He will be told that with a little inclination on his part, he will learn to reason on the republican debates of Greece and Rome, to comprehend the world in maps, to speak of numbers and surfaces, to recite the nomenclature of the arts and trades, and most especially to act with confidence in theatrical productions. But, in the end, the one necessary science will be missing from this universality of knowledge; and the young encylopedist will be ignorant of the geography of his own heart, and will not know the road he must take if he is not to miss the sublime destiny that religion assigns him.

43. The Prytaneum is divided into four

IN Brumaire of the Year VIII (November, 1799) a group of civilians combined with the young general Napoleon Bonaparte to replace the Directory with a new form of republican government having a stronger executive. They devised the Consulate, headed by three Consuls, with the authority and the initiative lodged in the First Consul, who was of course Bonaparte. At first Bonaparte had wide support among people attached to the republic on pragmatic rather than ideological grounds. Such people had no liking for popular democracy or neo-Terrorist radicalism on the one hand, or on the other for royalist and clerical reactionaries of the kind suggested (in Items 42 and 37 above) by the Abbé Proyart and the *Annales catholiques*.

The old argument over whether Napoleon saved, ended, or betrayed the Revolution has its counterpart in debates over what he did to education. Some have thought that the schools coming out of the Revolution were promising and innovative institutions which he crushed in the process of consolidating his own power. Others have thought that the schools coming out of the Revolution, and notably the Central Schools, were a failure, that they did not meet the needs or wishes of most families who desired secondary education for their sons, and that Napoleon in abolishing them prevented the relapse of education into the hands of the Catholic Church. In any case, it is a fact that in 1803 he replaced the Central Schools by a system of lycées, and that after 1806 he tried to regulate all education through his Imperial University, which was not a university in the usual sense but a highly centralized apparatus for standardization and control.

For the first few months of the Consulate Napoleon's younger brother Lucien was Minister of the Interior, and as such turned his attention to education. The following document contains his recommendations in March of 1800. It was at exactly this moment that J. F. Champagne wrote his *Views on the Organization of Public Instruction*, abridged as Item 54 below. A comparison of the two is highly favorable to Champagne.

The present report by Lucien Bonaparte is a far from candid statement. It makes no mention of the Central Schools, whose existence was the real issue. Since there were three Central Schools in Paris, it was less than adequate to say that the Prytaneum took the place of all former colleges in the city. The Prytaneum, with students from many parts of the country, was not a "local" institution, nor did "experience" teach everybody that a school should not have over 200 students. It was not true that a boy whose parents were in "comfortable circumstances" could be educated only at home; he could go as a day student to a Central School and pay fees, or he could attend, as many did, one of the private schools that were springing up in Paris and elsewhere, and that were "private" only in the sense that they were not maintained by the state.

Nevertheless, it could reasonably be argued that the Prytaneum had become too large for its purpose, and that it was time for boys needing financial aid and those from more comfortable families to be educated together.

The proposal as set forth by Lucien Bonaparte was adopted. The students at the Prytaneum, who now numbered about 700, were divided into four groups. One group stayed at the Prytaneum in Paris, and others went to "prytaneums" in Fontainebleau, Versailles, and Saint-Germain. The one at Fontainebleau was soon moved to the village of Saint-Cyr, where it became the nucleus of the national military academy. The "Prytaneum" became an amorphous concept, or a kind of funding agency for student aid until the introduction of the lycées in 1803. The Paris Prytaneum, in the rue Saint-Jacques, became less of a general residence hall and more of a compact teaching institution. It was renamed the College of Paris in 1800, and the Lycée of Paris in 1803.

[*Report
by Lucien Bonaparte,
Minister of the Interior,
to the three
Consuls of the Republic*]

1 Germinal An VIII
[March 22, 1800]

CITIZEN CONSULS:

The French Prytaneum has taken the place of all those public establishments for general education in Paris, which, under the name of colleges, formed part of the old University. After the violent shocks which have destroyed so many other institutions, we should be gratified to see, standing in the ruins, this last refuge open to public instruction; but the more fully we realize its utility the more we regret that the misfortunes of the times, which have set such great obstacles to the restoring of education in France, have allowed no more than this feeble effort.

Despite regulations to assure the placing of youth from the departments in the Prytaneum, we must admit that it can hardly be considered more than a local establishment. Moreover, the modesty of the revenue available for its upkeep, and of the sums granted to it by the government, restrict the benefit of its teaching to too small a number, and prevent its instruction from having any perceptible influence on the immense population of the republic. Since the suppression of the teaching bodies, education in France is almost nil. There are indeed in Paris, as also in the departments, some accomplished teachers who are zealous for the progress of their art; but these valuable men, scattered and dispersed, lend no support to each other. They are like sparks which, not joined in a common hearth, give off only a feeble and dying light. Ingenious theories and useful methods pass away with those who invented them; no tradition is formed, no system transmitted. . . .

The Prytaneum, as it exists today, cannot fulfill our objectives. First, it is the only such establishment, and hence cannot accommodate enough students. Experience has shown that the number assembled in one college should not exceed two hundred. Secondly, it is restricted to admitting only those having the right to a free education. Hence it comes about that the boy born with good abilities, whose family lives in comfortable circumstances, is deprived of the advantages of public instruction, and can only receive, in his parents' house, and under the discipline of a private teacher, the domestic prejudices and local habits which will later isolate him from the rest of his fellow citizens, remove him from affairs, and make him almost a foreigner among his neighbors and in his own country.

Haste must be made, citizen consuls, to remedy these inconveniences and to multiply establishments of public instruction, so far as we can, until it may be possible to have them in proportion to the needs of a numerous people, spread over the great extent of our territory. We might, for example, divide the Prytaneum into four colleges, one at Paris located at the present Prytaneum, one at Fontainebleau, one at Versailles, and one at Saint-Germain. There would be places set aside in these colleges for the exclusive use of those of small fortune, sons of soldiers who have died in battle or of government servants dying while exercising their functions. The revenues of the Prytaneum, and the subsidy of 200,000 francs granted to it for the year VIII, would be used to support government students [i.e., scholarship students]; but also, so as to favor so far as possible the propagation of enlightenment and the advancement of education, it might be decided to admit paying boarders, who would pay each year a sum representing the expense of each student. This sum can be set at 1,000 francs for Paris, and at 800 for the other colleges. . . .

44. A tour of inspection by Napoleon Bonaparte

A FEW months after the division of the Prytaneum the part remaining in Paris, known also as the College of Paris, was officially visited by the chief executive of the Republic, the First Consul, Napoleon Bonaparte. As Director, J. F. Champagne made a detailed report to his administrative board. Bonaparte was not yet emperor; it was still possible to have normal conversation with him, and the report is full of amusing sidelights as well as solid information on the state of the school.

Bonaparte as described by Champagne seems alert and inquisitive, able to make even the youngest boys talk without frightening them, and supremely confident in his own view of how a school should be run. His preference for military organization is evident, as is his liking for Saint-Cyr, the part of the Prytaneum that was to become the military academy. For the student uniform, to which reference is made, see Item 48 below. For the reference to exercise at Vanvres, see Item 41 above.

*Report
to the
Administration of the French Prytaneum
at its session of*

6 Prairial An IX

*by
Citizen Champagne, Director
of the
College of Paris*

The First Consul visited the Prytaneum on 2 Prairial An IX [May 22, 1801] at half-past four in the afternoon. Although a report has appeared in the public papers, the Administration will doubtless wish to have more particular details on this visit.

When the First Consul arrived at 4:30 the classes for the day were over, and the students were at recreation in the courtyards. The Director, on the First Consul's order, instructed them to go up to their study halls, which they did at once.

The Director rejoined the First Consul, who had remained in the Director's apartment examining some papers written by students, as well as maps and drawings made by them.

He remarked on leaving the Director's apartment, by way of conversation, that not everything seemed to be in good order, and especially that the exits and windows were in poor condition. The Director observed that he would find better order and tidiness in the rooms used by the students, which had been taken care of first.

He went up to the study hall of the mathematics students. On the way upstairs he asked the Director what the aim of the establishment was. The Director replied that its aim had not been clearly determined, and at the end of the course there was nothing to do with the students except to send them away.

The First Consul entered the hall of the mathematics students. He asked questions of several of them, proceeding along their ranks. Young Citizens LeCoq, Parisot, and one of the day students were questioned, and answered very well. The First Consul emphasized the necessity of the study and practice of mathematics for surveying, and spoke of the need of having a graphometer for representation of terrain. He noted, too, the importance of studying mechanics. The Director remarked that this subject was reserved for the Special Schools. The Minister of the Interior spoke up and confirmed this observation.

The First Consul noticed several students who were not wearing their coats, and asked the reason. The Director explained that his presence had required some of the day students to come into the study hall, that the coats of some students who were not in uniform had been sent away for mending, and that in any case the rest of their clothing was in uniform. The First Consul seemed to desire that all should wear the uniform so far as possible.

He then insisted on the importance of military discipline. He said that he understood that the Director could readily control instruction and the order of studies, but that it was difficult, without military discipline, for him to maintain any exactness in the external order and regulation of the establishment. The Director observed that a plan for military exercises had been announced, and a special regulation on this subject had been promised but not yet enacted. The first Consul recommended that this point of discipline be organized without delay.

He then announced to the students that they had been selected by him, and that he and the Government would provide for their wellbeing. That as a further benefaction by the Government, they would all be placed in good positions if they conducted themselves well.

He asked about the daily schedule, and the Director

showed it to him. He said that he saw no place for the afternoon snack. The Director answered that this was not an indispensable meal, that there was no evidence that it was useful for health, and that anyway the students could take all the bread they wanted at dinner and that their appetites would be enough to guide them on this point.

"Give them an afternoon snack," said the First Consul; "I think it is good for them at their age."

He then moved about the mathematics room. He asked the students their names. He particularly noted young Filangierry, young Abrial, and young Pitche and Petersen. He was delighted to learn that they came from the newly annexed departments, and had entered the Prytaneum since the conclusion of the treaty of Lunéville. He particularly recommended them to the Director.

He then went on into the second mathematics room, where he questioned the students Perie and Fanton-Mahon, and asked a few others their names.

On leaving, he observed to the Director that he expected students placed by the Government to give evidence of sound attitudes, good conduct, and hard work.

On leaving this classroom he expressed a desire to see the whole school. The Director led him into the second court-yard, to the big building where the younger boys are housed. To the right, he noticed a building in a state of dilapidation. He asked what the cause was. The Director explained that most of the buildings of the Prytaneum had been in that condition three years ago, as a result of having formed part of what was called the Plessis prison. That repairs had been made gradually, as funds were available. The First Consul paused a moment, but said nothing. Then he looked at the big building and observed that it had a fine appearance, but that Saint-Cyr had more to offer in this respect.

The Director remarked to him that, among such establishments in Paris, the Prytaneum still had the largest and most convenient buildings, and that it was fortunately located in a quiet quarter, without which it would in all probability have been converted to some other use.

The First Consul then entered the big building and went into the first study hall. He asked a question of young Leleu, of the elementary grammar class, who answered him very well.

It was in this hall that he gave his most positive order, that no student or boarder should leave the college under any pretext whatever. Turning to the Director, he said that no professor and no sub-director had the right to take a student outside. He alluded to something done by one of his own captains, who, in order to see his son, had issued an invitation to one of the sub-directors of the school, who had brought the boy with him. The father had mentioned the episode to the First Consul, who had told him that he should not have so taken the Director by surprise. He made this observation in a very affable way.

He then passed into the dormitory, which he found in good order.

Then he went into another study hall, where he questioned among others young Villars, who replied perfectly, giving a grammatical analysis from the first book handed to him.

"What is a gerund?" asked the First Consul at the end.

"It is a present participle," said the boy, "preceded by the preposition *en.*"

"Ah!" said he, "that is a solution that makes further discussion unnecessary."

"That is the solution offered by our modern grammarians," said the boy. "It is short, but it remains to be seen whether it settles the difficulty."

He also visited the dormitory here, and found it clean and in proper order.

In the third study hall he asked one of the boys about various grammatical principles, including the number of conjugations. The boy said there were four.

"And the verb in *ir*, such as *finir?*" asked the First Consul.

The boy persisted. "For some time now our grammarians have no longer counted these differences among verbs in *ir* as separate conjugations."

He glanced into the dormitory, saying it was all right, like the others.

At this point he remarked that the boys seemed in flourishing health, and carried themselves well. The Director replied that this was a matter of particular concern, and that the exercise they were getting at Vanvres contributed to their good physical condition.

He then asked to see the dining halls. In the large hall he noticed a smell, and remarked that it was a fault in college dining halls generally. He found the second dining hall better aired. The Director remarked that this one had been more humid than the other a year ago, but that the opening of a new door had made it more wholesome.

"You should burn some incense in there," said the First Consul. The Director observed that such perfumes were too expensive except for those, like the First Consul, who knew how to obtain them easily. The First Consul smiled, and took the Director aside. The Director wanted to say something about the rigid prohibition against leaving the college. The First Consul said that with such a policy he would be master in his own house, and that he should hold to the rule.

He shot several rapid questions at the Director.

"How many students have you?"—"368."

"How many boarders?"—"120."

"How many individuals in the house?"—"432."

"How many on the sick list?"—"Three. You will observe that in the last three years, out of 1,100 students, we have lost only one, which shows what good care they get."

"What is your cost per student?"—"830 francs all told, including instruction, food, clothing, paper, books, drawing materials, and medical care. It is the very minimum, reached by the Administration after many meetings and much calculation."

"How much income do you have?"—"200,000 francs." He turned to the Minister of the Interior and said, "Isn't it 260,000?" The Director said that he meant the sum effectively used for the students, and not for taxes and general overhead.

He asked the Director, "Do you use corporal punishment in your little world here?" The Director answered that he did not, that nowadays the youth of France could not be whipped, but that there were punishments of bread and water and that at present four students were serving such sentences.

The First Consul gave an order for a convenient parlor to be established for the students' relatives.

He ordered the Director to pay particular attention to economy and good quality in the matter of food.

He asked about the table service, and after hearing the details he added that it was like Saint-Cyr, and all right.

The Director proposed that they see the library. "How many volumes does it have?"—"18,000." He observed that it was late, and got into his carriage and returned to the Tuileries.

On the 6th, at the Institute, the Director saw Third Consul Le Brun, who told him that the First Consul had been well satisfied with the bearing, health, and performance of the students. . . .

45. The Lycée is introduced

ITEMS 45 through 49 illustrate the origin of the lycée, which in the nineteenth century became the distinctive element in secondary education in France. The term "secondary," however, though it had developed during the Revolution, had not yet become stabilized in its modern meaning. It is evident from Item 45 that the lycée was not at first thought of as a secondary school. It was to be at a somewhat higher level, and designed to stimulate the growth of a secondary system below it. The very word *lycée*, as used since the 1780's and in plans drafted during the Revolution, had hitherto always referred to advanced studies.

Louis-le-Grand—in its phase as the Prytaneum in 1800 and as the College of Paris in 1801—became the prototype, along with the Polytechnic School, on which Bonaparte and his advisers developed their system of lycées. In serving this purpose, Louis-le-Grand lost much of its special identity. It became one of a number of similar schools, though first among equals, and its history merged into the history of lycées in general, and after 1808 into the history of an even larger structure, the Imperial University, which after 1814 was called the University of France.

Item 45 presents excerpts from the speech by which A. F. Fourcroy presented the plan of the government to the legislative body of the Consulate, which promptly enacted it. It is remembered as the law of Floréal of the Year X. Fourcroy was an eminent chemist, teacher of chemistry, and author of textbooks widely used in England and America as well as in France. He had been active in the Convention at the height of the Revolution, and was the government's chief educational planner from 1802 until his death in 1809.

A number of points in Fourcroy's speech deserve special attention. The new system is to correct the weaknesses of the Central Schools. The new plan of studies is to combine the best in the Central Schools with the best in the old pre-Revolutionary colleges. (On this matter see also Item 46.) The loss of the old college endowments is deeply regretted. It is said that the government simply cannot afford to provide the funds to replace them. Not only can it not afford to pay for the universal primary schooling proposed during the Revolution, it cannot even afford to pay for secondary education, which must therefore be left to the initiative of local governments, private families, and philanthropists. The government hopes to receive "gifts, legacies, and endowments for education" of the kind accumulated for five centuries before the Revolution. Hence it promises that there will be no more confiscations. As is well known, however, such philanthropy never developed in France after 1800 as it did in America. It had been discouraged by the expropriations of the Revolution, and in any case no one makes donations to the state.

Fourcroy observes that schools are springing up by private and local initiative throughout the country. The purpose of the government in 1802 was to encourage them, since it could not produce them itself. After 1806 its purpose would be to control them. There was a danger that private schools, many of them under clerical auspices and reflecting royalist sympathies, would impart attitudes unfavorable to the modern régime.

In 1802 the main function perceived for the lycees was to accelerate the growth of secondary schools. Hence the lycées did not have to be very numerous, and by the end of the Empire, in 1814, there were only thirty-six in France, within the historic borders of 1792. There were hundreds of private or municipally supported secondary schools at that time, as there had been before 1789. There were only four lycées in Paris, and they were continuations of the Prytaneum and the three Central Schools of the 1790's. They received names of appropriate Napoleonic magnificence, with the Paris Prytaneum becoming the Imperial Lycée, the Central School of the Pantheon the Lycée Napoleon, the Central School of the Quatre-Nations the Lycée Bonaparte, and the Central School of the Rue Saint-Antoine the Lycée Charlemagne. In Paris as elsewhere the lycées occupied buildings inherited from the Old Regime, and most of their teachers, or at least those over forty years old, had taught in the colleges before 1789. There was no new building and not much new personnel; the innovations were curricular and organizational; and anyone familiar with the academic world may wonder whether, with the same men teaching in the same physical surroundings, the actual changes were as great as they were supposed to be.

The lycées were to encourage the secondary schools, or colleges, by providing grounds for emulation and competition for both students and teachers. They would offer a high quality of education to the keenest minds. Each lycée would have certain scholarships, for which bright boys in the secondary schools of its area would compete. If successful, these boys and young men would get a better and longer education at the lycée at the cost of the state. If they distinguished themselves at the lycée they might, after further competition, be singled out for further free education at the Polytechnic or other centers of higher education maintained by the government. Good teaching was to be encouraged—that is, teaching which enabled intelligent young men to rise into socially useful occupations—and hence fifty prizes for good teaching were to be awarded each year in the secondary schools.

The scholarships, as Fourcroy said, were the key to the new system. Not only were they to be a stimulus to secondary education in general, but in each lycée the funds received from the government for its scholarships would be enough to cover the base pay of the professors and other normal expenses. Paying students would then only defray incremental costs. The plan called for 6,400 government scholarships in the lycées (and higher schools), of which 2,400 were to go to the sons or orphans of war veterans and civil servants, and 4,000 were to be awarded competitively to boys in the secondary schools. It must be realized that (with the considerable exception of financing the Polytechnic, the College of France, and numerous other special and higher institutions) the funds necessary for these 6,400 scholarships were the sum total of what the French national government put into education during the Empire and for years thereafter. Nor was the figure of 6,400 actually attained. In 1813 there were only 14,492 students in all the lycées of France, and of these only 3,500 were scholarship holders. Many of the 3,500 held only half-scholarships, and the expense of many scholarships had been transferred from the national treasury to the local governments. At this time, in 1813, there were about 30,000 students in private secondary schools.

The lycées were by no means universally accepted. Some upper-class families did not wish their sons to mix with scholarship boys. Some feared the propagandizing and recruitment of their sons for a political system that they disliked. Some objected to the regimented and militarized atmosphere that the lycées favored. (See Item 48.) On the other hand, the lycées were attractive to many, and indeed more so than Napoleon himself at the end of his reign. Napoleon was blamed more for abusing his educational system than for the system itself. The idea of state-sponsored scholarships and of state-controlled education, with emphasis on careers open to talent, on selection of a few and elimination of others by a competitive system, on rewards for hard work and recognition of outstanding ability, remained characteristic of education in France. It was a form of élitism gladly believed in.

The Imperial Lycée remained the largest and most prominent of all the lycées of the Empire. It admitted day students as well as boarders, unlike its predecessors in the rue Saint-Jacques since 1762. By 1810 it had about a thousand students, of whom 40% were day pupils only; about half the remainder held scholarships and half were paying boarders. After the fall of Napoleon the number of scholarship students steadily declined. In this respect as in others the nineteenth century did not realize the expectations of the Old Regime, the Revolution, or the First Empire.

Fourcroy addressed the Legislative Body as follows:

In designing a new educational system, appropriate to the present state of knowledge and the genius of the French nation, the government has thought it necessary to depart from accustomed ways. Instructed by the past, it has rejected the old forms of the universities, which were no longer in accord with the progress of reason, and whose reform had been called for by half a century of philosophy and enlightenment. In the Central Schools it has seen institutions that are too few in number, and that are distributed too equally and organized too uniformly for departments of varied and unequal population, with differing resources and means. The government, nevertheless, has taken what is good in each of these two systems. . . .

It has thought that, to establish literary and scientific institutions on a solid basis, one must begin by giving them pupils. They must be peopled with students lest they be peopled only with professors. Such is our aim in creating a considerable number of national scholarships, the funds for which will suffice to support the lycées among which they are distributed. The whole foundation of the new system lies in this conception, whose grandeur is worthy of the French people, and whose suitability to the present moment will be easily realized by all those who appreciate the circumstances in which we live. . . .

The government regrets that the state of its finances has not allowed it to undertake the establishment of secondary schools or to recreate what was useful in the old colleges while avoiding their abuses. It is only after recognizing that the necessary means for such an important operation are not now at its disposal, that the government has found it necessary to adopt another arrangement. Since the suppression of the old colleges and universities, various old schools have taken on a new life, so that a large number of private establishments for the instruction of youth have been formed. . . .

The government believes that, if encouragement were given to what private initiative has already produced, the existing secondary schools would become more active, and new schools would soon be added to the old ones. It will be shown later how a system of examination and competition, set up to enable a certain number of students in these secondary schools to move on into the lycées, will constitute one of the most reliable means of such encouragement, and one whose success is already shown by the Polytechnic School.

The government proposes, as further means of encouragement, the allocation of buildings for new secondary schools, and annual awards for the fifty teachers in these schools who have most distinguished themselves.

In inviting the local governments which now lack such schools to form them at their own expense, the government, which has already received several requests to this effect, his grounds to hope that the towns which formerly had colleges, whose buildings remain at the disposal of the towns, will make haste to establish secondary schools. We can expect that the advance of funds necessary for this enterprise, which is more useful than it is costly, will soon be covered and repaid by parents wishing to place their children in a career of arts and letters. Those publicists who agree with Adam Smith that education should be left to private enterprise will find their ideas realized in this part of the project. Those, on the other hand, who think that the means of education should be offered to all by the government, will recognize that the government has done everything that it can do in the circumstances in which it is placed. It would require more than two million francs a year to establish 250 secondary schools at the expense of the public treasury, and yet this indispensable number would be less than the number existing in 1789, which in almost all cases owed their existence to private foundations.

In the lycées, what was formerly taught in the colleges will be reinforced by the subjects now taught in the Central Schools. The study of ancient and modern literature at all levels will be included, as well as the study of mathematics and physics so necessary in many professions. . . . The lycées will receive four kinds of students: those that the government places in them immediately, those from secondary schools who enter by competition, sons of parents who place them as paying boarders, and day students. Teaching will go by progression, from the first principles of the languages and literature of the ancients with which any liberal education should begin, up to the elements of the sciences which have been so developed in France in the last third of the eighteenth century. Students at all levels will find, in successive and graded classes, all the kinds of knowledge that can guide them in most occupations of society, or introduce a certain number of them to a more advanced study of the sciences.

One of the most important parts of our project deals with the national students. Out of 6,400 boarding students maintained by the government in the lycées, 2,400 will be chosen immediately from the sons of citizens who have served the Republic . . . and 4,000 will be chosen, by competition, from pupils in the secondary schools. The basis of the system, which constitutes the novelty of the plan and its difference from all plans proposed up to now, lies entirely in this arrangement. The experience of a school famous from its birth, as it has been in the seven years of its existence [the Polytechnic], has suggested the idea of having 4,000 students placed in the lycées by competition. It is to the Polytechnic School that we owe the great strides made in mathematics, the widespread taste for this science, and the formation over the past seven years of a host of private schools in which the science of calculation is emphasized. . . . The example is a great and useful lesson for the lawmaker. It allows us to hope that the creation of 4,000 places in the lycées will make our present secondary schools more flourishing, and arouse the desire of communes and individuals to establish new ones.

Thus the destiny of the lycées will stabilize and improve that of the private schools which today take the place of the old colleges. The lycées will become a powerful means of encouragment for the founding of new schools in places which still have none, especially in towns which once possessed one or several colleges, but which for ten years have been deprived of this source of education.

A final part of our project contains several general provisions . . . such as the upkeep of school buildings by the communes in which they are located, the prohibition against using the name of institute or lycée for any private establishment, the terms of retirement for school administrators and professors, and the acceptance by the government of gifts, legacies, and endowments for education. I must repeat here, on this last point, that the government, struck by the evils which followed the almost total destruction of the old endowments for education, and by the necessity of arousing again the spirit of philanthropy and the love of letters for one of its finest and most useful purposes, is determined to show the most profound and inalterable respect for endowments, which are the most precious fruit of philanthropy, and to consecrate in durable monuments the national gratitude toward those benefactors of mankind who make such a great and noble use of their fortunes.

46. The Lycée is to have older virtues

A FEW DAYS after Fourcroy's speech on the lycées, the following article appeared in one of the leading Paris newspapers, the *Gazette de France*. It was signed simply "A." It reads as if it had been planted by the authorities. Possibly it was written by Antoine Arnault, who had made a reputation as a writer of tragedies during the Revolution, then became connected with Lucien and Napoleon Bonaparte, and was chief of the division of Public instruction in the Ministry of the Interior from 1801 to 1808. The article gives an excellent statement of one line of criticism directed against the Central Schools, and of what the government hoped to accomplish in replacing them by lycées. We may note the rejection of certain educational ideas that would later be called progressive, and the belief that an organized teaching profession would be better than the mobile intellectuals by whom many courses in the Central Schools were being given. The *agrégation*, mentioned at the end, was restored in 1808. (See Item 4 above.)

The criticisms being made of public instruction will soon be without foundation. The Central Schools are to be replaced by lycées. These will not be so profusely scattered in the chief towns of all the departments, but will be established in places where one can count on a sufficient number of students to fill the classes and justify the expense.

The subjects of instruction will be less varied, but classified in a certain order; studies will be graded according to age and ability of the pupils; and teaching will no longer be, as some complain, a matter of diversion and amusement in which the pupils form only vague and mistaken ideas of what they are taught. There will be an end to the freedom to choose courses which most suit the student's taste, to pass from one course to another without reasonable purpose, or to follow one's own whim in deciding on what studies to undertake, a freedom ill-suited to youth, which was granted on the impossible premise that youth has a wisdom and discernment that are rare in mature years.

The public schools will go back to the discipline of the old colleges. They will no longer yield to the thoughtlessness of the young, but be concerned with their future advantage; they will not indulge idleness, but instil habits of work; they will not be satisfied with results that are more glittering than solid, with disciples reciting their masters' lessons from memory; they will demand more useful and positive results. A strict examination will verify the work of the students and the progress that they have made. In short, false knowledge and imperfect insights, which are worse than absolute ignorance, will no longer be the fruits of an education which the government will restore to its true aim.

The success of the new establishments will depend largely on the choice of professors. The teachers in the old colleges obtained their places only after excelling in their studies and passing several rigorous tests. Once they reached the rank of professor, they made it their life work. No ambitious plans turned them away from their duties, and since they were free from anxiety about the future they devoted themselves wholeheartedly to the tasks imposed upon them. Since the establishment of the Central Schools, on the contrary, the functions of teaching, especially in Paris, have been regarded as only temporary employments leading to better opportunities. Some professors, putting aside the serious and serene character so wrongly disparaged as pedantry, have been going out into society, neglecting their studies and their profession, and concerning themselves more with their own ambitions than with the progress of their students. The law which permits the holding of several appointments in public instruction at the same time has often allowed the same professor to occupy three different chairs, and this accumulation of *benefices*, which was rightly criticized in the Church, where it was less dangerous, has made it impossible for them to follow students of differing abilities with the attention that their duty prescribes.

From these two disadvantages have come the principal evils in our education. The studies have had no connection with each other; and for lack of attachment to a fixed position, some professors have fallen into an extremely dangerous carelessness in a kind of work where the most ardent zeal, limitless patience, and indefatigable exertion are the most essential qualities.

Hence it is to the selection of professors that the government will doubtless give its most serious attention. A name famous in the literary world will no longer make the decisions. We have had too many examples of highly educated men who are incapable of communicating what they know. Moreover, the habits and character of an author are rarely found along with the exactitude which the professoriate requires. Rollin, who did so much honor to the University of Paris, wrote no books while he was teaching. He composed his immortal works at a time when, in a retirement earned by forty years of labor, he still wished to render the same services to youth as he had done from his professorial chair.

It is believed that the new teachers will be drawn from former teachers dispersed by the Revolution, and from others who have marched in their footsteps since that time, and who especially have maintained that sobriety of life which is absolutely necessary to make an impression on the young. When the government applies itself to detailed regulations, it will probably decide to restore an institution that contributed powerfully to the improvement of the University of Paris, and could easily be adapted for the lycées. This is the institution of the teaching associate, or *agrégation*. Sixty young men were thus made teaching associates after passing a number of examinations, and the professors were chosen from among their number. The young men had the assurance of an occupation to which they might devote their lives; all their work was directed to this end; and the fear of failure made them as serious in their way of life as they were diligent in the important duties on which their future depended.

It cannot be too often repeated that in the social order we must avoid that fluctuation which keeps men in a continual state of incertitude, endlessly balancing on the choice of a career, trying several, and in the end unable to do well in any. This sound idea, which the government is now professing and has just applied to public instruction, is a

THE COLLEGE OF LOUIS-LE-GRAND

sure guarantee of the new organization and of the confidence which it will inspire. —A.

47. A solid curriculum

In 1803 two commissions were appointed to plan a six-year course of graded studies for the new lycées. One, of which the famous astronomer Laplace was a member, laid out a program in the sciences reaching as high as differential and integral calculus, and advanced physics, including optics and electricity. The other commission drew up a program for the humanities. Its members were Fontanes, who later became the first head of the Imperial University, Champagne as head of the Lycée of Paris, and Domairon, an experienced teacher and the author of a world history for students. Their plan, while making considerable room for history and geography, carried over the literary and rhetorical emphasis of the pre-Revolutionary colleges, with readings in Latin to the level of Horace and Tacitus, and in the French classics of the seventeenth century.

Both commissions defined topics to be studied year by year, and recommended books to be read. The following is simply the three introductory paragraphs and the concluding paragraph to the report of the humanities commission:

Report of the commission
appointed to select
instructional books for the
lycées in the Latin
and literature classes

25 Floreal An XI
[May 15, 1803]

The principles of literature are not subject to the same revolutions as those of the sciences; they are derived from imitation of an unchanging model. They can be neglected by laziness, misunderstood by ignorance, or insulted by pride and envy; but they are restored to their place of honor by reason as soon as it has the right to be heard. If forgotten, they are not destroyed; if attacked, new triumphs await them; and their finest privilege is to grow stronger with age. The teaching of these arts, whose essence is invariable, has therefore long been subject to rules which are certain, whereas the sciences, on the other hand, are obliged every day to give up their old systems in the light of new observations brought about by time or chance. It would be absurd today to cite the authority of Ptolemy or Epicurus in astronomy or physics; but the principles of Aristotle and Horace have not changed, and are still followed in eloquent or poetic expression.

These irrefutable observations have guided the commission charged by the government with choosing a plan of methods and authors most appropriate for literary studies. True principles have been published before us by the voice of twenty centuries; tested doctrines have formed several generations of illustrious men, so that we need only to restore the best traditions and pay our respects to experience. We must reflect here as elsewhere the wisdom of the government, which has found the materials for new schools in the ruins of the old.

Knowledge of the Latin language will always be the principal part of instruction, and we maintain this usage after thorough consideration. No other language combines so many advantages. Latin has given birth to a great many of the modern idioms; the Romans who spoke it are no more, but their language survives them, seeming as eternal as their name. Numerous sciences use it as a vehicle and spread themselves with it throughout the world; jurisprudence draws upon it, medicine does not abandon it, and religion consecrates it in its temples. Philosophers have sometimes raised the question of a universal language, but the question is answered in advance. Did not ancient Rome in a sense unite, under the domination of its language, all the empires of Europe which are only the remnants of this Roman rule?

. . . In any case, the founding of the lycées is a great benefit; we shall hear no more ignorant blasphemies against the world of letters. Vulgar minds will no longer inflict the laws of Crete and Sparta on this vast republic for which there is no model, and which should possess at the same time the martial virtues of Rome, the arts of Athens, and the commerce of Carthage.

FONTANES, CHAMPAGNE, DOMAIRON

48. Regulations for lycées
1803

THESE regulations of 1803 may be compared with those of 1769 in Item 5 above. In many ways there is a strong continuity. At both dates there is the same insistence on regulation as such, the same attention to levels of authority and subordination, the same prescribed daily schedule, the same cycle of class recitation, study hall, recreation periods, and supervised outings, the same silence at meals and the same air of seclusion from the protection against the outside world. There is a more humane atmosphere in the regulations of 1769, which show more concern for the feelings of the students, for the individual differences between them, for civility and considerate manners, and for personal warmth between masters and pupils. The tone in 1803 is more brisk and peremptory; there is an air of command and obedience; and the students are organized into squads and companies with student corporals and sergeants and are endlessly falling in and out of ranks to march in formation throughout the lycée at the sound of a drum. In short, the regulations of 1803 are more military.

In 1803 France had been at war for over ten years, and Bonaparte had a military man's ideas on organization. Yet it would be wrong to attribute the militarization of the lycées to these facts alone. Conservative educational writers before the Revolution, such as the Abbé Proyart in his book of 1785, had ridiculed the faddishness by which some private schools were advertising soldierly training. J. F. Champagne himself, in his plan of 1790 for the reform of education (see Item 53 below) stressed military exercises as desirable. Before the war began, or Bonaparte had been heard of, there was a taste for military virtues in schooling.

The uniform prescribed for students in 1803 was not actually military; that is, it was not the uniform of a soldier. Its cost was perhaps more significant than its martial connotation. The idea of the uniform was adopted, beginning at the Paris Prytaneum in 1800, to overcome the visible difference between the poor and the not-so-poor scholarship boys. But the uniform, or rather the outfit of which it was a part, as it developed by 1803, cost about 500 francs, nearly as much as a year's maintenance at the lycée. Attempts to assist poor boys to acquire it never became general and systematic, with the result that even the scholarship holders in the lycées came from families for which such an outlay was possible, to a greater extent than had been true of most colleges of the Old Regime.

It must also be remembered that in the time of Napoleon I forty percent of the students in the lycées did not live in the lycées at all. In Paris only two of the four lycées, the Imperial Lycée and the Lycée Napoleon, took in boarders. Day pupils were not allowed to wear the uniform, and they took no part in the life of the school.

It was not until the end of the nineteenth century that it became customary for day students to live with their parents. In Napoleon's time most of them lived in *pensions* or subordinate boarding schools which sent pupils to the professorial classes (that is, not even to the study halls) in the neighboring lycée. About a dozen such semi-schools were thus affiliated with the Imperial Lycée in 1810. Some of them harbored boys of well-to-do parents, but by no means all. One of them, for example, called the Institution Liautard, sent thirty pupils to the Imperial Lycée in 1809; the parents of nine of them were reported to be a cook, a cookshop owner, a blacksmith, a baker, a wig-maker, a porter, a water-carrier, a chambermaid and a "workman." If the lycée was a bourgeois institution, it was one patronized by bright boys from the working classes, and avoided by many of the bourgeoisie.

The regulations of 1803 begin by placing the prefect of the department on the governing board of the lycée, so that the educational structure would be co-ordinated with the governmental administration. This was done away with in the University of 1808. The regulations also create two new titles, the *proviseur* and the *censeur des études*, who are here called the director and the supervisor of studies; and they provide each lycée with an *instructeur*, which in French has the particular meaning of a military or tactical instructor. The one point in which these regulations carry out the more liberal innovations of the Revolution is the provision for non-Catholic students.

The regulations of 1769 were for one school only, Louis-le-Grand. Those of 1803 are for all lycées in France. The principle of standardization, or of geographical equality throughout the country, has prevailed. The basis is laid for the old joke in which, with some exaggeration, the minister in Paris can look at his watch and tell his visitor what every schoolboy in France is doing at that precise moment.

General Regulations
of the Lycées

21 Prairial An XI
(June 10, 1803)

The government of the republic, on report of the minister of the interior, orders as follows:

TITLE ONE. ADMINISTRATION

I. Administrative Board

1. The prefect of the department is the ex-officio chairman of the administrative board. . . .

II. Administrative Council

6. The director of the lycée is the ex-officio chairman of the administrative council. . . .

TITLE TWO. INTERNAL REGULATIONS OF LYCÉES

I. The Director

9. The director is head of the lycée; he oversees all services, and decides in all unforeseen and emergency cases, subject to an accounting to the administrative board. . . .

II. The Supervisor of Studies

13. The supervisor oversees the conduct, morals, work, and progress of the students.

14. The masters are subordinate to him.

15. He will report to the director every day on the state of the lycée. . . .

III. The Steward

[articles 21–33]

IV. The Professors

34. During class hours the students are subject to the authority of the professors.

35. If the professor finds it necessary to punish a student with one of the penalties authorized in article 26 of the government order of 19 Frimaire last, he will inform the supervisor of studies or the director, who will see to its execution.[a]

36. In classes where compositions on a given matter are appropriate the professors will have their pupils write such a composition at least once a month. The pupil winning the first place will deliver to the director a rank list signed by the professor.

37. A professor wishing to hold an exercise outside the time set for his class will make arrangements with the supervisor of studies.

[a] [The order of 19 Frimaire reads:]

25. Penalties imposed on students will be prison, penitence table, and arrest.

Arrest consists in being placed during recreation at the far end of the courtyard, under orders not to overstep a given circle.

26. Masters of quarters, the military instructor, the professors, and the supervisor of studies have the power to condemn to the penitence table or arrest.

Prison may be imposed only by the director, and may take place only during the daytime.

If the offense or the circumstances require prison at night, the director will report to the minister of the interior.

38. Every professor, every Saturday, will submit to the supervisor of studies, or to the director, his marks on the conduct and progress of his students. . . .

V. The Masters

42. There will be one master of quarters or master of studies for each class or company of twenty-five students over fourteen years old; for those under fourteen, there will be two masters for three companies.

43. Masters will not leave the students confided to them except during the time of lessons in class.

44. They will be informed by the students of assignments made by the professors, and see that these are fulfilled.

45. They will eat with the students.

46. They will sleep in the same dormitories and retain the keys.

47. Thy will accompany their students on outings, and in general on all collective excursions.

48. Two of them will take turns in being present at recreation periods.

49. They will conduct their students to the rooms for their respective lessons, as determined by the supervisor of studies.

50. They will examine their students' books, and take away those that may be morally dangerous.

VI. Drawing Teachers, Writing Teachers, Singing Teachers, etc.

[51–52]

VII. The Servants

[53–59]

VIII. The Students

60. Government students [i.e., scholarship holders] and those placed in each lycée as boarders by their parents will

be required to furnish the following outfit upon entry:

One blue cloth coat, with light blue collar and cuffs, lining *idem,* yellow buttons of solid metal bearing the word *lycée* in the middle; and around it the name of the place where the lycée is located.

Jacket and breeches of the same material, buttons *idem.*

Blue breeches

Two pairs of drawers

One under-vest

Two round hats until fourteen years of age, cocked hats thereafter.

Two pairs of sheets of eleven meters 80 centimeters each, in cretonne cloth.[b]

Six towels

Eight shirts, in cretonne cloth

Six handkerchiefs

Six neckties, four in double muslin, two in black silk

Four pairs of cotton socks

Three nightcaps

Two dressing gowns

Two combs

Two pairs of shoes

All must be new.

IX. Communication Outside the Lycée

61. It is forbidden for students to leave the lycée except with permission of the director, who will have them accompanied.

62. For this purpose there will be printed tickets on which the director writes the names of the student and of the person accompanying him. The latter on leaving will

---

[b] [It remains a mystery to the present editor why the sheets had to be 11.8 meters or almost forty feet long. One would suspect a misprint except for the fact that when the same regulations were reissued in 1811, the sheets were required to be *fourteen* meters long.]

give the ticket to the porter, who will return it to the director.

63. Students will have no correspondence except with their parents, or with persons having powers of attorney in place of the parents, and whose names will be made known to the director.

64. Letters arriving in the mail or brought by messenger will be delivered by the porter to the supervisor of studies, who will pass them on to the students.

65. Letters written by students will be placed in a conveniently located box, and the supervisor of studies will send them to the post-office.

66. Parents may give money to their children only by placing it in custody of the supervisor, who will oversee its employment.

67. No workman may be employed by students without the director's approval.

X. Movements of Students during the Day

68. The signal for all exercises will be given by the sound of a drum.

69. Masters will see that students are up and dressed at half past five in the morning, and at six on Sundays and holidays.

70. At 6:00, the masters will conduct the students to the study halls. Upon arrival, they will offer a prayer in common.

71. Study will last until 7:30.

72. The servant will bring breakfast to the study hall, and students will have a half an hour to eat it.

73. At 8:00 the master and the military instructor, or the student acting for this officer, will conduct the students to class.

74. Morning lessons will last for two hours.

75. At 10:00 the students will re-ascend in formation to the study hall, and remain at work until 11:30.

76. At 11:30, lessons in writing and drawing until 12:30.

77. Lessons in arms, or in music, etc., will be taken in recreation periods.

78. At 12:30, each company will be conducted in formation to its place in the dining hall assigned to it. Each sergeant will be at the head of his company, and each corporal at the head of his subdivision.

79. Dinner will last for three-quarters of an hour.

80. Students will rise from the table at a signal given by the supervisor of studies.

81. Recreation will follow in the courtyards for three-quarters of an hour, or in the study halls if the weather is inclement.

82. At 2:00, the students will be re-assembled and conducted to study in the formation prescribed for all movements.

83. Afternoon lessons will begin at 3:00 and last until 4:45.

84. Students will then return to the study hall and have an afternoon snack for a quarter of an hour; in fair weather this may occur in the courtyard.

85. Study will begin again at 5:00 and last until 7:00.

86. There will then be a half-hour of recreation in the courtyard; in winter or bad weather it will take place in the study hall.

87. Supper at 7:30, in the same order as at dinner.

88. After supper, there will be recreation as before, until 8:45.

89. There will be an evening prayer at 9:00, after which the students will be conducted in formation to the dormitories, where the masters will see that they retire immediately.

90. The masters will not go to bed themselves until assured that each student is in his bed first.

91. There will be a reading at meals, during which the students will observe complete silence. Breakfast and the afternoon snack are excepted from this rule, but students must speak without tumult or confusion.

XI. Holidays

92. There will be no classes on Thursdays, Sundays, and holidays.

93. There will be a study hall from 6:30 to 8:00 on Thursday. At 8:00, breakfast and recreation; at 9:30, study. At 11:00, military exercises until 12:30. The exercise will begin with an inspection of clothing by the military instructor and the supervisor of studies. Then will come dinner and departure for the outing. Students must return at the ordinary supper hour in the summer, and at 5:00 in winter, followed by study from 5:00 until supper.

94. On Sundays and holidays students will attend religious service immediately after breakfast, that is, at 8:30. After the service, at 10:30, there will be study until noon. At noon, dinner and recreation until 1:00; then, religious service, followed by departure for the outing.

95. By exception, there will be no outing on the principal holidays.

96. The director will determine the place of the outings.

97. These outings will not be omitted except when the weather makes them absolutely impossible.

98. No student will separate himself from his comrades.

99. They will purchase nothing except in the presence and with the consent of the masters.

XII. Religious Exercises

100. The chaplain of the lycée will be designated by the director and appointed by the bishop. He is responsible, under supervision by the director, for all that pertains to religious exercises.

101. Whenever possible there will be a chapel inside the lycée, for the celebration of divine service on Sundays and holidays.

102. If there can be no chapel inside the lycée, the students will be conducted to the nearest church, where the chaplain will celebrate divine service.

103. Students will proceed to church in the formation prescribed by article 22 of the decree of 19 Frimaire.[c] On the way, and in the church, they will observe an appropriate decorum.

104. If, in the town in which the lycée is established, there are one or more edifices used by different religious groups, and if the lycée has students of these religions, they will be conducted thereto in the same way.

105. If there are no such edifices, non-Catholic students will receive instruction in Scriptural morality while the others are at Catholic services.

106. The director will give information on the means available for religious instruction, according to the wishes of parents.

XIII. Examinations and awards

107. At the end of each trimester the director and the supervisor of studies, with the help of such examiners as they judge necessary, will examine the students and award prizes in each class.

108. At the end of the school year there will be literary exercises, which the students in each class must attend. They will be questioned in public, and in the presence of members of the administrative board, on matters to which they have applied themselves during the year. . . .

XIV. Vacations

115. Vacations will begin on 1 Fructidor and end on the following 15 Vendémiaire. [From about August 18 to about October 7.]

116. During this time the professors will be exempt from all work.

117. Students may spend the vacation with their parents,

[c] [The article reads:] When students go out in a body, they will have at their head the supervisor of studies, a master of quarters, and the military instructor.

but are required to return to the lycée on the day before the opening of classes.

XV. Penalties

122. Corporal punishment is forbidden.

123. Other penalties as designated in articles 25 and 26 of the law of 19 Frimaire Year XI can be imposed only in conformity with the provisions of that decree. [See Article 35 above.]

XVI. The Infirmary

[124–129]

XVII. Day Students

130. Boys or young men who desire simply to benefit from classes held at the lycée will be presented to the director by their parents or recognized correspondent.

131. They will receive an entry card, without which they cannot be admitted.

132. They must be properly dressed, but the uniform of the resident students is forbidden to them. They may not take part in the study halls or recreation periods. . . .

TITLE THREE. GENERAL PROVISIONS

137. The doors of the lycée will be opened at 5:30 in the morning, and closed at 9:00 at night. The keys will be kept by the director, or in his absence by the supervisor of studies.

138. No outsider may sleep in the lycée without express permission from the director.

139. No master, student, or servant may sleep outside the lycée without permission of the director.

140. Entry into the interior is forbidden to all persons of the female sex, except the mothers, sisters, aunts, or

guardians of the students, who may not enter without permission from the director.

141. All other women will be received in the parlor.

142. All dangerous games and exercises, and all card games and games of chance, are forbidden; it is likewise forbidden to let money be seen in any game whatever.

143. Students may not remove their coats during recreation periods without permission of the supervisor of studies.

144. All indecent or insulting language will be rigorously punished.

145. The introduction of any weapon, or of explosive powder, even fireworks, is forbidden.

146. Any kind of loan, exchange, or sale between students may take place only with permission of their respective masters.

147. The dormitories will be lighted at night.

148. One of the servants, in turn, will serve as a watchman to patrol the courtyards, stairs, and corridors to prevent disorder and fire.

149. Each professor and master in the lycée will receive a copy of the present regulations, which will be printed in sufficient number. . . .

150. The minister of the interior is charged with the execution of the present order.

Signed: BONAPARTE
H. B. MARET

49. Swimming lessons

DEVELOPMENT of the body was not overlooked by the new educational planners. Swimming, ridiculed by conservatives as a frill, was to be taught in the state-sponsored schools. It is not known whether this order had any immediate effect at the Imperial Lycée. In later years, by 1830, students at Louis-le-Grand were taking swimming lessons at a bath-house in the Seine.

30 Prairial An XII
[June 18, 1804]

The minister of the interior orders as follows:

1. The art of swimming shall be part of the education of youth in the lycées and secondary schools.

2. Swimming lessons will be given by recognized swimming teachers, in the presence of the masters of studies and the hall servants.

3. In rivers or suitable bodies of water a place will be chosen where the bottom can be verified every year, and beyond which the students may not venture on any pretext.

4. Students will wear bathing trunks at their swimming lessons.

> Signed: CHAPTAL, minister of
> the interior
> FOURCROY, state councillor in charge
> of public instruction

50. The Imperial University

THE University created by Napoleon was a large and composite institution, and only enough is said of it here to explain the place of the Imperial Lycée within it. In some ways the Napoleonic structure lasted until the middle of the twentieth century. In some ways it realized a desire for educational centralization that had been evident since the Old Regime. But the shape that it took, in the two funding decrees of 1806 and 1808, was also determined by the needs of the moment.

The lycées, which began to be organized in 1803, met with much criticism and opposition. One important purpose of the new University was to strengthen them against the competition of private schools. Some families found private schools that were more convenient, closer to home, more easy-going, or less expensive than the lycées. For others, or with other schools, the appeal of the private institution was that it taught more religion, or was preferred by the wealthy, or was patronized by families out of sympathy with Napoleon or with the whole French Revolution since 1789. Some objected that the lycées were full of ex-radicals and renegade or married ex-priests—as indeed they were. The government rarely emphasized this political aspect of the educational problem, because it did not want the feuds between Left and Right to be reopened. In the public statements of Fourcroy and others, the argument against private schools, which might well be true of many of them, was that after years of Revolutionary disintegration no one could know what they were or what they stood for—that their standards were low and their teachers unqualified, or in any case that families could not tell what these standards and qualifications were—that they might be here today and gone tomorrow—that some of them were run by educational cranks and some only for private profit without regard to public advantage—in short, that they were a heterogeneous lot against which the public should be protected.

One way to strengthen the state system, consisting in the lycées and the municipally supported secondary schools (called "colleges"), was to give the teachers in them a feeling of confidence, solidarity, collegiality, permanence, occupational status, pride in their work, membership in a large and important organization—in short, *esprit de corps*. Hence they were to be made into a *corps enseignant*, a Teaching Body. This was the purpose of the short law of 1806, which is printed in full below. The "special and temporary" obligations which it mentions were to be temporary in not being like the vows of the old religious teaching orders, and special in that they applied to teaching as a profession, involving such requirements as meeting one's classes, conforming to regulations, and teaching nothing of which the Emperor might disapprove.

The decree of 1808 was so long that only a sixth of it is translated here. It designed a University which, among other things, was to produce citizens loyal to Napoleon and the new dynasty that he hoped to found. As a bid for unity, it made a few concessions to Catholic sentiment. The "precepts of the Catholic religion" were to be the basis of teaching, but "precepts" is a vague word, and no exclusion of non-Catholics was intended. The celibacy requirement, stated in article 101, was also meant to be pleasing to Catholics, and its effect was to favor priests as teachers. But the actual professors in the lycées were excepted, and it was to become operative only "in the future." It was probably also a concession to public opinion, which often held that unmarried men had more concern and more time for their students, and to the practical needs of life in an all-male residential institution according to the proprieties of 1808.

In the first articles of the decree all educational establishments in the Empire, public and private, were declared to be part of the University. They were grouped in seventeen territorial units called academies, each under its rector. That the term "public instruction" was applied to all can be misleading, for actually there were still about as many students in private as in public schools at the end of the Empire. The state schools belonged to the University in the full sense, and their teachers were regarded as civil servants or *fonctionnaires*, who were trained, appointed, promoted, transferred, paid, and pensioned within the system. The private schools belonged to the University in a looser sense, in that they were subject to a complex of authorizations, requirements, and inspections. Both public and private schools paid certain fees to the University, by which the whole superstructure of Grand Master, councillors, inspectors, rectors, and deans was supported without cost to the state. Thus, since the fees eventually came out of the pockets of parents, the families which used private schools and the families which used public schools both paid for the system of public control.

As the scholarships were the key to the lycées, so the key to the University was the academic degree. These visible signs of achievement, abolished during the Revolution, were now revived from the Old Regime. Twenty years without them had made them more palatable, on condition that they should be a genuine means of assuring quality, maintaining uniform standards, and giving credibility to professional claims. To confer degrees, and conduct the necessary examinations, various "faculties" were created, in theology, medicine, law, science, and letters. The degrees, in descending order, were those of doctor, licentiate, and bachelor. The master key was the bachelor's degree, and especially that of bachelor of letters, or *baccalauréat*, which resembled the *maîtrise ès arts* of the Old Regime. It became prerequisite to higher degrees in the sciences, law, and medicine, to admission to the schools of science and learning maintained by the government, to a variety of appointments in the civil service, and even for anyone operating a private school, though this requirement was not successfully implemented in practice. The subject matter for the examination for the bachelor's degree was "whatever is taught in the higher classes of the lycées." The examination was conducted by the Faculty of Letters, hierarchically above the lycée; but in fact, since the Faculty did not do much except conduct examinations, many of its members were also professors in the lycées.

The lycées therefore held the master key. Anyone aspiring to a liberal, professional, learned, or governmental career had to attend them, at least for the last two years, or, under later developments, go to a private school which patterned itself on the lycée. From another point of view, the lycée became a shop for the manufacture of bachelors.

The competition of private schools remained so strong, and the disaffection of many parents so great, that Napoleon, in an even longer decree of 1811, attempted to compel the private schools to send their students into the state system. With his involvement in Russia in 1812, and subsequent reverses, the decree of 1811 went largely unenforced. As already noted, there were still only thirty-six lycées in France at Napoleon's abdication, and there were about as many students in private secondary schools as in all the lycees and public colleges combined.

As for the Imperial Lycée, the former and later Louis-le-Grand, it was a distinguished institution of learning, but it was also now a cog in a much larger machine.

(1)

Law on the formation of an Imperial University

May 10, 1806

Article 1. There shall be formed under the name of an Imperial University a body charged exclusively with public teaching and education in the whole Empire.

2. Members of the Teaching Body will contract special and temporary civil obligations.

3. The organization of the Teaching Body will be presented in the form of a law to the Legislative Body in the session of 1810. [This was in fact done by the following decree of 1808.]

(II)

Paris, March 17, 1808

Napoleon, by the grace of God and the constitutions Emperor of the French, King of Italy, Protector of the Confederation of the Rhine,

Considering the law of May 10, 1806, creating a Teaching Body,

Our Council of State having been heard,

We have decreed and decree as follows:

TITLE I

General Organization of the University

Article 1. Public teaching in the whole Empire is confided exclusively to the University.

2. No school, or any establishment for instruction whatsoever, may be formed outside the Imperial University or without the authorization of its head.

3. No one may open a school, or engage in public teaching, without being a member of the Imperial University, and having a degree from one of its Faculties. . . .

TITLE II

On the Composition of the Faculties

[Articles 6–15]

TITLE III

On degrees awarded by the Faculties and the means of obtaining them

16. Degrees in each Faculty are three in number, namely the baccalaureate, the licentiate, and the doctorate.

17. Degrees are conferred by the Faculties after examinations and public acts.

18. Degrees will not give the title of member of the University, but will be prerequisite to obtaining it.

19. To be successful in the examination for the bachelor's degree in the Faculty of Letters the candidate must (1) be at least sixteen years old, and (2) reply satisfactorily on whatever is taught in the higher classes of the Lycées.

TITLE IV

On the order to be established among members of the University; and on the ranks and titles attached to the several functions

29. The functionaries of the Imperial University will rank as follows:

Ranks

ADMINISTRATION	TEACHING
1. The Grand Master	
2. The Chancellor	
3. The Treasurer	
4. The Life Councillors	
5. The Ordinary Councillors	
6. Inspectors of the University	
7. Rectors of Academies	
8. Inspectors of Academies	
9. Deans of Faculties	
10. —	Professors of Faculties
11. Directors ⎫	
12. Supervisors of Studies ⎬ of Lycées	
13.	Professors of Lycees[a]
14. Principals of Colleges	

[a] Professors of Philosophy and of Rhetoric in the Lycées of Paris will rank after adjunct professors of the Faculties of Letters; they will have the right to wear the same robe and the same decoration, and may be called upon to act as examiners in these Faculties (University Council, October 31, 1809).

15. —   Associates in Lycées[b]
16. —   Instructors in Colleges
17. Heads of private schools
18. Boarding-school masters
19. —   Masters of studies

TITLE V

Basis of Instruction in schools of the University

38. All schools in the University will take as the basis of their instruction:

1. The precepts of the Catholic religion.
2. Fidelity to the Emperor, to the imperial monarchy as trustee of the welfare of peoples, and to the Napoleonic dynasty as preserver of the unity of France and of all liberal ideas proclaimed in its constitution.
3. Obedience to the statutes of the Teaching Body, which have the uniformity of instruction for their object, and whose effect is to produce, for the State, citizens who are attached to their religion, their prince, their country, and their family.

TITLE VI

Obligations contracted by members of the University

[Articles 39–49]

TITLE VII

Functions and powers of the Grand Master of the University

[Articles 50–63]

[b] [The French terms for the titles in ranks 15 through 19 are: 15 *agrégés*, 16 *régents de Collège*, 17 *chefs d'institution*, 18 *maîtres de pension*, 19 *maîtres d'études*.]

TITLE VIII

Functions and powers of the chancellor
and treasurer of the University

[Articles 64–68]

TITLE IX

The University Council

[Articles 69–84]

TITLE X

The Academy Councils

[Articles 85–89]

TITLE XI

Inspectors of the University
and Inspectors of Academies

Articles 90–91. The inspectors-general of the University
will be appointed by the Grand Master . . . and will make
visits in turn, on orders of the Grand Master, to ascertain
the state of studies and discipline in the Faculties, the
Lycées and the Colleges; to assure themselves of the exactitude and the talents of the professors, the intructors in
colleges and the masters of studies; to examine the students;
and to review the administration and accounts.

TITLE XII

Rectors of Academies

[Articles 94–99]

TITLE XIII

Regulations to be issued for Lycées,
Colleges, private schools, boarding schools,
and primary schools

100. The Grand Master will have the University Council review, discuss, and make decisions on the regulations as they exist today for lycées and colleges. Any changes and modifications that may be made will accord with the following provisions.

101. In the future, and after the final organization of the University, the directors and supervisors of studies in the Lycées, and the principals and instructors in the Colleges, as well as the masters of studies in those schools, will be required to be unmarried and to share in the communal life of the school.

102. Professors in the lycées may be married, in which case they will live outside the Lycée. Unmarried professors may live in the Lycée and benefit from its communal life.

No Lycée professor may open a boarding establishment, or conduct public classes outside the Lycée; but each may take one or two students to live with him while they are attending classes at the Lycée.

Title XIV

On the recruitment of University functionaries and professors

110. There will be established in Paris a residential normal school, designed to receive three hundred young men to be trained in the art of teaching the sciences and letters.

111. The inspectors will select each year, in the Lycées, by examination and competition, a certain number of students at least seventeen years old, from among those whose progress and good conduct have been the most constant, and who show promise of aptitude for administration or for teaching.

112. Students who enter this competition must be authorized by their fathers or guardians to follow a career in the University. They may not be admitted to the normal school unless they engage themselves to remain at least ten years in the Teaching Body.

113. They will take courses at the College of France, the Polytechnic School, or the Museum of Natural History, depending on whether their aim is for teaching in letters or in one of the various kinds of sciences.

TITLE XV

On emeritus status and retirement

123. Functionaries of the University in the fifteen higher ranks as listed in article 29, after thirty years of active service without interruption, may be placed in emeritus status and receive a pension to be determined, according to functions, by the University Council.

125. A retirement residence will be established, in which the emeriti may be received and maintained at the expense of the University.

126. Functionaries of the University who, during the exercise of their functions, are attacked by an infirmity which makes it impossible for them to continue, may be received in the retirement residence before the normal date of retirement.

TITLE XVI

Costumes

128. The common costume of all members of the University will be a black coat, with a palm embroidered in blue silk on the left breast.

129. Professors and instructors will conduct their classes in a robe of black muslin. On the left shoulder will be worn the band which designates the wearer's Faculty by its color, and his degree by its edging.[c]

_____

[c] [This band, *la chausse*, corresponded to the hood in the academic costume of other countries.]

TITLE XVII

Revenues of the Imperial University

[Articles 131–137]

TITLE XVIII

Expenses of the Imperial University

[Articles 138–142]

TITLE XIX

General Provisions

[Articles 143–144]

51. The new University receives what is left of the old endowments

THE reader may wonder what ever became of the pre-Revolutionary college endowments, used to support scholarships, of which so much was said in earlier pages of this book. The answer is, briefly, that they were lost. But such brevity must be qualified. And a distinction can be drawn between Paris and the whole country of which Paris was a part.

In Paris, the College of Louis-le-Grand, it may be recalled [Item 36], absorbed the decayed endowments of twenty-eight small colleges in 1763, and thirty-odd years later, now called the Central Scholarship Institute, it absorbed the endowments of the other nine full-program colleges in the city, so far as they had survived the extreme phase of the Revolution. The Scholarship Institute, renamed the French Prytaneum, thus became the heir to all the colleges of the Paris Faculty of Arts. But the Prytaneum was divided into four parts, geographically separated, and the government of the Consulate, which controlled the actual use of the funds, supported each part by annual grants. One part, located at Saint-Cyr, was converted into a military academy. For a time Saint-Cyr was financed from the income of the former Paris colleges. By the decree of March 24, 1808, however, printed below, Napoleon trans-ferred Saint-Cyr to the budget of the War Department, and in recognition of the claims of the abolished Paris colleges, granted an "endowment" of 400,000 francs a year to the Im-perial University, consisting in effect of the interest on govern-ment bonds. A sum of 400,000 francs a year was not very much for a national system, being less than the endowed income of Louis-le-Grand alone at the time of the Revolution.

For France as a whole, all income-producing properties of the colleges, including those of Paris, were confiscated, along with church properties, late in 1789. In principle the colleges continued to receive the income for three years, but in March 1793 these properties were ordered sold, and many were in fact sold to private buyers. In 1797, by the law of 25 Messidor of the Year V, these sales were stopped. What then happened is not altogether clear. Some sales probably continued for a while, but in general these properties remained in the national domain, and their income constituted revenue for the govern-ment. Champagne, in his book of 1800 (Item 54 below), dis-cussed the problem of the lost endowments. Fourcroy, in intro-ducing the lycées in 1802, regretted that the old endowments had disappeared. What had not been alienated had probably melted beyond recognition into the general mass of government income.

In 1808, by the decree of December 11, reproduced below, Napoleon conveyed what was left of the pre-Revolutionary properties to the Imperial University. So far as this meant the buildings actually used for educational purposes, the Em-peror's gift was far from munificent, since such buildings had been excepted even from the confiscatory law of March 1793 (Item 27). So far as it meant income-producing properties, such as farms and house rentals, very little could have been left. The budgets of the Imperial University, as reconstructed for each year beginning in 1809, show the endowment income of 400,000 francs a year, but only a microscopic sum of from 20,000 to 40,000 a year as income from its own properties. We can only conclude that the decree of December 11, 1808, was insignificant, and that there was nothing left of the pre-Revolutionary educational endowments, in the whole of France, to convey to the Imperial University.

As for scholarships in the lycées, Napoleon's government granted between one and two million francs a year from the central treasury for this purpose. Public funds for student aid then declined for seventy years, and next to nothing came from private donors for new endowments. In 1842 the Minister of Public Instruction, Villemain, estimated that there were only 7,567 secondary-school students in France whose parents did not pay the full cost of their education, compared to a figure of 40,621 for such students in 1789.

(1)

Decree on the endowment of the University

March 24, 1808

Article 1. The perpetual income of 400,000 francs, which was transferred by the sinking-fund to the Prytaneum of Saint-Cyr in conformity with our decree of March 5, 1806, will constitute the endowment of the Imperial University.

2. The University will enter upon the receipt of this income on July 1 next.

3. On the same date the Prytaneum of Saint-Cyr will be entirely at the charge of the War Department.

(11)

Decree assigning to the University the available properties of former establishments of public instruction

December 11, 1808

NAPOLEON, Emperor of the French and King of Italy Having heard our council of state, we have decreed and decree as follows:

1. All property, real, movable, or in the form of funded income, which used to belong to the former French Pry-

taneum, or to universities, academies, and colleges of either the old or the new territory of the empire, and which has not been alienated or definitively assigned by special decree to another public service, is granted to the Imperial University.

2. In towns which used to have universities, where there may still exist enough property to endow and maintain a lycée or a college, the Imperial University will maintain one or the other of these kinds of establishment; and scholarships in them will be given by us, in line with the terms set by the founders and by preference to members of their families; without derogation, however, to the particular arrangements made in our preceding decrees for the universities of Genoa, Turin, Geneva, or others.

These universities will simply take the name of academies.

3. Our ministers are charged, each in his own area of responsibility, with the execution of the present decree.

Signed: NAPOLEON
H. B. Maret, Secretary of State

52. The Imperial Lycée—or Louis-le-Grand old and new

IN 1814, when the Napoleonic empire came to an end, the Imperial Lycée was in many ways very different from what the College of Louis-le-Grand had been in the generation before the Revolution. Mathematics and the sciences were taught to a higher level. Religion was less pervasive. The students were more mixed; not all were scholarship students, as they had been until 1800. The students were also younger, for the lycée had become a "secondary" school; there were no longer those who went out to professional schools for their studies, as there had been at the old Louis-le-Grand, Equality College, the Scholarship Institute, and the Prytaneum. Resident students were in uniform. Drums beat every hour or so. The classes were invaded by several hundred day pupils from satellite boarding schools. All told, there were about a thousand students, twice as many as before the Revolution. Classrooms were overcrowded.

In other ways the lack of change is surprising, considering all that had happened. In physical accommodations the school was larger, having annexed the buildings of Plessis College, but all buildings were inherited from the Old Regime. Teaching methods had changed very little; the old scholastic disputation was not revived, but supervised study, recitation, declamation, and written and oral examinations went on as before. The same spirit of competitive achievement prevailed. Pupils moved forward in graded annual classes. The daily schedule of getting up, eating, studying, reciting, mingling in the courtyards, and going to bed was much the same in 1814 as in 1774. And while younger teachers and masters came and went, the basic professorial staff remained remarkably stable.

The following item shows the names of the three chief administrators and the titular professors at three different dates from 1798 to 1810. It is clear that, after the low point of 1793–95, the reconstruction of the senior teaching staff took place in the years from 1798 to 1800. It was not the reorganization as a lycée that made the difference. When J. F. Champagne retired in 1810, he had had the same men as colleagues in the same establishment for ten years or more. Most of them had taught in the colleges of the Old Regime. When Le Prevost d'Iray left the Lycée to become an inspector in the Imperial University, he was replaced by Guerle; but Guerle, though new to the Lycée, had been a master at Lisieux College before the Revolution, and then a professor in the Central Schools. When "philosophy" was reintroduced as a final year of the plan of study, somewhat on the model of the Old Regime, it was J. B. Maugras who was appointed at the Imperial Lycée; but Maugras had taught philosophy at Montaigu College from 1778 to 1792, and even substituted as professor of philosophy at Louis-le-Grand in the 1780's. When J. B. Jumelin died in 1807 he was succeeded by Thillaye as professor of physics. Thillaye had not taught before the Revolution, but he was a young man, born in 1776.

233

The lesson seems to be, if we were to generalize from the case of Louis-le-Grand, that even in time of revolution, with innovations in education proposed and demanded on every side, with new laws and new forms of organization enacted, and even with new people setting up experimentally as schoolmasters or professors for a few years, it is the professional teachers who expect to spend their lives in the schools, and whom it is difficult to replace, that will carry on through all attempts to modify the system.

The Senior Staff

1798–1810

Title	At the Prytaneum 1798–1800	At the Imperial Lycee 1804	At the Imperial Lycee 1810
Director	*J. F. Champagne	same	same
Supervisor of Studies	none	Le Prevost d'Iray	*J. N. Guerle
Steward	*F. P. Lesieur	same	same
Professor of Philosophy	none	none	*J. B. Maugras
Professors of Sciences and Mathematics	*M. B. Duport	same	same
	*J. S. Landry	same	same
	*P. A. Laran	same	same
	J. B. Jumelin	same	J. B. A. Thillaye
	— Dubourget	same	same
Professors of Rhetoric and Humanities	J. C. Luce de Lancival	same	same
	P. L. R. Castel	same	(died 1809)
	*E. C. Dubos	same	same
	*E. E. Mollereau	same	same
	*J. A. Roussel	same	same
	*— Adam	same	same
	— Goffeau	same	same

* Known to have been active at Louis-le-Grand or another college before 1789. The word "same" means same as to the left.

II

JEAN FRANCOIS CHAMPAGNE
AS AN EDUCATIONAL PLANNER

53. "Ideas on Public Education Presented to the National Assembly"

October 22, 1790

HARDLY was it realized by the French that they were in the midst of a revolution when a great many people began to submit plans to the Constituent Assembly for the reform of education. Many of these plans came from teachers in the schools. One such as Audrein's (Item 17 above), written in 1790 and published in 1791. Another was drawn up by J. F. Champagne and his two colleagues and friends, the brothers Guéroult. It was never published, but was presented on the floor of the Assembly on October 22, 1790.

The fact that the manuscript is in Champagne's hand, with his own emendations, suggests that he may have been the most influential of the three in determining its contents. The other two, however, were not insignificant persons. In age, all were about forty in 1790. All had taught for years in the Paris colleges. The elder Guéroult later became the director of the Lycée Charlemagne, a councillor of the Imperial University, and head of the Ecole Normale Superieure, from which he was removed at the Bourbon restoration. The younger Guéroult was employed by the police during the Terror, then became professor at the Lycée Napoleon, and finally professor at the College of France until his death in 1816.

The plan was referred by the Assembly to its Committee on the Constitution, and so became part of the materials from which the Talleyrand report on education of September 1791 was developed. On the manuscript, in a different hand, it is noted that the plan was also submitted to the Legislative Assembly, and hence presumably to its Committee on Public Instruction, so that it was probably among the sources available for the Condorcet report of April 1792. It is not possible to say that the Champagne-Guéroult plan had any particular influence on either of these justly famous reports. Many of its ideas were not very unusual. Both Talleyrand and Condorcet moved in social and intellectual circles in which professors in the colleges were seldom seen and not highly regarded.

The plan, however, and others like it, might give them the feeling that extensive changes in the educational system would be acceptable to many teachers.

Nevertheless, there are a few verbal similarities between the unpublished Champagne-Guéroult plan and the far more comprehensive report presented by Talleyrand to the Constituent Assembly and published in 1791. They are sufficient to prove that someone on Talleyrand's committee worked with the Champagne-Guéroult text. They are most evident in the discussion of scholarships in the Paris colleges, but may also be detected in what is said of primary schools, and in the idea that older students, as a practical exercise, should play the roles of judge, prosecutor, and attorney as if in a courtroom. Talleyrand said forty years later, when he wrote his memoirs, that he had consulted Lavoisier, Laplace, Lagrange, Monge, Condorcet, La Harpe, and Vicq d'Azyr. Probably our three professors had as much to do with the report as some of these scientific and intellectual notables.

It is in being typical rather than original that the plan is of interest, and the identity of the authors is as significant as the content. We have here three professors who begin by quoting Rousseau, not from the *Emile* but from the tract on Poland in which Rousseau prescribed education as means of nation-building. Our professors are in fact, like Rousseau in his *Poland*, more nationalistic than either the Talleyrand or Condorcet reports, in their fervid insistence that the regenerated French should be different from other peoples. For the general idea of "national education," as for the use of the words "gymnasium" and "lyceum" in the Champagne-Gueroult plan, the reader may recall what is said in the Introduction to the present book.

The emphasis in the plan on practicality, and the avoidance of theory, are characteristic of Champagne, or of men actually involved in the daily business of dealing with boys in the classroom. The three authors define the levels of primary, secondary, and higher education very much like Talleyrand and Condorcet. Like them, they put all the highest education in Paris. They assign no role to the church or the clergy in schooling, but they do not express the acrimonious anti-clericalism of Condorcet, the *philosophes*, and the *idéologues*. They commit the schools to control by the national and local governments, and even anticipate the Napoleonic University (and echo ideas of the Old Regime), in proposing that every private schoolmaster should be licensed by the state, and be required to send his pupils to the public school for some kinds of instruction. The emphasis on drawing and military exercises was usual at the time. The three authors agree with other reformers that the archaic Latin Quarter should be broken up, and the colleges distributed more evenly throughout the city of Paris.

The "lyceums" in four sections, each pursuing advanced studies in its field, and all located in Paris, prefigure in a way certain elements in the Talleyrand and Condorcet reports, and anticipate the Institute of France as it was organized in 1795. The thought that they need cost no more than was already being spent was an observation commonly made during the Revolution, and is a reminder of how much the French government was already contributing to the highest levels of science and scholarship in the last years of the monarchy.

While maintaining the pre-eminence of the capital, the plan is very much concerned with providing an equal quality of education for all parts of the country. It thus proposes a National Committee on Education to promote uniformity in instruction and textbooks. Its powers are to be only advisory and informative. But it is noteworthy that this committee is to be composed of teachers, not bureaucrats, and of teachers at all levels from the primary to the highest. Neither Talleyrand nor Condorcet nor any other planner envisages so much influence for teachers in the ordinary schools.

To equalize opportunities geographically, the authors favor a drastic re-arrangement of the scholarships for study in the Paris colleges. Individual colleges will no longer be endowed with their own scholarship funds. Such funds will be combined in a common pool, to be administered by the department of Paris, which will allocate it among all the other departments of France, and determine to which Paris college each scholar will be assigned. No fear is expressed that the endowments will be lost. The feeling is, rather, that with the distinctions between rich colleges and poor colleges done away with, and with separate colleges no longer autonomous, education as a whole will remain endowed by the existing endowments, with wise government officials distributing the income. This principle was widely agreed upon, and something of the kind happened with the creation of the Central Scholarship Institute in 1797 (Items 34 and 36 above), but in fact the department of Paris, late in 1791, forbade further appointments to scholarships in the Paris colleges.

Neither the Champagne-Gueroult plan, nor the more official plans for which Talleyrand and Condorcet were the spokesmen, were even enacted. Except for some ineffective legislation on primary schools, the three revolutionary assemblies, Constituent, Legislative, and Convention, produced nothing for general education until the law of 3 Brumaire of the Year IV (October 1795), whose most notable creation was the Central Schools of the Directory period. But if little was actually established, a vast range of educational questions had been intelligently canvassed, so much so that educational thinkers made reference to the French Revolution for well over the next hundred years. As Champagne said in his book of 1800 (Item 54 below), the debates in the revolutionary assemblies, reinforced by a flow of plans volunteered by private citizens, had constituted a grand National Rostrum on the subject.

Paris, October 22, 1790

Ideas on Public Education, presented to the National Assembly by MM. Guéroult the elder, Professor of Eloquence at Harcourt College, Guéroult the younger, Professor of Eloquence at Grassins College, and Champagne, Professor of the Second at the College of Louis-le-Grand

"It is education that must shape the minds of youth in the national mold, and so form their tastes and opinions that they are patriots by inclination, by passion, by necessity."—
Rousseau, *Government of Poland.*

Such no doubt is the aim to be kept in mind by those concerned with education, this powerful stimulant in the hands of law-makers, an instrument more effective than the laws, since laws can do nothing without moral attitudes and habits. Good citizens will regret that Rousseau did not develop his ideas himself, or trace for us a plan of national education. What he did not do a host of writers have tried. But their works offer fewer useful views than declamations against our present system of studies. No great perspicacity is needed to discover that these studies are indeed inadequate, and even pernicious in several respects. We will observe in general that most modern plans have the inexcusable fault of being impracticable.

Even the wisest, says the philosopher we have just quoted, often emphasize in education what is important for men to know, without considering what children are in a condition to learn. We shall at least try to avoid those brilliant theories which are seductive by their appearance of usefulness, but which offer neither facility of execution nor simplicity in method.

We have asked ourselves first what is to be understood by national education. It has seemed to us that an education is truly national when young people bring into society, from the public schools, a knowledge of the history, laws, customs, and products of their own country; when they feel respect and enthusiasm for the constitution of the state and see no higher honor than that of being French; when in a word they have contracted from an early age the habit of doing what a Frenchmen should do all his life, so that their minds have a definite character and physiognomy, and the country can recognize them as truly French from the moment they present themselves for registration on the civic list.

It is in this spirit that we think education should be directed, if it is to be really national. Doubtless its form cannot be the same for all citizens. Doubtless it must be modified according to the students' needs and abilities, and to the professions to which nature and fortune appear to call them. But it is none the less necessary for maintenance of the constitution, and the good of the empire, that all should have true principles impressed upon them from infancy, and that while following different studies for the different functions of society, all should be made to know their duties as citizens, and be formed in patriotic virtues.

Until now it has been thought that, for the children of rural districts, it was enough to establish schools for reading and writing. This was a good deal at a time when the government was afraid to enlighten the people. Let us today make these institutions doubly useful, by having the children write nothing but what is relative to the French nation. Their earliest studies should bear on the laws and products of their own country. In beginning to know it they will learn to love it.

The best and surest method would be to compose a national catechism for the use of schools, to contain the principles of religion and morals at the level of the pupils' understanding, the essential points of the constitution, the local laws that need to be known, and the elements of rural economy suited to the industry and products of the locality. A few examples of virtue and patriotism should be added, drawn so far as possible from the district and the department; this will be their course in history. The names of towns, villages, and marketplaces of the canton, district, and department will be their geography. It is evident that, with these ideas, what they learn from older people and their own experience will be enough to guide them in their private conduct, and even to equip them later for local government functions.

Such an education would be suitable also for the children of the poorer classes in the towns. One need only substitute a knowledge of the arts and trades for rural economy. It would be a great benefit to these children to teach them drawing. It is well known how much the arts and manufactures would be improved if such knowledge were more ordinary and usual. It could become so, if a date were set after which no one could be accepted as a schoolteacher unless he understood the elements of drawing and design.

This education as we have described it cannot suffice for

all citizens. While all have an equal right to public employment there are some who, more favored by nature or fortune, should find the road to further education more open. For them more schooling is necessary. It is not enough to cultivate their minds by the study of ancient and modern languages, history, general geography, rhetoric, mathematics, physics, and natural history. Such an education would contain nothing to distinguish them from other nations. There would be nothing in it to identify them as French citizens, or to qualify them to serve the country usefully in various parts of the new administration. They must also have a thorough knowledge of the history of France, and of the sources of its wealth, products, commerce, population, military forces, and relations with neighboring countries. They must not be ignorant of matters relating to their own department or any of the constitutional laws. They must be trained to discuss the great questions of law and right and learn how laws are applied. They must know how to manage arms and execute military maneuvers. With such knowledge, the country on receiving them as citizens may be assured of finding in them competent administrators, judges, and defenders.

These reflections lead us naturally to propose the creation, in the chief towns of the departments, and other places as the administrative assemblies may judge, of establishments to be called national gymnasiums, which will offer a complete course of study. For many towns such establishments would doubtless be too large. Departments in their wisdom will modify the pattern according to their resources and population, subject to the provision, however, that in no part of France will there be any town without one or two public teachers, charged with teaching matters of local importance and all parts of the constitution of which no Frenchman should be ignorant.

. . . To give our work more clarity and precision we have divided it into several sections to be developed in the following order:

1. Primary Schools
2. National Gymnasiums
    I. Organization
    II. Public Instruction
    III. Daily Schedule
3. National Education in Paris
    I. Primary Schools
    II. National Gymnasiums
    III. Lyceums
    IV. National Committee on
        Education
4. Foundations existing in Paris
    for public education

* * * *

Title One

Primary Schools

1. Three shall be placed in every parish, according to the new administrative division of the country, a primary school to which all children without distinction should be admitted.
2. They are to learn (i) to read both print and script, (ii) to write from models drawn from the national catechism, (iii) the rules of arithmetic, (iv) land measurement.
3. The national catechism will contain the rights of man, the civic oath, the principles of religion, morality, and the constitution made understandable to children; the elements of rural economy appropriate to the locality; acts of virtue or patriotism performed by the common people; and so far as possible, according to district and department, the names of towns, villages, and market-places of the canton, district, and department.

[The succeeding articles 4 through 11 largely repeat what was said in the introduction, and provide that these schools, including the qualification and appointment of teachers,

244

should be controlled by elected officials of the new local governments as set up in the constitution of 1789–91. No mention is made of church or clergy.]

TITLE TWO

National Gymnasiums

Before proposing an organization for the national gymnasiums we should submit to the wisdom of the National Assembly some reflections on the number of these establishments, and on the modifications that they should undergo according to locality. We think that there should be at least one gymnasium for each department, but that the number cannot be equal in all departments. The population and wealth of towns, and the state of their present endowments, must lead to variety. Thus, large establishments are needed at Aix, Arles, and Marseilles in the department of the Bouches du Rhone, and at Valenciennes, Douai, and Lille in the department of the Nord. They are less necessary in the departments of the Haute-Marne, the Doubs, or the Mayenne, where there are few important towns. On the other hand, endowments for education are distributed very unequally. Vendôme, La Flèche, Billom, Tournon, Brienne, and Sorrèze have magnificient colleges, while many of the more populous cities are absolutely lacking in this resource. Let us add that in many places the colleges were operated by religious orders, even mendicant orders, while in others the teachers are paid at the expense of the municipality. These difficulties prevent the adoption of a system of equality for all educational houses. It is to be hoped that each department may combine all these diverse revenues into a single fund, so as to distribute such useful institutions according to population. It is for the National Assembly to decide this question, into which we shall not enter.

We content ourselves with outlining the organization of a national gymnasium having a complete course of study.

The organization of others will naturally follow, because derived from the same principles, and requiring only the cutting out of this or that feature, according to population and locality.

CHAPTER I

Organization of National Gymnasiums

1. One or more national gymnasiums will be established in each department.
2. The inspector [i.e., principal] and the professors will be appointed by the department.
3. No one may be an inspector unless he has served at least five years in one of the gymnasiums of the realm. No one may be a professor until twenty-five years of age and after passing an examination in public teaching. The content and mode of the examination will be determined by special regulation.
4. The inspector will take care that regulations established by law are observed inviolably by teachers and students.
5. The inspector and the professors before entering upon their functions will take the civic oath at the hands of the municipality.
6. Leading citizens named by the commune will be specially charged with overseeing the national gymnasium, occasionally attending the classes, and inspecting the boarding facilities. They will refer to the municipality if any fault is to be found; the municipality will report to the directory of the department.
7. The inspector and the professors can be removed from their positions only by the department, and after being heard orally or in writing.
8. At the end of each year a report will be sent to the department on the state of education and teaching in the gymnasium.
9. The provision of meals, and in general all matters of income and expense, will be entrusted to a steward, who

will submit an accounting monthly in the presence of the inspector, the professors, and the leading citizens above mentioned. These accounts will be approved once a year by the municipality.

10. If income exceeds expense, the surplus will be used to establish positions giving free board, or free half-board, for needy students who have shown notable conduct or talents.

11. All citizens being equal before the law, there will be no distinction among students. They will all be subject to the same rule, eat at the same table and be treated together in the same way.

12. Corporal punishment is abolished. No student may be dropped from the gymnasium except by a council composed of the inspectors and the three senior masters.

13. A teacher wishing to set up a private educational establishment may do so only after passing an examination and obtaining the consent of the department. He will be required to send his pupils to the classes in the gymnasium.

14. A regulation will be issued for the examination and selection of assistant masters in the boarding facilities.

15. Lesser gymnasiums established within the department will be organized in the manner described above. Appointment, jurisdiction, and supervision will lie with the district assemblies.

CHAPTER II

Public Instruction in the Gymnasiums

Section 1

Public instruction will be divided into three courses embracing all knowledge necessary to prepare young men for the functions needed by society.

The first course will last for three years under the same professor.

First Year

Morning	Afternoon
Elements of the French Language	Sacred history, and mythology
Reading and principles of pronunciation	Elements of geography; division of parts of the world, and of Europe by states with their capitals. Names of cantons and districts of the department
Catechism of religion, morals, and the constitution	
Simple arithmetic	

Drawing twice a week
Military exercises likewise

Second Year

French Grammar	Abridged ancient history
Greek and Latin Grammar	Detailed geography of France by departments; division of European states by provinces
National catechism	
Algebra	Ideas on products and manufactures of the department

Drawing and military exercises twice a week

Third Year

General Grammar	Roman history
French, Latin, and Greek languages	Abridged history of France to the third race
Poets and historians	Review and completion of geography
National catechism	
Rules of proportion and review of arithmetic	Ideas on the arts and commerce of France
Elements of Geometry	

Drawing and military exercises twice a week

The second course; two years under the same professor.

First Year

Morning	Afternoon
Principles of logic	History of France under the third
Public speaking	race to Henry IV
French versification	Elements of natural history
Greek and Latin poets and orators	Famous men of the department
Analysis of the national catechism	The sphere; cosmographies

Second Year

Further study and analysis of French, Latin, and Greek authors	History of France from Henry IV to our own time, particularly the relations of the French nation with other peoples of Europe
French moralists	Natural history, mainly that of the department
Eloquence for deliberative and forensic purposes, written and oral	
Constitutional decrees of the National Assembly	

Third course; one year under two professors.

Morning	Afternoon
Moral philosophy and French legislation	Mathematics and experimental physics

The students will practice the application of the laws by forming, by themselves, a kind of courtroom. They will take turns in discharging the functions of judge, royal prosecutor, juryman, and attorney. Each will be obliged to substantiate his opinion publicly. They will practice the treatment of the major questions of law. After discussion there will be a vote, and no one will give his vote without developing his reasons.

For the last three years, that is the second and third courses, a textbook will be composed to include the rights of man, the duties of the citizen, the detailed laws of the constitution, and the principles of rural economy, commerce, and the useful arts.

249

Since the students in these two courses are engaged in more serious studies they will have no military exercises during the week. On every second Thursday there will be a general drill. On that day a martial spirit will prevail throughout the gymnasium. The drills will take place under the master at arms in the public square. Officers will be named every six months by majority vote.

To complete the course of public instruction there will be created, at the option of the department, chairs in the arts and sciences of local importance. Thus in maritime regions there will be teachers of pilotage, hydrography, and modern languages. In the interior of France there will be chairs in mineralogy, commerce, agriculture, etc.

Each gymnasium will have a library, a cabinet of experimental science, and one for the natural history of the department.

Section 2
Reasons for Proposed Changes

1. We have divided the studies by courses to continue under the same professor, and proscribed the old usage by which the student had a new teacher each year. It is the only way to teach with method. The teacher will see his instruction as a whole. He will follow the progress of his students, have a better knowledge of their talents and characters, and give them closer attention because he will feel more affection for them, and be better liked by them himself. He will also have more incentive, fearing that his colleagues may outdo him in the general opinion.

2. Latin is excluded from the first year. Reason has long protested against the old practice, which was vigorously opposed by the Abbé de Fleury, Locke, Rousseau, and La Chalotais.

3. We put logic and rhetoric together in the same course. These studies are indivisible and should never have been separated. It is absurd to have boys write and speak before they have learned to think.

4. The form we propose for the study of moral philosophy and law is used at Berne with great success. In England young men of mature years do not disdain to take part in such literary and political "games," to which they attribute the prodigious facility that we admire in their orators.

5. We have assigned different hours to the teaching of languages, literature, eloquence, and politics on the one hand, and history, geography, and physics on the other. We have had two reasons. First, we think that the lessons will be more useful if presented connectedly, without distraction. Second, we consider the interests of many young persons who are not able to devote themselves to all areas of instruction, but wish to be able at least to acquire the knowledge that they find most essential.

CHAPTER III

Daily Schedule of the Gymnasiums

6:00 A.M.	Rising. Prayers, followed by study.
8:00	Recreation
8:30	Classes
10:30	Recreation
11:00	Study hall. Pupils in the first course will have drawing lessons and military exercises, on alternate days from 12:00 to 1:00
1:00 P.M.	Dinner and recreation
2:30	Study hall
3:30	Classes
4:30	Recreation
5:30	Study hall
7:30	Supper and recreation
9:00	All in bed

By this distribution the students will have eight hours of sleep, ten of study, and six of recreation. There will be time off on Tuesday and Thursday afternoon each week.

On Sundays and holy days the students will attend religious exercises and receive parish instruction.

TITLE THREE

National Education in Paris

CHAPTER I

Primary Schools

1. A primary school will be established in each section of the capital in the manner described above.
2. The national catechism will include, besides the matters noted above, (i) a special section on commerce and the useful arts, (ii) simple ideas on weights and measures, money and exchange, (iii) simple and precise instructions on the duties of citizens and the municipal laws, (iv) examples of civic spirit and obedience to the law, chosen from actions of the common people.
3. Schoolteachers will be required to teach drawing.
4. A regulation will fix the conditions of eligibility. [It is not clear whether this means the admission of pupils or the qualification of teachers.]

Note: In this immense city it is especially necessary to instruct the people. Their minds must be put on guard against those wrong opinions and incendiary slanders that spread so rapidly among the multitude, are accepted so eagerly, and by suddenly bringing together blind and mistaken crowds produce such terrible explosions. It would be desirable to have the national catechism distributed free even to parents.

CHAPTER II

National gymnasiums in Paris

1. What are called the full-program colleges will be reorganized on the pattern of the departmental gymnasiums.

252

2. These gymnasiums will be distributed in the various quarters of Paris.

3. The inspectors and professors will be named by the department. What concerns their qualifications, installation, and responsibilities will be determined by regulations.

4. The teaching and order of studies will be as in the gymnasiums of other departments, except that students in the several gymnasiums of Paris will assemble before vacation to take part together in military formations.

5. Every year there will be a general distribution of prizes, for which students may compete only at the end of each of the three courses.

6. Students who have obtained the free places known formerly under the name of scholarships, of which we shall speak in a later article, will be divided equally among the gymnasiums of the capital.

CHAPTER III

Lyceums

We have proposed above to establish a few chairs for the arts and sciences in each department according to locality. It seems indispensable to bring all these branches of knowledge together in a single whole. It is by such knowledge that France has risen to the first place among the nations of Europe. Could we wish to renounce such glory at the very moment of reconquering our freedom? It befits the majesty of a free people, and should be its policy, to preserve this precious treasure and increase it if possible. Paris must naturally be its depository. Its population, its monuments, the presence of the royal family and now of the legislative body assembled within its walls, all make it impossible for other cities to begrudge it this advantage.

1. Four lyceums shall be established in Paris to facilitate the study of the arts and sciences by those who devote themselves to them by taste and profession.

253

2. In the first will be taught the ancient and modern languages, political and moral philosophy, history, and all branches of literature.

In the second, mathematics, geometry, physics, astronomy, natural history, geography, and the exact sciences in general.

In the third, botany, chemistry, anatomy and all that concerns medicine.

In the fourth, painting, sculpture, architecture, and in short all that concerns the fine arts.

3. The chairs will be filled by competition.

However considerable these establishments may be, they will place no new burden on the public treasury. Most of them exist already, and few new chairs need be founded. It is only a matter of combining chairs at the College of France, the Jardin du Roi, the Apothecaries' Garden, the Louvre, the school of surgery, the observatory, the chairs in mathematics and physics now established in the Oratory and at Mazarin and Navarre Colleges, the chair in Greek at Grassins College, in Hebrew at the Sorbonne, etc.

CHAPTER IV

National Committee on Education

1. A Committee on Education will be formed, composed of teachers chosen from all branches of public instruction.
2. Its members will be elected from a simple list by all persons teaching in primary schools, gymnasiums, and lyceums.
3. The Committee will elect, by majority vote, its chairman and two secretaries for three-month terms.
4. Half the members will be renewed each year by election.
5. The Committee will have no powers of jursidiction.
6. It will be charged, under the authority of the department, with all that concerns the competitions for chairs

and the examination of persons wishing to set up houses of education.

7. It will assemble and publish the observations and methods that seem most likely to improve public education and teaching; it will concern itself with the means of obtaining the best elementary books, and may offer prizes for works that it judges most useful.

8. It will carry on a continuing correspondence with all educational establishments throughout the realm, so as to maintain unity of teaching and unity of sentiments and principles among all citizens of the same empire.

9. The departments are invited to transmit to the Committee on Education the information they have received from teachers and from gymnasiums within their territory.

10. The Committee will prepare a general report on education and public instruction throughout the realm, and submit it to each new legislature for such legislation as may be thought necessary.

TITLE FOUR

Foundations Existing in Paris for Public Education

There exist in Paris a great many foundations or endowments for public education. Until now they have been associated with provinces and dioceses; but the former boundaries of provinces and dioceses are now dissolved. Power of nomination [to the scholarships, which are actually the subject of this discussion] has lain with abbots, canons, chapters and religious orders; but ecclesiastical bodies and titles are now destroyed.

Hence we must find a new method of nomination and distribution. We propose to put all these endowments into one mass, from which free places [in the Paris colleges] will be formed and divided among all the departments. Such free places would be both a recompense for parents, and

255

an incentive to emulation for their children. To this advantage is joined another, no less valuable. This existence in common, this rallying of young citizens from all parts of the empire, educated under the eyes of our legislators, would help to tighten the bonds of fraternity, strengthen the public spirit of all inhabitants of France, and make them into one family of Frenchmen.

The funds destined for public education in Paris reach at least 1,300,000 livres of annual income. If the following list is not quite exact, we at least think we cannot be accused of exaggeration.

COLLEGE OF:

Louis-le-Grand	520,000 livres
Mazarin	120,000
Harcourt	40,000
Lisieux	30,000
Cardinal Le Moine	18,000
Montaigu	35,000
Plessis	6,000
Grassins	6,000
Lombards	18,000
Scots'	18,000
Sorbonne	90,000
Navarre scholarships	20,000
Seminary scholarships	100,000
TOTAL	1,039,000[a]

We have not included the reveneus pertaining to the University as such, nor to the four nations that compose the Faculty of Arts, which together reach 70,000 livres. It is from these revenues, we think, that several expenses relative to national education should be drawn, such as prizes, up-

[a] [The total for the column as shown should be 1,021,000. The discrepancy is therefore 18,000. Possibly, at the time the manuscript was written, the authors had not decided whether or not to include the Lombards or Scots' colleges, neither of which was a regular full-program college of the Paris Faculty of Arts.]

keep of the library and the cabinet of natural history, office expenses and correspondence, and the cost of printing the reports to be expected from the Committee on Education. The National Assembly will dispose of the surplus.

The seminaries of Paris are carried for only 100,000 l. in our calculation, though their endowments run much higher. Saint-Sulpice alone has more than 80,000 l. a year. But we have supposed that these funds would be needed for ecclesiastical education in the diocese.

It should not be surprising that we have included the revenues of the houses of the Sorbonne and Navarre in our reckoning. These houses were really founded for poor students, represented nowadays by the bachelors [of theology] who reside there. With degrees abolished by the new organization of the clergy, and with the Assembly announcing its intention to locate theological studies in the seminaries, it is not evident what the utility of these two houses is. Their property should therefore be returned to its original purpose and be used for education according to the will of the founders. The same is true of the revenues of many seminaries which are useless today, now that the borders of the diocese are practically confined to the walls of Paris.

All these properties will be combined under a single administration. The suppression of separate administrations will produce a great economy. The mass of endowments for what are called "scholarships" will be augmented by the funds we have indicated, with the result that all parts of the realm will participate in the advantage, which will be truly national, without the former provinces which were richest in scholarships having anything to complain of. In the redistribution of free places there will be two for each district, and probably even three. In addition, those former provinces which will at first experience some loss will be compensated by the power to name, themselves, the students to receive these places, and to distribute them throughout their borders, whereas in the past they have been a kind of patrimony of certain individuals attached to the nominating authorities by birth or status.

We add only one reflection. There would be a manifest injustice if such a redistribution were not made.

The diocese of Autun, for example, has several scholarships. But the episcopal city is now separated from almost all the old diocese, and forms part of a new one with Châlons and Macon. These two towns have no scholarships. If the scholarships remained identified with dioceses, with boundaries as newly drawn, Macon and Châlons would have an advantage, but those who used to benefit would be deprived. The same kind of spoliation would take place in many other dioceses.

In line with these observations we have the honor to present the following proposals to the Assembly.

1. All existing endowments for public education in Paris will be combined under a single administration.
2. The free places for students that will be formed from them will be equal in value.
3. They will be divided equally among the departments, which will apportion them among the districts within their jurisdiction according to population. An exception will be made in favor of the Department of Paris.
4. Those obtaining such free places will be called national students.
5. With every vacancy or resignation, the Department of Paris will notify the attorney-syndic of the department having the right of appointment, and the vacancy will be filled without delay.
6. Income accruing during the vacancy will be reserved for the travel expenses of the young man to whom the place has been accorded.
7. Those named will present themselves to the directory of the Department of Paris, which will register their appointment and assign them to the gymnasium which they are to attend.

8. National students will defray none of their own expenses except clothing and incidentals.
9. Present holders of scholarships will retain them until the end of their studies.
10. Family scholarships will continue to exist as long as any member of the founding family is alive.
11. The administration of the gymnasium will report once a year to each district on the work and conduct of national students.

54. *Views on the Organization of Public Instruction in Schools Destined for the Young,* April 1800

IN 1800, with the consolidation of a new government under Bonaparte, it was generally expected that further changes would soon be made in the schools. A first step was taken with the recommendations of Lucien Bonaparte, set forth in Item 43 above. J. F. Champagne entered the discussion with a little book of one hundred small pages, of which about half are translated here.

The book, or perhaps one should say pamphlet, was hastily written for a practical purpose; the title page bears the date Germinal An VIII, yet the text mentions a date as late as 19 Germinal. It was thus put together in mid-April 1800, and it shows the signs of speedy composition. The author likes figures, but the figures do not always correspond; he is interested in foreign examples, but his references to them are hazy; and he throws in as footnotes various afterthoughts which might better have been woven into his text. Not many copies could have been printed, for the book is relatively rare. The copy in the Croker collection at the British Museum bears Champagne's autograph as a gift to P. L. Ginguené, who like Champagne was a member of the National Institute. In 1800 Ginguené also belonged to the Tribunate, which was part of the legislative apparatus newly set up under the Consulate. Known as one of the *idéologues,* Ginguené had been active in educational affairs since 1794, and had served as first head of the bureau of public instruction in the Ministry of the Interior from 1795 to 1797. Probably Champagne gave copies of his book to persons that he thought would have influence in the coming reorganization.

Like others, Champagne in 1800 was in a less exuberant mood than he had been early in the Revolution. He now hopes for stability from the Consulate after the repeated fluctuations of preceding years. In the schools, he means only to "improve or modify what is not quite right," not to offer another whole new plan. He still uses the phrase National Education, as in 1790; but it is now a fairly tame conception, connoting universal literacy and social efficiency rather than a grand transformation into a new era. As always, he wants to be practical, and is impatient of theory.

The book is a defense of the principle that the state is responsible for education. It recognizes that the primary and secondary schools produced by the Revolution have not come up to the expectations of those who launched them. It accepts, as facts of life, that the old pre-Revolutionary endowments are gone, and that neither the government nor the taxpayers are going to finance a comprehensive educational system. Champagne thus now differs from Condorcet and others who, from 1792 to 1794, had urged that education at all levels should be supplied by the government without cost to students or parents.

Given this situation, he somewhat paradoxically argues that the government must look to private and local initiative. He even offers England as his main example, surprisingly enough since France and England had been locked in an ideological struggle for seven years. He admires and exaggerates the success of English voluntary societies in spreading popular education. For France, he argues that philanthropic giving can be revived under appropriate legal safeguards. He even suggests a kind of alumni fund. But he does not suppose that voluntary initiative or philanthropy will be enough. Even if they were, he does not want the state to surrender control. He proposes that the government, with its limited resources, use subsidies to generate voluntary activity. In more modern terms, he proposes to use the public sector to stimulate the private sector; and in this he anticipates the ideas in Fourcroy's speech of 1802. (See Item 45.) At the primary level, he sketches an arrangement by which a national subsidy, small fees, local civic spirit, and individual philanthropy may combine to make it possible for every boy and girl to attend school through the age of eleven.

The legislation of 1802, following Fourcroy's speech, set up two levels of schools above the primary: a large number of "secondary" schools and a smaller number of higher schools or "lycées." Champagne, more gradualistic, proposes only to readapt the hundred Central Schools which nominally existed in 1800, drawing from them about 150 "colleges" which would be truly secondary institutions, and maintaining twenty-nine of the Central Schools as higher-level establishments like the later lycées. Another common objection to the Central Schools was that they had no boarding facilities, and so could not serve boys outside the particular towns in which they were located. Champagne, therefore, like Fourcroy in 1802, proposes to have residential schools which he calls prytaneums.

He is most emphatic, naturally enough in view of his position and background, on the need for scholarships. Liberal student aid, he thinks, is necessary to uphold the Revolutionary principle of equal rights, to prevent the moneyed class from monopolizing the best governmental and cultural positions, and to recruit the best talent wherever it may be found. He thus insists that access to education should depend upon merit, that is, upon aptitude for education and promise of usefulness, and not on the financial circumstances of the parents. He is moderate in proposing only 1,600 scholarships for the whole country. It must have gratified him when the legislation of 1802 called for 6,400 scholarships in thirty-six lycées.

Champagne's book of 1800 thus anticipated the legislation of 1802 in important respects—the critique of the Central Schools, the delineation of a secondary and a super-secondary level, the use of a state system to activate local and private initiative, and a provision for scholarships. It does not follow that Fourcroy or Bonaparte was influenced by Champagne, but only that there was a significant convergence of ideas in educational and governmental circles during the first years of the Consulate. Or, in more general terms of historical argument, the lycées were not introduced simply for political purposes, but also reflected the thinking of professional schoolmen for educational reasons.

There is one striking idea in Champagne's book which had no future. "Public instruction," he said, "in one way or another must be endowed." It must be protected from the vagaries of taxation and the competing fiscal needs of the government. He proposes endowment of the entire educational system by a gigantic land grant. What he means here is far more than restoration of the pre-Revolutionary properties of the colleges. His idea is to set aside for public instruction a large portion of the whole national domain, which consisted in what the government still retained of former ecclesiastical, royal, and émigré estates. An endowed annual income of over 20,000,000 francs for education would result. The figure contrasts sharply with the 400,000 francs with which Napoleon endowed the University in 1808. (Item 51 above.) The idea of a really large endowment was not preposterous; it was advanced by others in 1800, and even reflected ephemerally in a law of 1801; but in the end nothing came of it, the schools remained mainly dependent on students' fees and the parsimony of taxpayers, and it was half a century before the French national and local governments spent as much as 20,000,000 francs a year on all forms of public instruction. In this respect France was not very different from other countries. But is is curious to speculate on what might have been, if a large portion of the Revolutionary confiscations had been used to support education.

Champagne's final pages are a ringing expression of a more permanent consequence of the Revolution, and indeed of an idea that antedates it. Refuting those who would rely on "private" schools, he proudly dismisses the Greeks and Romans, the English and Germans, as irrelevant to the new France, in which the state and its public instruction are to provide an arena for the career open to talents. He issues the challenge of ability against birth in a final celebration of open rivalry and competitive tests, *l'émulation* and *les concours*, by which talented youth of obscure origin will prove their equality with the upper classes, and their indispensability to modern society.

Views on the Organization of Public Instruction

by CITIZEN CHAMPAGNE,

member of the National Institute
and Director of the French Prytaneum

Paris, Germinal An VIII
[April 1800]

A wise and enlightened government now watches over the destinies of France; the political and civil powers are now constitutionally organized; Education and Public Instruction will soon be the subject to attention by the government. This is a natural consequence of the regular establishment of social order, for it is needless to demonstrate that something is lacking for the constitution of a state if the instruction and education of the young are not coordinated with the political system and the national character.

This truth has been recognized by our successive legislative assemblies of the past years. All have understood that in changing the system of government it was necessary to modify the principles of education. Never among any people, perhaps, has the theory of education been treated with so much grandeur and philosophy as in our National Rostrum. The reader will recall the plan of Talleyrand-Périgord, where methods of instruction and the improvement of human knowledge were set forth with clarity and order. He may read the reports of Mirabeau, Condorcet, Rabaut Saint-Étienne, Lacépède, Fourcroy, Daunou, and many others. All either recognized the vices of the old education, or pointed to sounder methods, or sought to unify the teaching of all sciences, to the point where today we can add nothing to theory.

From this great impulse new creations have resulted for teaching the exact sciences, and these have perhaps even exceeded the hopes of their founders. The Polytechnic and other schools of public service, the schools of music, of medicine, of natural history, in short all those recently established for the advancement of the sciences have been completely successful, thanks to the ability of their teachers, the merit of their methods, and the progress of their students.

But however important these schools may be, they have more to do with higher learning than with Public Instruction in the proper sense. True public instruction means first of all the primary schools; then, the secondary or Central schools. It is in the former that the people, from childhood, learn their interests and duties. In the latter, youth finds the general and introductory knowledge that constitutes liberal education for all ages and conditions of life. It is this education, difficult to supply if neglected in younger years, that has contributed to making France the mother country of arts and letters, and to render the rest of Europe tributary to its talents and its genius.

Hence the need of instruction has been generally felt, and after the total destruction of educational establishments among us, there has been a serious effort at reconstruction. Six or seven thousand primary schools, and ninety-eight Central Schools in operation, attest to the concern of our legislators for these essential needs.

Why, then, with so much effort, is Public Instruction so languishing among us? Why do we have complaints everywhere that elementary education is neglected and almost non-existent, that the youth of France is sunk in dangerous ignorance, a deadly sickness which a wise government cannot move soon enough to cure!

The truth is that, having explored *only* the theory of education, we have supposed the task to be completed. The art of organizing education, an art almost as important as theory, and which alone assures its success, has not been adequately considered. Men who little suspect the need and importance of this art have been irritated at the small success and virtual isolation of the new schools. They have attributed it to the indifference of parents and to hatred of the Revolution, and these causes may indeed have some influence. Then they tried to correct the evil by prohibitive laws, ordering parents to send their children to the primary schools, threatening those who would not use the Central Schools with exclusion from public employment. A disorder that repelled rather than attracted students to the public schools has been called "organization."

Want of real organization is the hidden vice that arrests the development of instruction and education among us. There is a defect of organization in our plan of studies as a whole. There is a defect of organization in the lack of incentives, especially for teachers in the primary schools. There is a defect of organization in our lack of institutions to excite the emulation and progress of our youth. . . .

. . . Without pausing for the theory of education, which is not my subject, and which in any case I regard as sufficiently elaborated, I shall concern myself only with the organization of our schools.

I shall treat rapidly:

1. The organization of primary schools.
2. The organization of secondary or Central Schools.
3. The organization of national boarding establishments or Prytaneums.
4. Ways in which plans can be financed and executed, which I will touch on summarily, since only the government has the positive data and the right to make these decisions.
5. Institutions suited to our form of government, to give incentive to youth in the public schools.

I shall remember that success depends on harmony between the parts of the educational system; and that after so much devastation and ruin it is wise simply to improve or modify what is not quite right, without precipitating too much confusion.

Organization of Primary Schools

Primary instruction, said Condorcet, *is what is necessary for all citizens in various conditions of life.* If the men who first invented signs for ideas gave us the key to knowledge, those who teach the value and use of such signs render us a service almost as great. They are the ones who form our early habits, correct our earliest ideas, and put us into relation with our fellow men. *Whoever knows how to read,* said Duclos, *knows the most difficult of all the arts.* The primary schools, the true schools of National Education, should thus be the first object of consideration by a wise and enlightened government.

Until now the organization of these schools has been almost nil. The law of 3 Brumaire ordered the teaching of reading, writing, elementary arithmetic, and moral ideas. But there have been no elementary books to guide either the teachers or pupils, no incentives for the teachers or rewards for the children. The supervision that has been called organization has hardly consisted in more than municipal visits, official minutes, and denunciations. It is as if the rod had been taken from teachers to be used against them. So teachers have been abandoning an arduous occupation which they found to be a source of irritation and disgust. In these disorders what has become of the three million children who should have been receiving primary education every year?

Now the number of children, prodigious as it is, is not exaggerated. The population of France is estimated at thirty millions.[a] Condorcet estimated that a tenth of the population is composed of children of primary school age. Other calculations, based on life expectancies, and assuming a population of 30,000,000 give the following approximations:

571,908 seven-year-olds of both sexes
560,700 eight-year-olds
553,713 nine-year-olds
548,192 ten-year-olds
544,419 eleven-year-olds

Or a total of 2,778,732 children of both sexes who should be taught in the primary schools.

I consider it a constant that one-sixth of families are suf-

[a] From the table of departments inserted in the *Bulletin des Lois* for Germinal of last year, the population of France was 31,933,043, without counting the four departments on the left bank of the Rhine not fully annexed. [I.e., Champagne's figure does include Belgium and Luxembourg, fully incorporated with France from 1795 to 1814.]

ficiently educated and prosperous either to give their children primary education themselves, or to pay private teachers. I assume also, that the average number of children will be 60 per school. We must therefore have 46,312 teachers, men and women, to carry on primary education throughout the Republic.

If the government undertakes so gigantic an enterprise itself:

1. It will be condemned to make a thousand unfortunate mistakes before finding and organizing such a huge number of teachers who are sufficiently instructed themselves.

2. The state of finances will not permit for a long time, and will perhaps never permit, the procurement of the immense sums necessary to pay teachers' salaries and the expenses of so many pupils.

3. It will be incapable of direct supervision of so many teachers, and of these millions of pupils, the quality of whose education must have a noticeable influence on the public prosperity or adversity.

4. If the government today should want to risk the execution of this vast program, given the state of opinion, it would get no support from the public, it would carry the whole enormous burden alone, and it would fail—as has happened to the transient governments that preceded it.

It should therefore content itself with establishing a general system with interconnected parts, and give partial aid by any means that its enlightenment, its resources, or public confidence will suggest.

After much reflection, I judge that nothing will be more favorable to the sound organization of elementary schools than the establishment of societies such as they have in England, where they are called voluntary associations. Let us have no fear of borrowing from our jealous but thoughtful neighbors. Thus the Romans prudently adopted the arms of their enemies when they found them advantageous, and soon defeated their opponents.

At the time of the English Revolution the instruction and education of youth were at first debated in Parliament. There was much discourse on this important matter, but no action. Then toward the end of the last century philanthropy, that public spirit that has often been observed in England, gave birth in several counties to private societies for the education of the poor. The government soon recognized their utility; it encouraged them, and let them alone to do their work.

[Twelve pages are here omitted, in which the author describes the activities of these English societies, remarks on their provision of elementary textbooks, notes the importance of these primary schools for the economic development of England, and cites also the examples of Sweden and Austria.]

. . . The French government should aid in the establishment of elementary schools by wisely distributed subsidies. The largest cantons, with small population, are usually the poorest. They present all kinds of difficulties for the establishment of schools, which are the only means of removing the ignorance and prejudices that go with poverty. I estimate that a sum of 5,000,000 or 6,000,000 francs, wisely distributed by the government, in a proportion of 12,000 to 15,000 for each of the 398 arrondissements, would be enough for basic needs. For France as a whole, I estimate the total sum necessary for elementary education at about 20,000,000. I assume that of the 2,778,732 children to attend these schools (a figure lower than Condorcet's), only one million will pay the modest sum of one franc a month toward the teachers' salaries. This will produce 12,000,000 francs. Contributions by the communes, in buildings and other facilities, can be evaluated at 1,500,000. Another 1,500,000 might be furnished by voluntary gifts. The 5,000,000 or 6,000,000 provided by the government would thus complete the necessary funds. We should not think that this sum, which seems so large, is entirely a net cost to the State. If we consider how much elementary education will promote individual industry, commerce, and the arts, we will be convinced that, to a large extent, the more that is paid for education the less need be spent, as today, on the suppression of vagabondage and begging.

A few ideas may be offered on how the needed sum can be raised. We used to have a tax on the personal property of unmarried persons, but this tax was considered only as a fiscal expedient. Let us give it a moral dimension, and use the proceeds exclusively for education; the tax might be levied at a decreasing rate, from the unmarried man to the father of three children, who would be exempt; a small tax might also be levied on collateral inheritances received by the unmarried. It would be only fair that he who gives no children to the State, and has neither the burdens nor the anxieties of a family, should make compensation by a small indemnity. The justice of such a tax would protect it against complaints.

And why should not the government encourage donations in favor of Public Instruction, through regularizing them by law so that they may be neither ridiculous nor excessive? Let us hope that we have seen the last of those ruinous confiscations which have deprived future generations of their educational heritage. Let us still count on the vast resources which philanthropy, gratitude, and even vanity have offered in all past times.

It is necessary to provide incentives to elementary-school teachers. Such a measure will be less a reward for useful labors than an act of public policy, to attach teachers to the principles of the government. We have at least 50,000 clerks in the different branches of the administration in France. A quarter of these positions, excepting the principal ones, might be reserved for primary-school teachers who had taught for ten years. They would have the qualities necessary for these functions, a good handwriting and a good knowledge of spelling. Only a few favorites would lose by such an arrangement. But the prospect of an easier and more lucrative employment would multiply the number of teachers, give them the desire to do well, and attach them to the government, which would obtain a powerful influence on elementary education by such effortless generosity.

Rewards should also be offered to arouse a competitive spirit among pupils. If, as Citizen Chaptal has reasonably urged, we were to establish apprenticeships in the trades, some of these places might be open to competition in the primary schools. Other pupils, showing a germ of real talent, might be appointed to free places for board and room in secondary schools. Rewards of this kind would double the activity of the pupils and the zeal of parents aspiring to such precious advantages for their children. . . .

Secondary and Central Schools

Our present law makes instruction in the Central Schools follow immediately upon that in the primary schools. But the two levels of instruction are not co-ordinated, so that a great interval remains between them. This gap was to be filled by secondary schools in the plans of Talleyrand, Condorcet, and many wise lawmakers. Their wisdom has been proved by the sad experience of the last five years, during which thousands of young Frenchmen have remained lost in ignorance, because deprived of the proper kind of primary instruction.

In fact, since our primary schools are now limited to teaching the elements of reading, writing, and arithmetic, all that a child knows, on leaving them, is to read and write rather badly, and hardly more than the four basic arithmetical rules. He has no idea of grammar, hardly any of spelling, and above all none of that auxiliary knowledge that prepares for the development of his faculties.

A father wishing his son to have a liberal education looks

about him and, seeing nothing but the Central School, sends the boy there. The professor of ancient languages is the first to receive him. I do not know which is the more embarrassed, teacher or pupil. The former is supposed to teach ancient languages in one year, for he is the only teacher of the subject. The latter must learn them in about the same time, since the beginner's course is repeated the following year. Does the teacher wish to discharge his assigned function? He explains Latin and Greek to his pupil, but the pupil does not even know French, and so is ignorant of the preliminary medium of understanding. There is therefore no means of communication between teacher and taught. So what does a good teacher do? He gives up the teaching that is prescribed for him, and offers the teaching that is necessary. He takes the pupil back to the first elements, and gives him what in former times would have been called a weak Seventh. That is the scope of the instruction.

This disorder arises from the fact that the law, in establishing the Central Schools, conceived of them as relatively advanced institutions. But it is in the nature of things that advanced instruction can only follow upon elementary; and this elementary instruction does not exist. The same nature of things has condemned the professors in the Central Schools to either not being understood if they give the courses designed for them, or reducing their courses to the level of their students if they wish to be useful.

Both reason and general utility show the need of a gradation in three levels. We had such a gradation before the Revolution, under the names of petty schools, colleges, and universities. Instruction in the petty schools, indispensable for all, in all conditions of life, was enough for those citizens obliged to work with their hands for a living. Instruction in the colleges was necessary for a great number of children without fortune, to enable them one day to exercise one of the liberal professions, which are as difficult as they are indispensable for the social order. Finally, university instruction was for the small number who desired to make a deeper study of the arts and letters and sciences.[b]

The establishment of secondary schools or colleges [between primary and Central schools] is demanded by reason and experience and the opinion of parents, and should be the object of solicitude by the government, which should organize them immediately. Let us note that the general interest is here in accord with public opinion. A State does not organize education at great cost, except to obtain for itself a number of adequately educated men for a host of important and difficult services which it requires. Now almost all such men are unable, by their own fortune, to pay the cost of their education. To those who can pay the State owes very little; it would be a misplaced generosity for the State to spare them an expenditure which they can make from their own surplus, without disturbing their own comfort. If this is true, it follows that the government should tend to the utmost to disseminate a liberal secondary education, and to bring it as close as possible to the huge number of children whose education is necessary to the government, but who have not the resources to go away for it far from their own homes.

Now *secondary schools* or *colleges* will fill this important purpose. Only in them can enough instruction be given to many who are needed by the government for its public employments. In this immense empire we must have at least 60,000 officers and under-officers in the army and navy; at least 50,000 agents and employees in all parts of the financial administration; several thousand judges, as many professors, and 18,000 or 20,000 primary-school teachers, and we know that these latter, in choosing such a difficult occupation, are forced to it by a degree of poverty which

[b] Though never exactly fulfilled, this was the original purpose of the universities. I regard the Central Schools as designed to replace them today. The wisdom and liberal views of the government assure us that our youth will soon receive an improved education in the Central Schools.

hardly allows them to seek their own education except in public secondary schools. Nor need I mention the throngs of other equally useful men, those in business affairs, merchants, and artists for whom it is important to have the elements of a liberal education, from the point of view of the public prosperity. And it is in large families of modest income that many of these individuals originate. Men of talent and small furtune are the ones who in all governments, and especially in France, carry on the daily work of political administration. The son of a rich man will never become, for a small salary, a lesser government servant, a clerk, or primary-school teacher. He will raise his sights to higher positions, and possibly indeed to more difficult ones, even though they pay nothing.

Formerly we counted in France, when it was smaller than it is today, 320 colleges, great and small. If we look at the present state of society, we see that nineteen-twentieths of the men now filling, not only secondary employments, but even the most eminent functions, which they honor by their intelligence and their talents, owe their first education to some obscure but useful little college in their own part of the country.

In place of these 320 colleges we have established a hundred Central Schools, according to the political division of the country into departments. If we consider them from the point of view of education, their number is insufficient. If we think of them as replacing secondary schools and colleges, their program of study is too advanced. If we note that these schools, including a librarian in each case, are each composed of ten teachers, we see them as an almost useless scientific luxury for two-thirds of the towns in which they are established. I shall try to demonstrate this statement.

It is estimated from life expectancies that a town of 8,000 inhabitants has only 880 persons of both sexes from twelve to eighteen years old, and hence only 440 boys. It is known that at most, only a sixth of the boys are intended by their parents to have a liberal education. Hence a town of 8,000 provides only 73 pupils for such studies. A town of 10,000 has only 98, a town of 15,000 has 131, a town of 20,000 has 161. Finally, a town of 25,000 provides only 220 students for regular courses.[c]

Such in fact is about the number of students who, on the average, have taken courses in the Central Schools. In many of these schools the number is well below the figure I have given, so much so that the ratio of students to teachers is less than six to one. The point is that education, like commerce, does not lend itself to political subdivisions, but only to those arising from nature and locality. For example, when a father decides to send his son away from home to give him a good education, he will not send him to the central town of his department unless it offers the advantages he desires. He will place him in a town which is a commercial center or has some connection with his own affairs, and especially one which offers better teachers and more facilities for education. A difference of ten or twenty leagues is of no importance in this family arrangement. Now, however France may be divided politically, Paris will always be the educational center for the children of parents in easy circumstances, living within a radius of thirty or forty leagues. Rennes and Nantes, rather than Vannes or Quimper, will attract those of what used to be Brittany. Those of the former Franche-Comté will go to Besançon rather than Dole or Lon-le-Saunier. Bordeaux, Montpelier, Toulouse, Strasbourg, Lyon, Dijon, Rouen, Caen, Angers, Lille, Brussels, and Nancy will necessarily draw crowds

[c] [Champagne's figures are deceptive at this point, since each Central School was intended, by the law of 3 Brumaire, to draw students from its whole department, and not merely from the town in which it was located. Using his figure of a sixth of the age group, he might have given a much larger number of the boys available for each Central School. Use of the larger number would have strengthened the point made in the following paragraph, on the failure of the Central Schools to attract the enrollments to be expected.]

of students, because a more thorough education will always be given there, and most especially because fathers have in mind, in sending their sons to school, the opportunities for advancement and improved fortune that come after the course of studies, and which are to be found exclusively in the larger cities.

From another point of view, a faculty of ten in the Central School is surely a useless apparatus to set up at Gap, Charleville, Saint-Girons, Aubusson, Fontenay-le-Peuple, Bruges, Tarbes, Epinal, Colmar, Luxembourg, Saint-Sever, Roanne, Mende, Porentruy, and many other places equally unimportant. Unless special circumstances attract students, these schools will be reduced to a handful and almost deserted. Ask the family heads: almost all will prefer to have the present over-extended curriculum replaced by a small college with a simple program more suited to their sons' needs and their own expectations. Most of them in fact want only a limited instruction to develop their sons' minds for a few years, because they do not want to make scholars out of them, but want to educate them enough to place them without delay in commercial or other similar occupations.

It seems to me proved, therefore, that (1) the number of Central Schools is now too great, and (2) the establishment of secondary schools or colleges is indispensable. It follows that we should reduce the number of the former, and organize secondary schools or colleges as a first step in elementary liberal education.

The location of the remaining Central Schools, in this case, is clearly indicated by our new social compact. It will be, as I have said, in the larger towns, which offer real resources for the education and advancement of youth. These advantages are found in the 29 cities in which the judicial system has placed our appellate courts.

That is where I put the Central Schools, reduced in number to 29, with an exception for Paris because of its huge population.

There remain 71 Central Schools, each with ten teachers, which as I have shown are only an educational luxury, because of the small populations of the towns in which they exist.

I replace them with 140 or 150 small colleges, each with five professors. I locate them in towns of the second rank, in such a way that population and the real needs of education are the only things considered, regardless of political subdivisions.

1. It is unnecessary to demonstrate that the expense of these small colleges would be about the same as for 71 Central Schools, each of which I divide in two.

2. The buildings of these colleges are fortunately preserved, by the foresight of the law of 25 Fructidor An V, which forbade their further alienation.[d]

3. The necessary teachers also already exist. If professors in most of the Central Schools have tried to be really useful, their teaching must be no different from what should be set up in the colleges. Why would they hesitate to continue the same functions in the new establishments? They might have the inconvenience of moving, but they will be sufficiently devoted to their country to agree that the new order is as necessary as it is universally demanded.

[Thirty-two pages are here omitted, giving details of the teaching program in the proposed colleges, a critique of the existing Central Schools and proposed means of their improvement. Combining his long experience at Louis-le-Grand with his ideas of reform, as developed since his plan of 1790, Champagne sets forth a seven-year program for boys of ages eleven to eighteen. The first year will be devoted mainly to French; the second and third to French, Latin, Greek, and geography; the fourth and fifth to literature and geography; the sixth and seventh to mathematics

---

[d] [Champagne meant to write 25 Messidor (July 13, 1797), referring to the law forbidding the further sale of buildings of the pre-Revolutionary colleges. See Item 36 above.]

for all, with some students also studying physics and chemistry, and others natural history and modern languages.]

National Boarding Schools, or Prytaneums

If the government wishes to have a direct influence on the instruction and education of youth, it should immediately set up a number of free national boarding schools, to rear children of fathers who have deserved well of the country, and those of recognized abilities, but of poor parents, whose services and talents it will one day employ to its advantage.

One reflection arising from the nature of our government is enough to demonstrate the need for such institutions.

Our social pact has the equality of rights for its basis, without other distinction than virtue and merit. If a thorough education is given only to the rich boy who can buy it, would this not be a privilege in favor of wealth? Of course we should call to public position only those citizens who are most distinguished in knowledge and enlightenment; but if fortune alone gives the means to acquire these precious advantages, the man of moderate circumstances will be forced to renounce a too-costly education, and reduced to seeing these honorable employments as the exclusive preserve of the opulent. A line of demarcation would be drawn between citizens; then would come distinction of ranks; and the base of our social pact would be overturned.

It is by opening national boarding schools for talented sons of poor citizens that the balance can be restored. If some can have high aspirations because their own fortune provides resources for a liberal education, careers will be equally open to others by the beneficent action of government. In the distribution of honors, which will be the rewards of education and merit, the well-to-do will always have the advantage, because all without exception can receive a careful education, whereas the government will never be able to give a careful education to more than a small number of the children of less affluent citizens.

In the second place, if it is true, as was said by an ancient,[e] and by Rousseau after him, that a wise government should favor an education that has its own character, and so to speak a national physiognomy, it is mainly by means of national boarding schools that this result is to be obtained.

It is in these institutions that the government will awaken love of country in children who are naturally attached to it by a feeling of indebtedness; organize institutions by which youth is to be formed; experiment with methods of education and adopt those that are proved to be advantageous. Soon, when the superiority of the education given in these schools is evident from its unquestionable successes, the force of example will begin to work on other educational establishments. Families will favor the institutions created by the government, because, whatever their prejudices or opinions, they will act prudently in plans for their children. Thus without violence, and without prohibitive regulations, by means of national boarding schools the government will achieve the real aim that it should have in education, which is to direct and shape it while leaving it entirely free.

The utility of such national boarding schools has been recognized by many European states in this century. Austria has its national military cadets, Russia its gentlemen cadets, England its naval cadets. Our own old government gave the example. It created military schools where young men received an excellent education, whose only fault was to be reserved exclusively for one class of citizens. The former College of Louis-le-Grand, today the French Prytaneum, where almost 600 young men were educated gratis, was an institution of the same kind. Many old colleges also had free places. In them was formed that numerous, active, educated, and competitive younger generation which, pressed

[e] Aristotle.

278

by the prod of necessity, has overcome all obstacles. The learned societies, the law courts, the administration, the public schools, the army, the legislative bodies have been filled by these youngsters, now grown men, who have rendered enormous services to their country—and, to dispense with all other praise, let it be remembered that it was in the military schools that was formed the youth of *Bonaparte.*[f]

There is another reason why, in the present state of France, it is wise to establish such boarding schools. Belgium, the departments of the left bank of the Rhine, those of the Mont-Terrible, the Mont-Blanc, and the Alpes Maritimes [adjoining Switzerland and Italy], even of Corsica, and above all of the West [Brittany] need more than ever to merge into the general body of the Nation, from which they are separated by customs or opinions or language. Education is the most powerful means of joining these almost isolated parts. By using it the government will introduce the French spirit and manners in its new acquisitions, where otherwise the peoples will remain what they are, that is foreign, and nothing but their territory will belong to the Republic. A certain number of children from these regions, after giving evidence of promising aptitudes, should be carefully brought up by the government. Assembled in national boarding schools, where they will find rivals as well as schoolmates, with what a spirit of emulation will they not launch into careers in the letters and sciences? With the annual renewal of students, education will be carried to all parts of France. Soon the government will find enlightened men everywhere, who have a feeling of gratitude, to fulfill the many important functions, especially the secondary ones, which the rich man disdains, but which are

[f] [This flourish is a reminder that Bonaparte, First Consul for the preceding six months, was a product of the military school at Brienne, one of eleven founded by the French government in 1776, which, as Champagne remarks, had been designed for boys of noble family. The Bonapartes were considered noble in Corsica.]

solicited and performed with intelligence by those with talent but without fortune.

This policy was not overlooked by the First Consul when he was in command of the Army of Italy. Hardly had he conquered the three departments of the Ionian Sea when he ordered that thirty of their young men should be sent to Paris, to receive our education and learn our ways.

Louis XIV had the same idea, after his conquest of Alsace, Flanders, Franche-Comté, and Roussillon, when he founded Mazarin College, which gave free education to boys born in those countries.

By the same principle, in 1775, the empress Maria Theresa forbade the Belgians to study elsewhere than in her own states, under penalty of disqualification from public office. She feared the influence of French education, since at that time many Belgians went to school in Paris.

Finally, strict justice requires that the government restore the free places in colleges created in former times by the liberality of our fathers. The property that supported them has been partly sold off. The belated law of 25 Messidor An V has returned what little is left. A series of solemn laws and acts has promised to replace what has been so imprudently alienated.

The French Prytaneum has gathered to itself what remains of the endowments that used to exist in Paris. Those in Belgium have fortunately been preserved. If a survey is made in France, as the Minister of the Interior in his zeal for education has invited the prefects to do, a considerable fraction of these funds may yet be recovered.

A wise decree of the Consuls[g] has ordered that free places in the Prytaneum should be given exclusively to the chil-

---

[g] Dated 1 Germinal An VIII. [See Item 43 above. It cannot be known whether Champagne really agreed fully with this decree. Where Lucien and Napoleon Bonaparte meant to use scholarships for the sons of men who had served the government, Champagne always saw them as opportunities for talented but poor boys, of whatever origin, who will later become useful to society.]

dren of defenders of the country dead on the field of honor, or of civil servants dying in the exercise of their duties. Some recompense to the children of such deserving citizens is indeed due, and none is more precious than education. How often have we seen mothers who have lost their husbands, and are in hard financial circumstances, shed tears of joy on presenting a son at the Prytaneum, and showing the certificate by which a benevolent government assumes the charge of his education! They look forward hopefully to a time when such sons, when well educated, can take the father's place, and be an honor and a support to their old age; the very thought helps to relieve the grief and regret they feel.

The same decree, which I have cited, divides the Prytaneum into parts, to make room for the children of prosperous citizens who, as paying students, will share in the thorough education which the government plans to give its own students, or rather its own children whom it has adopted in the country's name.

Another decree of the Consuls, dated 19 Germinal, is organizing a Prytaneum at Brussels for the children of the annexed departments. Fairness demands that the government do the same for the whole of France. Formerly Paris alone had 950 such free places, with a revenue of 844,000 francs. At Toulouse there were over 200 free places in the colleges, and there were others at Douai, Rouen, Caen, Angers, La Flèche, Bordeaux, Auch, Tarbes, Montpelier, Reims, Lyon, Bourges, etc., and in all the old universities. The total number of free places was almost 3,000 in France, without counting at least 2,000 reserved for studies in Philosophy and Theology. It must be noted that very few of these foundations belonged to the government, but that they resulted from the philanthropy of a host of private persons, who had established them in part for their own families and in part for children of their own province or part of the country. Hence almost all regions of France participated in these precious establishments.

They still have a right to do so. The government, strictly as an act of justice, should not hesitate to replace, at least partly, the alienated property of these endowments, which represent a philanthropy quite as useful as in the case of the hospitals. But in recreating them it should redirect them in a way more advantageous to the public than they formerly were.

To attain this end, I would establish eight Prytaneums in which, given the present difficult circumstances, it will be enough to set up half as many free places as the number promised. Each Prytaneum should comprise the territory of four appellate courts, and each department would have the right to send twelve students. The Paris Prytaneum, with its new subdivisions, would be destined, by the wise decree of the Consuls, to receive four hundred sons of fathers dead on the field of battle, or of civil servants dying in office. It would also admit children from departments within the jurisdiction of the appellate court of the Department of the Seine. Thus the allocation of free places would extend to the territories of all twenty-nine appellate courts into which France is divided.

One of these Prytaneums, by decree of the Consuls, should be established at Brussels.

A second, at Rouen or Caen.

A third, at Rennes.

A fourth, at Bordeaux.

A fifth, at Montpelier or Toulouse.

A sixth, at Lyon.

A seventh, at Nancy.

Finally, the eighth already exists at the center, that is at Paris and the places designated by decree of 1 Germinal.

There would thus be 1,600 national students in these various Prytaneums. This would be only half the number of those existing before the Revolution, and proportionately even less, considering the recent augmentation of the territory of the Republic.

These national students would be appointed by the prefects. Qualification for admission would be: 1. That they are children of parents of modest circumstances. 2. That they are from ten to fourteen years of age. 3. That they are selected from among the pupils of the secondary and Central schools, who have given proof of aptitude and talent, since the state should have some assurance that it will not lose the product of its expenditure.

These Prytaneums would thus have each 150 national students,[h] and would also be open to children of more prosperous citizens, who would pay full fees.

Instruction would be much the same as in the Central Schools. Some physical education would be added. Music would also be taught, not only that which pleases the ear, but of the kind that develops the vocal organs for speaking. I would like to add instruction in the art of reading well, which is so necessary and so rare among us. Above all, the boys' bodies should be developed by gymnastics. In short, all these establishments should follow uniform principles, tending to the greatest possible improvement of the intellectual, moral and physical faculties of youth.

I shall say nothing on the internal regulation of these schools. The one being prepared by the Minister of the Interior for the French Prytaneum will be adopted, and become the model for all.

I will give only one example to show the utility of such establishments. In the past six years during which the French Prytaneum has been gradually reorganized, over 150 graduates have come out of it, of whom three-fifths are now advantageously placed in the army, in the Central schools, in the schools of applied sciences, and in other parts of the public service.

[h] [This reconciles with the figure of 1,600, mentioned above, because Champagne is counting 150 scholarship students for each Prytaneum, including Paris ($8 \times 150 = 1,200$) and adding for Paris the 400 orphans of deceased military personnel and civil servants.]

THE COLLEGE OF LOUIS-LE-GRAND

On the Replacement of Former Revenues

Under the old government [before the Revolution] education cost little to the State, because almost all establishments of this kind, and especially their boarding facilities, were supported by property of their own which assured the continuing of their existence. Similar foundations or endowments existed in most states of Europe. If it were possible to question the wisdom of such philanthropy, I would cite in its favor the highly respected authority of Washington, who, after winning liberty for his country and governing it with such prudence, has just bequeathed to it a large part of his property to endow Public Instruction.[i]

The sale of educational properties with a promise of replacement which no government has yet been able to effect, and which has left our studies so enfeebled, is a new proof of the need of making good on the promise. By dissipating in an instant the gifts accumulated by the benevolence of four centuries, a precious part of future generations has been disinherited from its education. The damage has been done; we must try everything possible to repair it. To do so:

1. It would be useful to authorize gifts made for public instruction, by a law which would regularize them. Philanthropy and above all the gratitude felt for the benefit of education would gradually produce great resources. Although public spirit and benevolent giving seemed extinct

---

[i] [Champagne alludes to the fact that Washington, when he died in 1799, left 20 shares in the Bank of Alexandria, Va., to the Academy of Alexandria to assist in the education of "poor and indigent children"; 50 shares in the Potomack Company, "towards the endowment of a university to be established within the limits of the District of Columbia"; and 100 shares in the James River Company to Liberty-Hall Academy in Virginia. Washington's will was well publicized in France. The National University, then much discussed in the United States, was never in fact established.]

among us in the last few years of the monarchy, never-theless many citizens, who owed their own fortune and advancement to their education, continued until 1789 to create endowments to procure the same advantages for others.[j]

2. I should wish that all who have completed their course of study in a public school, and especially those who had been students in the national boarding schools, should be invited, if their circumstances permitted, to give to the school in which they received their education, in the year following their marriage or their establishment in a profes-sion, a sum of no less than 50 francs for the secondary schools, or of 100 francs for Central Schools and national boarding schools. The admissions register of the school would be rigorously preserved, and the gift would be later entered beside the student's name, to perpetuate its memory. There is no doubt that most would acquit themselves liber-ally in recognition of their indebtedness. These funds would be assembled and deposited once a year in the Bank of France, and converted into bank shares. When the sum reached two or three thousand francs the government would give the school real property from the national domain in return for the shares. In this way the educational system would gradually be endowed with real property, which at the same time would continue to belong to the government.

3. Today, if the government, as the laws have solemnly promised, wishes to restore the alienated wealth of our na-tional boarding schools, old foundations which are to be

[j] In 1768 Collot, who had been a scholarship student and became a canon of Notre-Dame, founded a great many free places in Plessis College. In 1784 Bougault, who had been a scholarship student, and amassed a large fortune in the building of the Pantheon, likewise founded a number of free places. I know a citizen, who unfortunately died last Nivôse, who wanted to give a very fine property to establish six free places, if only the laws would guarantee the security of such a foundation. I could cite other cases from very recent times.

highly respected because they were the heritage of youth, it can do so with practically no sacrifice.

The government now possesses 8,000,000 *arpents* of forests.[k] Such property is too immense to be well managed; it will be dissipated in the government's hands. In any case it is a bad thing when wood, a primary consumer's need, belongs almost exclusively to the government. The government is obliged to sell it in large lots, and the poor citizen must buy it from third parties. The profits do not go to the Republic, which does not sell at a high price, but by contract; and in many places the sale of wood, for inhabitants obliged to buy in small lots, constitutes a tax almost as onerous as the old salt tax used to be.

The 8,000,000 *arpents* of wood bring in 28,000,000 francs a year, of which four are absorbed by the costs of administration. There remain 24,000,000, from which it follows that each of the 8,000,000 *arpents* yields only three francs a year to the State.

Add further, that this forest land now pays no tax, or only a fictitious tax, and that the state does not receive, at the time of cutting, the ten centimes per franc authorized by the law. It is doubtful, therefore, that the state would lose much by ceasing to be the proprieter of this land, if we calculate what it would produce in taxes and in cutting fees. The alienation of this part of the national domain would be hardly noticeable to the state, and would be of great advantage to the educational system, which, without

[k] [The *arpent*, which was then in process of replacement by the metric *hectare*, was equal to about an acre. The reason why the government owned so much forest is that, from all the properties confiscated from the church, the émigrés, and the crown during the Revolution (the "national domain" or *biens nationaux*), it was the agricultural and urban properties that were most readily sold to new buyers, so that woodlands remained in the hands of the state. Champagne's proposal of course never went into effect, and it seems that much of this woodland was later recovered by the émigré, and mainly noble, families.]

bearing the cost of exploitation, would sell in small lots and so obtain a good income.[1]

4. If the state feels that it cannot make this sacrifice, there is another way in which, without cost to itself, it might create an endowment. Land in the national domain is selling today at hardly more than five or six times its annual revenue, and even less in the Western departments. We have proposed the establishment of eight Prytaneums. Let the government appoint five experienced and zealous administrators for each of them, as it has already done for the Prytaneum of Paris. Let it sell to each of these administrations, at current prices, a quantity of the national domain sufficient to endow that particular Prytaneum. Let each administration be held to pay the price in six years. There is no doubt, given enough security, that the zeal of the administrators would soon liquidate the debt, using voluntary contributions made by the local departments, or loans at low interest or at no interest provided by local philanthropy. Youth would soon find the endowed Prytaneums open.

I have limited myself to suggesting resources. The government, well knowing the resources of this mighty Republic, will easily find others which may be more sure and decisive. But public instruction in one way or another must be endowed, to shelter it from financial embarrassments in which the state may find itself, and to relieve the state of a burden that is as heavy as it is indispensable. Of course, the old foundations cannot be restored today in their integrity. They can be supplemented by the educational system itself, by wise management and good organization. Let the

[1] These woodlands would still be subject to forest law for their management and exploitation. Here is the advantage, not counting receipt of taxes and cutting fees. The government sells wholesale, on terms payable in eighteen months. Well-managed hospitals and other public institutions sell wood today in very small lots. Big purchasers are thus kept out, and citizens buy small amounts directly for their own consumption. Wood is paid for in cash, and ordinarily sold for a price about a third above what the Republic gets.

state make a beginning; let it protect and encourage; it will then see small endowments,[m] under effective administrators, grow into very considerable sums.

Some Institutions to be Created for the Teaching of Youth in the Public Schools

If the government wishes the public schools to be frequented, fathers to send their sons there, a lively competition to prevail in them, youth to be devoted ardently to literature and the arts and sciences by which France has flourished and should still flourish; if it wishes to have a gentle but powerful influence on the rising generation and deserve its gratitude and attachment, it should create institutions in conformity with our age. For our youth these institutions should consist of various rewards and enjoyments.

1. If we wish to arouse rivalry, the mother of success in secondary and Central Schools, let the twelve free places set up in the Prytaneums for each department be granted in a competition; if the son of a rich man wins out over the other contestants he should receive an award that shows his success, but he should generously cede the place to a worthy competitor who needs it.

2. Military glory is the greatest of all. A certain number of young men distinguished for good conduct and talent in their studies should obtain, by competition, appointments as second lieutenants in the army. . . .

3. The government sends many ambassadors and com-

[m] The early endowments for public instruction were at first of little importance. They grew continually by order and economy. The former College of Louis-le-Grand, today the French Prytaneum, was established in 1762 and composed of a great many small foundations whose success had been nil, because they were so isolated. In 1762 there were only 250,000 francs of income, and fewer than 300 students. By 1792 a sound administration and wise investments had raised the income to 520,000 francs and the number of students almost to 600. In ten more years there would have been much more growth, so much so that a new school would have been formed as a sort of colony, as numerous and as flourishing as the first.

mercial commissioners to foreign peoples. I should like to see young men designated every year, by a competition, to the Ministry of Foreign Affairs, which would assign them to representatives of the Republic. They would be given the task, according to their specialized knowledge and the modern language they have learned, of translating foreign books for the enrichment of French literature, or natural sciences, or commerce, or agriculture, or political economy.

As means of advancement, there are the competitions already established for the Polytechnic School, the schools of mining, roads and bridges, artillery and engineering; such encouragements are both worthy of the government and suited to inflame the spirit of emulation among our youth.

There are arrangements of another kind, in which the rewards must correspond not only to the talents but even more to the inclinations of individuals.

4. The public schools will often be in need of professors. Those whose taste is for this kind of work, and who are judged worthy after examinations, will be designated to the committees charged with making such appointments.

5. We have in France several large administrations, such as Finance, Customs, Forests, and the Post Office, in which employments are granted to friends and relatives by a kind of patronage, and a proper education is not always required of the candidates. Nevertheless, in time, men often rise in them step by step, and acquire an experience with details that often brings them to high positions in the state. I would like to see those administrations required to include, among the new appointees, a certain number of young men desig- nated by a competition. These organizations would gradu- ally be filled with employees of recognized intelligence, who would render important services on reaching the higher levels.

6. Others may wish to study medicine, chemistry, natural history, liberal arts, or mathematics. I would like to see a competition opened for them also, and a certain number of those in financial need obtain grants of five or six hundred

francs a year, to enable them to pursue such important studies for three years.

Aid accorded to outstanding young men without fortune is only an act of wisdom and foresight. Paternal care and government subsidy may have provided for their needs until completion of ordinary studies. But then, at what may be the most difficult moment in life, if the young man is not supported by a benevolent hand he may be exposed to hardship and poverty. He is troubled by the fact that, despite his inexperience, he must find a means to support himself without delay. So he snatches at the first chance that offers itself, however foreign to his own inclinations or to the knowledge that he has acquired. Aid to such men was provided in the old military schools and the former College of Louis-le-Grand. It should be rigorously preserved. . . .
[Two pages are omitted on positions in law and teaching.]

No doubt my ideas will not find favor with those who say that the government should leave education to private initiative, and not burden itself with the expense or the busy and troublesome supervision that it entails. Do such people then approve of what was done in 1793, when public instruction was so brutally deprived of its own resources? They forget that our social pact, in establishing the equality of rights, requires us to offer the means of education to citizens without fortune, because they have the same right as the wealthy to public positions.

The government also knows that in this vast Republic it needs a great host of employees at secondary levels, which it can find only among the class of people in modest circumstances.

Those who object cite the examples of the Greeks and Romans. But among the ancients it was a handful of people who, under the name of a Republic, kept the rest in oppression and slavery. The main part of their education (and the government gave it to them) was for war, to provide their security and maintain their usurpation.

The example of Germany or England may be quoted

against me. But in Germany the noble class is destined to command, and the rest of the nation to obey. Policy in that country therefore holds that the people should not be too educated, lest they learn their rights. In England, the man who works with his hands receives as good an education as his condition allows, and other citizens live in such opulence, as a result of trade, that the state can dispense with paying the cost of public liberal education.

It is said too that individuals should pay for the education of their own children; but for six years an unhappy experience has shown that we cannot count on this resource. Except for three or four fairly flourishing colleges, whose existence depends on the abilities of a few men, no one can cite a single establishment of public instruction created by public spirit or parental zeal. Such indifference, whose cause I do not ask, seems always to have existed among us; and if public instruction received aid in earlier times, it owed it exclusively to the benevolence of a few individual citizens.

It is said that the government can burden itself with such expense only with very great difficulty. I believe it! Hence I have suggested means by which public instruction will gradually cease to be an expense to the state. But in a country so shaken and torn apart, with so many factions dividing the French nation, the government has no means more potent than education for attaching the rising generation to a common center. To abandon education to individual wishes, to the prejudices and opinions of so many parties, would merely prepare for us new storms in the future.

The government will be too wise to adopt such hazardous principles, or rather such dangerous sophisms, which would compromise the destinies and the prosperity of the Republic. It will remember that, in the present state of political societies, it is not merely the strongest people, but the one most widely educated in the arts and sciences, that holds the first rank among nations.

Bibliographical Note

ANY study of Louis-le-Grand must begin with the monumental work of Gustave Dupont-Ferrier, *Du Collège de Clermont au Lycée Louis-le-Grand, 1563–1920*, 3 vols., Paris 1921–25. The third volume contains a minute index, statistical matter, and classified biographical data. The first and second volumes, divided at the year 1800, contain masses of information, with thousands of references which offer a ready-made guide to the archives.

There are four important printed source collections, listed below. The first three are so rare that indications are given for finding them. The fourth, being a French government publication, is more common in American libraries. Some items for which archival references are given below may also be found in one or more of these collections.

1. *Recueil de toutes les délibérations importantes prises par le bureau d'administration du Collège de Louis-le-Grand*, Paris, 1781. At the Archives Nationales, H 2406.

2. *Recueil de plusieurs des ouvrages de M. le Président Rolland, imprimé en exécution des délibérations du bureau d'administration du Collège de Louis-le-Grand des 17 janvier et 18 avril 1782*. Paris, 1783. At the Bibliothèque Nationale, R 6074.

3. *Recueil de lois et règlements concernant l'instruction publique, depuis l'édit de Henri IV en 1598 jusqu' à ce jour. Publié par ordre de son Excellence le Grand Maître de l'Université de France*, 8 vols., Paris, 1814–27. In the United States, at the Library of Congress, New York Public Library, and Cornell University Library.

4. A. [Marais] de Beauchamp, *Recueil de lois et règle-*

ments sur l'enseignement supérieur, 6 vols., Paris, 1880–93. The first volume is on the years 1789–1847.

Among printed sources there is also, for the years 1792–95, M. J. Guillaume, *Procès-verbaux du Comité de l'instruction publique de la Convention Nationale*, 6 vols. plus 2-vol. index, Paris, 1889–1957. Much of value can be learned from the *Archives parlementaires*, a huge compilation of legislative debates and allied materials of which publication began in the 1860's. The first series, on the years beginning in 1789, has indexes in volumes 33 and 51 for 1789–92. The second series, on the years beginning in 1799, has an index in volume 14-*bis* for the years 1799–1815. The daily newspaper, the *Moniteur universel*, has an index for the years 1789–99. It must be remembered that the nineteenth-century reprint of the *Moniteur* is incomplete for the years after 1795, for which the original must be used. The Croker collection at the British Museum contains, on educational subjects, about 500 pamphlets, tracts, leaflets, offprints of speeches, etc., originating during the French Revolution. They can be readily consulted through the catalogue prepared by G. K. Fortescue.

The most thorough historical treatments are disconcertingly old. For the period before the Revolution nothing replaces Charles Jourdain, *Histoire de l'Université de Paris au XVIIᵉ et au XVIIIᵉ siècles*, 2 vols., Paris, 1862–66, and second edition, 1888. The first edition is more valuable, since it contains a 300-page appendix of documents; it is far rarer than the second, but may be found at the Newberry Library, Chicago. For the colleges before 1789 there is also much of value in M. Targe, *Professeurs et régents de collège dans l'ancienne Université de Paris, XVIIᵉ et XVIIIᵉ siècles*, Paris, 1902.

For the years of the Revolution there is nothing as comprehensive as Jourdain on the Old Regime. L. Liard, *L'enseignement supérieur en France, 1789–1893*, Paris, 2 vols., 1888–94, deals with colleges and lycées only incidentally.

The recent history of education in France by Antoine Prost begins with the year 1800. Félix Ponteil, *Histoire de l'enseignement en France*, Paris, 1966, begins with 1789, and is very helpful, but unavoidably brief on the Revolution. More monographic, full of information, and powerfully argued, are the old works of E. Allain, Albert Duruy, and Louis Grimaud, but they all express anti-Revolutionary or anti-republican attitudes, which the reader can allow for as he judges best. For the Napoleonic years the standard work remains Alphonse Aulard, *Napoléon et le monopole univesitaire*, Paris, 1911, reinforced by the book of his student Charles Schmidt, *La Réforme de l'Université Impériale en 1811*, Paris, 1905.

Of the life of Jean-François Champagne not much can be known. There is nothing in his personal dossier in the Archives Nationales, from the Ministry of Public Instruction, except a bare record of his pension and death. He received some attention as a deceased member of the Institute, within which, when the class of moral and political sciences was abolished in 1802, he became a member of the class (after 1814 academy) of inscriptions and belles-lettres. Quatremère de Quincy pronounced his eulogy after his death; a copy exists as a 3-page leaflet at the British Museum under the title, *Funérailles de M. Champagne le 16 Septembre 1813*. At the public sessions of the academy on July 15, 1815, the perpetual secretary, Baron Joseph Dacier, read a notice on Champagne's life and work. It showed considerable ignorance of or indifference toward Champagne's actual career in education—or perhaps only discretion, since it was delivered in the atmosphere of royalist triumph only a month after Waterloo. See *Histoire et Mémoires de l'Institut Royal de France: Académie des Inscriptions et Belles-lettres*, vol. V, Paris, 1821, pp. 189–97. Gleanings may be picked up from G. Emond, *Histoire du Collège de Louis-le-Grand depuis sa fondation jusq' en 1830*, Paris, 1845, pp. 387–89, and from J.E.J. Quicherat, *Histoire de Sainte-Barbe: collège, communauté, institution,* 3 vols., Paris, 1860–64, II, pp. 241–42. See also the index, appendices, and references in Dupont-Ferrier.

Champagne soon dropped from historical memory. The article in the *Biographie nouvelle des contemporains,* vol. IV, Paris, 1822, was seriously misinformed. He was briefly and favorably noted by Louis Maggiolo in the first edition of Ferdinand Buisson, *Dictionnaire de pédagogie et d'instruction primaire,* 2 vols., Paris, 1882–87; but in the second edition, Paris, 1911, one enormous volume in 2,087 double-column pages, the article on him was deleted.

References

REFERENCES are given only for location of documents translated in this book, and are numbered accordingly. Locations cited more than once are abbreviated as indicated; particulars are given in the preceding Bibliographical Note.

AN   Archives Nationales, Paris
A-UP   Archives de l'Université de Paris
AP   *Archives parlementaires*
BM-Croker   British Museum Croker Collection
Dupont-Ferrier The history of Louis-le-Grand noted above
Jourdain   The history of the University noted above
Recueil 3   The *Recueil* numbered 3 above
Recueil 4   The *Recueil* numbered 4 above

1. Jourdain, ed. 1862–66, II, pp. 215–20. See also AN H3 2528.
2. Dupont-Ferrier, I, 363–66.
3. J. J. Garnier, *De l'éducation civile*, Paris, 1765, 146–50.
4. Jourdain, ed. 1888, II, 348–53.
5. Jourdain, ed. 1862–66, II, 238–52. See also A-UP carton 16.
6. A-UP, carton 16.
7. Louis-Ernest Hamel, *Histoire de Robespierre, d'après les papiers de famille, les sources originales et les documents inédits*, 3 vols., Paris, 1865–67, I, 19–20.
8. A-UP, carton 16.
9. Recueil, 3, I, 133–36.
10. Louis-Sébastien Mercier, *Tableau de Paris, Nouvelle édition corrigée et augmentée*. 12 vols., Amsterdam, 1782–88, I, 252–57.
11. Dupont-Ferrier, III, appendix F 3.
12. L. B. Proyart, *De l'éducation publique et des moyens d'en*

réaliser la réforme projetée dans la dernière Assemblée générale du clergé de France, Paris, 1785, 98–127.

13. AP ser. I, VIII, 303.
14. BM Croker, R 374–3. See also Jourdain, ed. 888, II, 468.
15. AP ser. I, XI, 331–32.
16. BM Croker, F 499–18.
17. Yves-Marie Audrein, *Mémoire sur l'éducation nationale suivi d'un projet de décret présenté à l'Assemblée Nationale le 11 décembre 1790*, Paris, 1791, *passim*.
18. Derived from Dupont-Ferrier, III, appendices B and C.
19–21. AN H 2546 B
22. Adolphe Schmidt, *Paris pendant la Révolution, d'après les rapports de la police secrète, 1789–1900*, 4 vols., Paris, 1880–94, IV, 164–66.
23. AN H 2546 B
24. AP ser. I, XLVII, 269, 292.
25–26. AN H 2546 B
27. AP ser. I, LIX, 710–11.
28. AN F17 1037, no. 618. Also printed in Guillaume, *Procès-Verbaux* (see above), I, 499–501.
29. A-UP carton 26, dossier 2, cahier 9, pp. 103–18.
30. AN F7 3688ª, dossier 2.
31. AN F17 2546 B.
32. AN F17A 1081.
33. AN H3 2563, liasse A.
34. AN F17 1143, no. 6.
35. AN F17 6722.
36. *Moniteur universel* (original), 26 Messidor An V, 1183–84.
37. *Annales philosophiques, morales et littéraires*, Paris, 1800, I, 49–57.
38. Jean-François Champagne, *La Politique d'Aristote, ou la science des gouvernements*, 2 vols., Paris, An V, I, lxii, and II, 4, 6, 208.
39. AN F17A 1021 B.
40. AN F17 6724.
41. BM Croker, F 495–14.
42. L. B. Proyart, *Louis XVI détrôné avant d'être roi, ou Tableau des causes nécessitantes de la Révolution française et de l'ébranlement de tous les trônes*, London, 1800, 130–138.

43. Recueil 3, ii, 1–4.
44. AN H3 2558 dossier 26.
45. AP ser. 2, iii, 476–85.
46. *Gazette de France*, 8 Floréal An X.
47. Recueil 3, ii, 378–98.
48. Recueil 3, ii, 418–37.
49. Recueil 3, iii, 82.
50. Recueil 4, i, 156, 171–88.
51. Recueil 4, i, 189, 206.
52. Derived from *Almanach National*, An VIII, 480–81; An XIII, 711–12; 1810, 798–99; and from Dupont-Ferrier, iii, appendices B and C.
53. AN F17 1007, no. 1223.
54. *Vues sur l'organisation de l'instruction publique dans les écoles destinées à l'enseignement de la jeunesse, par le Citoyen Champagne, membre de l'Institut National, et Directeur du Prytanée francais.* Paris, Germinal An VIII.

Acknowledgments and References
for Illustrations

1. Principale cour intérieure du Collège de Louis-le-Grand. Bibliothèque Nationale, Cabinet des Estampes, Va 26oh 51A3893

2. Bretez, Louis: Plan de Paris commencé l'année 1734. Dessiné et gravé sous les ordres de Messire Michel Etienne Turgot, Paris, 1739. Sectional plan No. 7. Beinecke Library, Yale University.

3. Plan du Collège [1793] Archives Nationales, C 295 dossier No. 5, 989.

4. Lithograph: Lycée de Louis-le-Grand [1860] Bibliothèque Nationale, Cabinet des Estampes, Va 26oh 52C8429

Library of Congress Cataloging in Publication Data

Palmer, Robert Roswell, 1909-
  The school of the French Revolution: a documentary history of the College of Louis-le-Grand and its director, Jean-François Champagne, 1762-1814.

  1. Paris. Lycée Louis-le-Grand—History.
2. Champagne, Jean-François, 1751-1813.   I: Title.
LF2395.P34P3413   378.44'36   74-25625
ISBN 0-691-05229-8